MANAGING INFORMATION
SYSTEMS FOR PROFIT

John Wiley
INFORMATION SYSTEMS SERIES

Editors

Richard Boland
Case Western Reserve University

Rudy Hirschheim
University of Houston

MANAGING INFORMATION SYSTEMS FOR PROFIT

Edited by

Tim Lincoln

John Wiley
INFORMATION SYSTEMS SERIES

JOHN WILEY & SONS
Chichester · New York · Brisbane · Toronto · Singapore

Copyright © 1990 by John Wiley & Sons Ltd,
Baffins Lane, Chichester,
West Sussex PO19 1UD, England

Other Wiley Editorial Offices

John Wiley & Sons, Inc., 605 Third Avenue,
New York, NY 10158-0012, USA

Jacaranda Wiley Ltd, G.P.O. Box 859, Brisbane,
Queensland 4001, Australia

John Wiley & Sons (Canada) Ltd, 22 Worcester Road,
Rexdale, Ontario M9W 1L1, Canada

John Wiley & Sons (SEA) Pte Ltd, 37 Jalan Pemimpin #05-04,
Block B, Union Industrial Building, Singapore 2057

Library of Congress Cataloging-in-Publication Data:

Managing information systems for profit / edited by Tim Lincoln
      p.   cm. — (John Wiley information systems series)
   Includes bibliographical references.
   ISBN 0 471 92554 3
    1. Business—Data processing.   2. Management information systems.
 3. Efficiency, Industrial.   4. Chief executive officers.
 I. Lincoln, Tim.   II. Series.
 HF5548.2.M2965   1990
 658.4'038—dc20   89–70529
                                            CIP

British Library Cataloguing in Publication Data:

Managing information systems for profit.
   1. Information services. Management
   I. Lincoln, Tim
   025'5'2'068

   ISBN 0 471 92554 3

Printed and bound in Great Britain by
Courier International Ltd, Tiptree, Essex

To Ann and Robin

CONTENTS

CONTRIBUTORS

Bill Amos *Senior Systems Management Consultant, IS Strategy and Organisation. SMC, IBM UK Ltd, 389 Chiswick High Rd, London W4 4AL*

A mathematics graduate of Edinburgh University, Bill worked in a major life assurance company for six years before joining IBM in 1966 at Greenock, where he held various management positions, including Application Development and Computer Operation, before becoming plant IS Manager in 1975. In 1977, he was appointed UK Manufacturing IS Manager with overall responsibility for IS support to the plants at Havant and Greenock. From 1978 to 1981, Bill was Manager for Manufacturing IS for IBM Europe in Paris; responsible for giving IS direction to all of the European plants. At the end of 1981, he returned to the UK and joined the Systems Management Consultancy Department where he worked on a wide variety of consultancy projects specialising in Strategic and Organisational issues. Bill joined IBM Europe IS in December 1985, as Manager of IS Skills and International Education based in Brussels, and rejoined the Systems Management Consultancy Department in 1989.

George Bauer *Professor of Information Systems, Georgia State University. 4456 Chattahovehee, Plantation Drive, Marietta, GA 30067, USA*

George joined IBM in the United States in 1956. He gained extensive marketing management experience before moving to financial and IS management. He has held the positions of Chief Financial Officer of Information Records Division, Director of IS US Marketing and Service Group, Group Director of IS for Office Product Divisions, Group Director IS IBM Europe, Middle East and Africa and, finally, IBM Corporate Director of Administration Operations. In 1985, George was assigned to the Systems Management Consultancy Group in the UK where he specialised in working with chief executives on IS issues. In 1987 George returned to the US and retired from IBM. He is currently Professor of Information Systems at Georgia State University, holds non-executive directorships of several US banks and manages a private investment banking company.

Raphe Berenbaum *Systems Management Consultancy Manager. SMC, IBM UK Ltd, 389 Chiswick High Rd, London W4 4AL*

Raphe joined IBM in 1962 after gaining a PhD in low-energy nuclear physics. He has held a number of management positions within IBM UK and IBM Europe which included responsibility for Systems and Technical Training in IBM UK and Systems Engineering Planning and Services for IBM Europe. He has held the position of IS Manager for IBM UK Ltd where he was responsible for initiating major online systems in finance and administration. More recently he was Manager of Host Systems and Planning at the IBM Europe Installation Support Centre. Raphe's present responsibility as Manager of Systems Management Consultancy involves him with the full range of issues facing business management today; particularly the identification of those issues relating to the successful use of IT.

Michael Clark   *Independent Business Consultant.*
Belsize House, Plough Lane, Sarratt, Rickmansworth, Hertfordshire WD3 4NP

Before joining IBM in 1963, Mike had eleven years of industrial experience within the aircraft and nuclear industries. Within IBM, his career encompassed three areas: marketing, where he held a number of management positions; education, working in IBM's Advanced Marketing Institute in Belgium and, subsequently, as the UK Manager of Customer Executive Education; and consultancy, helping develop IBM's Intensive Planning Programme, and working with customers helping them to develop comprehensive IS stratetic plans. Mike retired from IBM in 1989 and is currently an independent consultant working with large UK organisations on strategic planning issues.

Steve Davis   *Systems Management Consultant, Installation Management and Planning.*
SMC, IBM UK Ltd, 389 Chiswick High Rd, London W4 4AL

Steve joined IBM's Bristol Data Centre in 1966, specialising in manufacturing control systems. In 1970, he moved to the IBM Manufacturing Plant in Havant, where he led a number of developments in the area of manufacturing support and control, subsequently moving into computer operations management. Since then, he has held management posts covering the strategic planning, development, and operation of IS, first within IBM and then with Southern Gas where he was responsible for managing computer operations and, later, for the definition of an office systems strategy. Steve entered management consultancy in 1984, and became involved in the development and implementation of IS management methodologies. In 1985, he joined IBM Systems Management Consultancy where he specialises in operations issues.

Brian Edwards   *Senior Systems Management Consultant, IS Policy and Projects.*
SMC, IBM UK Ltd, 389 Chiswick High Rd, London W4 4AL

Brian entered industry in 1956 at the Ford Motor Company, beginning his computing career there in 1959. He moved to IBM in 1961. For fifteen years he undertook systems design and consultancy with many manufacturing companies, notably in the aerospace industry. He helped to write and edit the IBM COPICS books, and was involved in IBM education. In the later 1970s Brian moved into retail systems consultancy and became interested in the general problems of systems management. In 1980, this led to his joining Systems Managment Consultancy. Brian's work focuses on the issues of IS policies in complex organisations, and on the requirements for effective IS implementation projects. In each of these topics he has conducted research with the support of the Oxford Institute for Information Management, of which he is a Research Affiliate.

Bob Jones   *Senior Systems Management Consultant, Networks and Operations.*
SMC, IBM UK Ltd, 389 Chiswick High Rd, London W4 4AL

Bob is a mathematics graduate who has been a Fellow of the British Computer Society since 1969. He gained extensive experience as an applications programmer in four companies before joining IBM's Hursley Development Laboratory in 1961. At Hursley he managed a wide variety of software development projects before becoming IS Manager in 1972. He was appointed Manager of the European Laboratories Computation Network in 1979 with responsibility for both IS and the European Development Network. In 1984, he was appointed Director of the International Network Centre in Zoetermeer, The Netherlands, responsible to Information Network Europe for the service delivery and network strategies, development of the network and systems software, delivery of international services to customers in 53 countries and management of computer centres in 15 European countries. In 1987, he joined Systems Management Consultancy where he specialises in organisation, operational and networking issues.

Tim Lincoln *Senior Systems Management Consultant, IS Investment Appraisal and Strategy.*
SMC, IBM UK Ltd, 389 Chiswick High Rd, London W4 4AL

After obtaining a PhD in low-energy nuclear physics, Tim joined IBM in 1968 and for six years worked on IS projects under contract to IBM customers. This was followed by three years at IBM's European System Research Institute in Brussels; initially as a lecturer in IS and subsequently as Planning Manager. Since then he has been a consultant working primarily in the areas of IS strategic planning, investment appraisal and IS management effectiveness. Tim was a Visiting Fellow at the Oxford Centre for Management Studies for 10 years, and is a member of an IFIP Technical Committee on Information Systems. He is on the editorial board of the journal *Information and Management* and has been a member of the UK Government working party on 'computer systems investment appraisal'.

Mike Parker *Senior Systems Management Consultant, Applications Development.*
SMC, IBM UK Ltd, 389 Chiswick High Rd, London W4 4AL

Mike qualified in accountancy and business studies and started his career as a product accountant in an electronics company. In 1967, he joined IBM's manufacturing plant in Havant and became Systems Development Manager in 1969. In 1971, Mike became Information Systems Manager and subsequently UK Manufacturing Information Systems Manager. In 1974, Mike was assigned to IBM headquarters in White Plains, New York, as Europe Manufacturing Information Systems Liaison Manager. On returning to the UK, Mike held various senior management appointments including Systems Architecture and Strategy Manager. From 1981 until 1985, Mike was UK Development Manager responsible for such developments as the National Office Support System (NOSS, and a Common Intercompany Accounting System (CIAS)—installed in 19 countries. He set up the first Development Centre in the UK to support a group of over 300 staff. In 1985, Mike joined the Systems Management Consultancy Group, where he specialises in system development and organisation issues.

David Shorrock *Senior Systems Management Consultant, Business and IS Planning.*
SMC, IBM UK Ltd, 389 Chiswick High Rd, London W4 4AL

David joined IBM as an Instructor in the Customer Education Department in 1959. He then gained field experience in the publishing and food industries, followed by several management positions in Education for the Marketing and Product Development Divisions. David has worked in IBM's International Development Department in Belgium as a Programme Manager where he was responsible for introducing a number of middle and senior management training programmes for European executives of IBM. Since returning to the UK in 1980, David has put his experience in training management into practice in two different areas. As a Quality Manager, he was responsible for introducing quality circle techniques into a Marketing Division. As a Planning Consultant, David initiated a programme of executive information planning studies. David joined Systems Management Consultancy in 1986, where he specialised in executive planning and investment appraisal.

Julian E. Smith *Systems Management Consultant, Office Systems.*
SMC, IBM UK Ltd, 389 Chiswick High Rd, London W4 4AL

Julian joined IBM in 1964 as a Systems Engineer from a consumer electronics development laboratory. He worked initially with the automotive industry and subsequently was Product

Manager for banking terminals and cash dispensers. After extensive experience with the banking industry he was appointed Banking Industry Manager, responsible for product launches, sales support, training, and the progress of business. In 1982, Julian became UK Manager for Office Systems Announcements and Sales Support. Since joining Systems Management Consultancy, Julian has been helping IBM's customers to clarify the business dimensions of IS investment decisions and to plan the achievement of projected benefits.

Bryan Ward *Senior Systems Management Consultant, Business IS Strategy. SMC, IBM UK Ltd, 389 Chiswick High Rd, London W4 4AL*

A graduate of the London School of Economics and Political Science and Fellow of the Institute of Chartered Accountants in England and Wales (ICAEW), Bryan joined IBM in 1963 after working as an auditor and within the Finance Department of British Airways. Since joining IBM, he has had extensive field and staff experience within the marketing function. A member of the Systems Management Consultancy Group since the late 1970s, he has specialised in consultancy work with 'top teams' (both IBM and IBM's large customers), assisting them to formulate business strategies, associated IS strategies and to define the major projects required to implement strategies. As a member of ICAEW working groups, Bryan has contributed to the publication of Information Technology Statements entitle *Good Accounting Software* and *Costs and Benefits of Information Technology Projects*. He has described his consultancy methodology in a recent Harvard Business Review paper and is a Visiting Fellow at the Department of Accounting and Management Science, Southampton University.

SERIES FOREWORD

In order for all types of organisations to succeed, they need to be able to process data and use information effectively. This has become especially true in today's rapidly changing environment. In conducting their day-to-day operations, organisations use information for functions such as planning, controlling, organising and decision making. Information, therefore, is unquestionably a critical resource in the operation of all organisations. Any means, mechanical or otherwise, which can help organisations process and manage information presents an opportunity they can ill afford to ignore.

The arrival of the computer and its use in data processing has been one of the most important organisational innovations in the past thirty years. The advent of computer-based data processing and information systems has led to organisations being able to cope with the vast quantities of information which they need to process and manage to survive. The field which has emerged to study this development is *information systems* (IS). It is a combination of two primary fields: computer science and management, with a host of supporting disciplines, e.g. psychology, sociology, statistics, political science, economics, philosophy and mathematics. IS is concerned not only with the development of new information technologies but also with questions such as: how they can best be applied, how they should be managed and what their wider implications are.

Partly because of the dynamic world in which we live (and the concomitant need to process more information) and partly because of the dramatic recent developments in information technology, e.g. personal computers, fourth-generation languages, relational data bases, knowledge-based systems and office automation, the relevance and importance of the field of information systems have become apparent. End users, who previously had little potential of becoming seriously involved and knowledgeable in information technology and systems, are now much more aware of and interested in the new technology. Individuals working in today's and tomorrow's organisations will be expected to have some understanding of and the ability to use the rapidly developing information technolgies and systems. The dramatic increase in the availability and use of information technology, however, raises fundamental questions on the guiding of technological innovation, measuring organisational and managerial productivity, augmenting human intelligence, ensuring data integrity and establishing strategic advantage. The expanded use of information systems also raises major challenges to the traditional forms of administration and authority, the right to privacy, the nature and form of work and the limits of calculative rationality in modern organisations and society.

The Wiley Series on Information Systems has emerged to address these questions and challenges. It hopes to stimulate thought and discussion on the key role information systems play in the functioning of organisations and society, and how their role is likely to change in the future. This historical or evolutionary theme of the Series is important because considerable insight can be gained by attempting to understand the past. The Series will attempt to integrate both description—what has been done—with prescription—how best to develop and implement information systems.

The descriptive and historical aspect is considered vital because information systems of the past have not necessarily met with the success that was envisaged. Numerous writers postulate that a high proportion of systems are failures in one sense or another. Given their high cost of development and their importance to the day-to-day running of organisations, this situation must surely be unacceptable. Research into IS failure has concluded that the primary cause of failure is the lack of consideration given to the social and behavioural dimensions of IS. Far too much emphasis has been placed on their technical side. The result has been something of a shift in emphasis from a strictly technical conception of IS to one where it is recognized that information systems have behavioural consequences. But even this misses the mark. A growing number of researchers suggest that information systems are more appropriately conceived as social systems which rely, to a greater and greater extent, on new technology for their operation. It is this social orientation which is lacking in much of what is written about IS. Research has also shown that it is the organisational rather than technical aspects of IS which lead to their success. This is a theme explored in the current volume, *Managing Information Systems for Profit*, where Lincoln and his colleagues seek to show how information systems provide organisational benefits. This volume, based on practical experiences, relates practice with theory.

The Series seeks to provide a forum for the serious discussion of IS. Although the primary perspective is a more social and behavioural one, alternative perspectives will also be included. This is based on the belief that no one perspective can be totally complete; added insight is possible through the adoption of multiple views. Relevant areas to be addressed in the Series include (but are not limited to): the theoretical development of information systems, their practical application, the foundations and evolution of information systems, and IS innovation. Subjects such as systems design, systems analysis methodologies, information systems planning and management, office automation, project management, decision support systems, end-user computing, and information systems and society are key concerns of the Series.

Rudy Hirschheim
Richard Boland

PREFACE

The past few years have seen a marked shift in the attitude of senior executives towards the use of information technology. No longer are expenditures seen as low and investments 'acts of faith'. Now executives require that their information systems are both profitable and can be shown to be profitable.

However ensuring that information systems provide an overall return to the business requires the right balance to be struck on a series of complex issues. Cost control is important and necessary but so also is benefit achievement; short term actions may be required for survival but a healthy organisation will also bear in mind longer term goals; user requirements are important but business process integrity must be maintained. The decisions required demand comparision of a variety of 'hard' and 'soft' data under conditions of great uncertainty. To many executives faced with this challenge it can seem an impossible task.

Perhaps, at some stage, a single unified approach to these issues will emerge. At the current time however there is a variety of techniques which are used at different stages in the process of building and operating information systems and these rarely seem to link together in a coherent fashion. Such techniques often have their own unique jargon and attract disciples who argue their case with evangelical fervour. Executives do not have the time or motivation to find their way through this maze and it is not supprising therefore to find many organisations managing some elements of the IS profit equation well while handling others poorly. Too frequently this results in unprofitable systems acting as a constraint on the business.

Discussions with executives about these problems identified a need to pull together the best practical experience across the full range of IS management processes and to present this clearly and with the minimum of jargon. It was felt to be important that the techniques described were based on a common approach and used, wherever possible, common terminology. It was recognised that this was a distinct challenge since the range of experience required far exceeded that achieveable by any one person. However the collective experience gained by my colleagues in the *Systems Management Consultancy* function within IBM UK, covered the required range and, after some persuasion, they agreed to collaborate on this venture. In total twelve consultants have contributed to this book and while each has his own specific area of expertise they all have worked closely together over a number of years to evolve techniques which are supportive and coherent. Their experience includes line management experience of IS and related functions both within

IBM and other companies. Each consultant has more than 20 years experience in his field and collectively they have extensive consultancy experience with virtually all large UK companies as well as many European organisations. They have distilled this experience into chapters which provide a coherent thread of techniques but which can, if someone is interested in a specific topic, be read in isolation. Their views, as expressed in this book, arise from their experience and cannot be taken necessarily as representing those of IBM.

The book is addressed to both IS and executive management of large and small companies in the public and private sectors. Its purpose is to analyse the problems likely to impact the major processes used to build and operate information systems and to offer practical and proven approaches to these problems. The focus of the book is pragmatic and down to earth. It is designed to help the practising manager directly rather than make the case for employing expensive consultants. It focuses on proven techniques rather than latest theory. It is essentially a 'how to' book written on the basis of the best available practical experience.

The underlying theme of the book is that the key to managing information systems for profit lies in closely integrating the management processes associated with IS with those of the business. This theme is developed in detail in Chapter 1 *Integrating Information Systems With The Organisation* where the five fundamental IS processes required for effective management are discussed and ways are suggested of ensuring that these processes are fully integrated with the business. Each of these IS processes is then dealt with in turn by two complementary chapters which review different dimensions of the process.

Setting information systems direction and policies is addressed in Chapters 2 and 3. Chapter 2 focuses on the role of top management, specifically that of the chief executive, in the IS planning process while Chapter 3 analyses the policies and strategies required for effective IS management in large, particularly multidivisional, organisations.

Identifying and prioritising applications is covered in Chapters 4 and 5. Chapter 4 deals with determining business priorities and describes a number of techniques for appropriately involving top management. Chapter 5 develops this theme by describing a specific approach for executive committees which identifies potential information systems by forging links between critical success factors and business processes.

Implementing applications is addressed in Chapters 6 and 7. Chapter 6 examines the challenges application development managers face during the life cycle from initial request to system implementation. Chapter 7 deals with the specific issue of the development of office systems where successful integration demands the active involvement of relatively large numbers of clerical and professional staff.

Providing service is addressed in Chapters 8 and 9. Chapter 8 describes the management processes and measurements which ensure effective service is delivered by the operational departments. Chapter 9 addresses the issue of securing IT services and provides a framework which allows senior management to select the level of security investment appropriate to the risks involved to the business through loss of service.

Ensuring benefits is addressed in Chapters 10 and 11. Chapter 10 reviews the problems inherent in cost-justifying specific information systems and in preparing business cases. Chapter 11 looks at the issue of demonstrating to senior management the contribution made by the IS department to achieving corporate objectives and recommends an approach which draws together quantifiable costs and benefits and user assessments into a consolidated report.

I would like to give particular acknowledgement to Raphe Berenbaum, the manager of the *Systems Management Consultancy* group, who provided invaluable guidance and support during the preparation of this book. Acknowledgement is also due to Sylvia Palias and Diane Allision who provided the office support to the team. Finally I must stress that the book could not have been written without the close collaboration of the consultants involved. Individually they all have national and in many cases international reputations and as a group they represent a unique combination of consulting experience. It has been a pleasure and privilege to work with them on this venture.

Tim Lincoln
January 1990

Chapter 1

INTEGRATING INFORMATION SYSTEMS WITH THE ORGANISATION

Raphe Berenbaum and Tim Lincoln

1 INTRODUCTION

The 'Information Society' has been so extensively (perhaps excessively) heralded that it has been easy to overlook, or take for granted, the real changes which are taking place in developed countries in the use of information technology (IT). Whole industries have emerged which supply services rather than human power or energy (Bell, 1973). The use of IT has become all pervasive and in so doing has transformed almost all facets of our society including schools, banking, transport, etc. It has been claimed (Colombo, 1982) that 'it is highly likely that by the end of the century information technologies will have replaced, wherever possible, all the more traditional technologies in every sphere of activity in the industrialised countries and to some extent also in the developing nations'. Two obvious examples of these trends are the emergence of industries which market information rather than physical products or services and the establishment of the world-wide financial services market place in the 1980s.

Because of these massive and obvious changes it is easy to lose sight of the steady evolution of the use of IT in more mundane ways in every modern organisation. This has been summarised in a framework (Gibson and Hammer, 1985) characterising the first era of application of computing as achieving benefits of efficiency and effectiveness for functional units within an organisation, and the impact of the subsequent spread of personal computers as providing similar efficiency and effectiveness for individuals. However, the usage of IT is now developing in ways which enable entire organisations to improve their efficiency and effectiveness and, probably more importantly, facilitates the 'transformation' of individuals, functions and organisations. These transformations enable individuals to undertake new roles and whole organisations to move into new areas of profitable activity. In addition to its use as an internal resource, information is increasingly recognised as having external value. Thus inventory systems can both minimise inventory costs and

Managing Information Systems for Profit. Edited by T. J. Lincoln
© 1990 John Wiley & Sons Ltd

provide product availability information to potential customers. Accordingly, many companies are appraising the potential of corporate information to add value to their base product or perhaps to form a product in its own right.

As the nature and use of corporate information changes, the associated planning and control processes must also evolve. It has been long accepted that companies who manage computing technology successfully tend to involve their top management in key decisions relating to computers (McKinsey, 1968). As information becomes a key competitive weapon, corporate strategic planning will need to take IT developments into account (Benjamin *et al.*, 1985). As information becomes one of the most important corporate assets, successful management of that asset is of vital importance to future success.

Although the potential importance of IT is commonly accepted there is still widespread dissatisfaction with what has actually been achieved. In many organisations the benefits attained are not seen as commensurate with the costs incurred; IT and profit are not seen as compatible. This chapter is concerned with why this is the case. The fundamental weaknesses are exposed and ways available for improving the situation suggested.

2 IT MANAGEMENT PRESENTS UNIQUE PROBLEMS

2.1 IT Failures Can Be Traced to Management Inadequacies

A recent case in which IT was perceived by top management as failing provides a valuable insight into the type of issues which require exploration.

An insurance company was experiencing consistent difficulty in implementing computer applications which met user requirements and which were delivered within required and committed time frames. Senior management were baffled by the lack of agreement between users and Information Systems (IS) staff as to where the problems lay and suspected that the technology was defective. However, a structured, one day review, set up to examine the issues, clarified the different perceptions of the key difficulties. It showed that the computer department felt that the main issues were:

— Lack of user education
— Poor relationships between users and DP department
— Lack of user involvement, commitment and support
— Lack of business skills in DP department

while the users felt that the principle problems were:

— Insufficient analysis of requirements by DP department
— Inability of users to provide support requested by DP department
— Lack of mutual understanding and respect

When these issues were tabled and compared it became apparent that the key problems did not lie with the technology but centred on poor communications between users and IS staff. Historically in this organisation communications had been given a low priority, were taking place at too low a level and were based on poor mutual understanding.

Most departments had found informal ways of dealing with this but these methods failed when applied to IS management processes, with the result that although required roles for project development had been defined they were not being performed effectively.

This example is by no means unique. The development and use of IT within most organisations is impeded by constraints that are associated with IS management processes. Technological advances are unlikely to remove these constraints; indeed it appears likely that increasing opportunities for cost effective deployment will create even greater stress on management processes designed for a more limited environment. To understand why this is the case, and to identify the changes required for managing IT successfully, it is necessary to probe deeper into the issues which make the management of IS resources particularly difficult.

2.2 IS Skills and Attitudes are Difficult to Manage

Successful management of sophisticated technology seems to demand increased numbers of experts with evermore esoteric skills. In the 1970's it was still common to find only two basic IS functions, 'development'— responsible for writing the programs—and 'operations'—responsible for running computers. Each typically covered a relatively narrow range of skills and responsibilities with systems analysts and programmers in the former and systems programmers and operators in the latter. Today things look very different. In addition to the two basic functions, it is common now to find 'plans and controls' and 'architecture' functions. The development area will house staff who specialise in business analysis, information analysis, project management, quality control, fourth generation languages, relational and hierarchical data bases, office automation, etc. Operations will similarly contain staff specialising in data storage management, network administration, telecommunications, testing, backup and recovery, data security and privacy, etc. These lists are not exhaustive and new specialities emerge every day.

This diversity of highly technical skills presents difficult management problems and these problems are compounded by the nature of people who tend to work with IT. A study of the personality profiles of data processing people (Woodruff, 1980) showed that DP staff tended to have a lower need for affiliation and a higher need for autonomy than the general population. This supported earlier findings (Weinberg, 1971) that computer programmers tended to be detached, i.e. they wished to be left to themselves to be creative. These characteristics are often reinforced by organisational reward structures which recognise individual achievement as opposed to contributions to group effort. In the light of these personality and motivational pressures it is not surprising that different IS skills groups all seem to develop their own jargon and work practices which are often incomprehensible to users and even to fellow professionals.

The effect on the rest of the organisation has been particularly well summarised by David Butler (Butler, 1985).

> At present, the systems function is often thought of by its host organisation as rather like a small group of aliens living on a hostile Earth. The aliens can, through powers the Earth-men barely understand, make themselves look and talk like Earth-men but they have no emotions, no hopes, no fears and they breed in unconventional ways! Eventually they might take over the world. Until then, they should be ignored as much as possible.

Groups containing a wide variety of skills, jargon and work practices present coordination problems. These problems can become acute when the group is required to produce structured solutions for other business functions. A study of the ability of teams to solve problems (White, 1984) found that heterogeneous teams, containing a wide variety of skills and experience, had difficulty in reaching a consensus on a structured problem definition whereas homogeneous teams reached consensus quickly and completed the task rapidly. White comments: 'In such structured task situations, it is possible that homogeneous groups are able to work together to complete the task quickly. Heterogeneous groups may have to deal with the tension created by their different perceptual viewpoints and be unable to rapidly complete the task'. Support for White's findings is offered in the research of group work; Aamodt and Kimbrough (1982) found that heterogeneous groups were not as successful as homogeneous teams in completing structured debugging tasks.

Thus IS work brings together people who have a wide variety of highly technical skills, each with their own jargon and work practices and who tend to prefer working in isolation rather than in groups, and requires them to work on structured cross-functional problems. To this extent IS work is unique and it is little wonder that management problems arise!

2.3 IS–User Interaction Growing More Difficult

There is, however, an additional dimension to the issue of IS management which compounds the problems—that of the interaction of IS with the rest of the organisation. In the early days of computing the DP department was relatively isolated. This was partly because computers were a new subject and users were apprehensive about the technology and its implications. However, it was also commonly because computer systems were then developed for very few areas of the business, typically finance, and most users saw little need to get involved. The outcome was often a self-contained, 'fortress', DP function with its own independent, technology related management processes with relatively little external contact.

The situation is now very different. Computer systems are becoming more central to business operations and the IS function is assuming a key role in helping users meet their business objectives. This can only be achieved if IS and users are able to interact successfully. Self-contained management processes are therefore no longer adequate. It is instructive to look at the two major IS functions, Operations and Development, to see the ways in which they are evolving to meet these needs.

2.3.1 Operations

In the early days of computing, data was primarily input via written documents which were then transcribed to machine readable format. The operations department exerted complete control over all aspects of processing, up to and including the production of finished listings of documents. Operations staff accepted time constraints within which work had to be completed and took responsibility for accurate processing and for the checking and control of performance. Agreements with users related solely to these input and output markers; everything in between was a 'black box'.

In these circumstances a self-contained structure of procedures, schedules, operating instructions and practices evolved. In many respects the task resembled any other production process and similar disciplines were adopted. However, the fact that the production environment was in a continuous state of flux caused by the on-going development of new applications and the regular installation of new equipment made it difficult to maintain adequate control and provide a really high level of performance.

In recent years the operations function has been opened up to the rest of the organisation. Their task is now not simply to carry through a predetermined process behind closed doors but is to provide hundreds or perhaps thousands of users with minute-to-minute capabilities and services which may be called upon in any combination of sequence. Thus not only are the service requirements essential but the implications of short term failure of service are significantly more severe than they used to be. The impact on the business of any IT catastrophe means that enormous effort and expense must be devoted to planning for this possibility. This has introduced a new dimension into the problems associated with operations management, and new management processes such as service level management and capacity management are emerging to cope with the situation.

2.3.2 Development

Application development in most organisations has been marked by growing complexity and proliferation. Early systems development usually concentrated on mechanising existing administrative procedures and users were merely required to specify what they actually did. The interface with users was thus both narrow and repetitive with the result that IT experts showed little understanding of the business processes they were working with and the business people showed even less understanding of the capabilities of IT.

The vast range of alternatives now available to users has changed the position. Managers and professionals have acquired sufficient understanding of IT to enable them to select solutions to address their specific business needs. This has resulted in the acquisition of personal computers or departmental 'minis' together with standard packages. Although not always successful the success rate has been high enough to make users increasingly impatient with traditional IS lead times.

However this piecemeal approach has introduced its own problems with considerable fragmentation of systems. The inability of departments or functions to communicate with each other effectively or share data, the inability to integrate office and data applications within a single department and the inability of business modelling developed unilaterally on personal computers to make use of corporate data bases all ultimately limit the successful development of new uses of IT. The development function has had to respond to this situation by broadening its role to cope with buying packages and helping users implement their own solutions. New management processes embracing techniques such as information centres and prototyping are emerging to cope with these issues.

2.4 Change Is Needed

The management of IS resources presents unique problems. These stem from the need to use a wide variety of highly specialised skills, the personality profile of a typical IS person and the need for close IS–user interaction. These pressures are not getting easier; if anything they are getting worse. The failure to manage these issues has been the underlying reason why IT is frequently perceived as failing to support the business effectively.

3 THE NEED FOR NEW APPROACHES

The failure of IS management processes even in companies which have been using computers for many years suggests that something more fundamental than inadequate managers is to blame. The clues as to what this might be are to be found in established organisational theory.

3.1 IS Creates Differentiation

Lawrence and Lorsch (Lawrence and Lorsch, 1967) discussed the differences between different parts of an organisation in terms of cognitive and emotional orientation and formal organisational structure. They argued that the culture and management structure in any part of an organisation should match the degree of uncertainty faced by it. Thus an R&D division faces considerable uncertainty compared with a manufacturing division and must adopt a totally different style and structure if it is to be successful. The more uncertainty a function faces the less formal structure is appropriate and the longer the time horizon of interest has to be. Lawrence and Lorsch found that these considerations directly affected the ways in which organisations functioned to the extent that high performing organisations had structures and cultures which were appropriately differentiated.

These concepts are particularly relevant to the management of IT because of the sharp differences between IS experts and users in most organisations. Frequently the introduction of IT brings a level of differentiation into the organisation not previously seen before and management have little experience in coping with it. The case below illustrates the problems that can arise when this happens.

A small newspaper company was steadily introducing computers into their printing and publishing process. The level of reliability of the computer systems was a continuing source of complaint and investigation showed that the complaints centred more on the unexpectedness and the unannounced nature of failure than on the lack of availability itself. It was pointed out that whereas if there was failure of the printing presses alarm bells rang throughout the building, a failure of the computers (now almost equally essential to the successful publication of the paper) was accompanied by no public warning. Users concluded that the IS staff lacked the necessary commitment and seriously questioned whether the use of the system was worth the risk. The computer manager did not have a background in the newspaper industry and consequently he had failed to appreciate the critical impact that even a short interruption of service would have on the print run. However, senior management on their part had failed to appreciate that the introduction of computers into the newspaper industry required people with very different skills and backgrounds. They saw the people recruited with these skills as a separate function, located them in a remote area and made little attempt to assimilate them. It was hardly surprising that problems arose and that users were dissatisfied.

3.2 Integration Is Essential

Lawrence and Lorsch (Lawrence and Lorsch, 1967) found that while appropriate differentiation is necessary for an organisation to function effectively it can introduce problems in terms of friction, lack of understanding and lack of coordination. Reducing differentiation by standardisation is not the answer to these problems. What is needed is the introduction of some form of coordinating or integrating mechanisms. Lawrence and Lorsch analysed the integrating mechanisms used within organisations and showed that the most common are:

— Line management structures
— Cross organisation teams and committees
— Individual coordinators
— Coordinating departments
— Plans and procedures

Other authors (Thompson, 1967; Galbraith, 1977) have identified alternative classifications of integrating mechanisms but the above classification is particularly relevant when considering IS issues.

The importance of these concepts has recently been discussed (Feeny, 1987) where it was pointed out that the key criteria for establishing the success of the use of IT in any organisation is the extent to which it is successfully integrated within the organisation as a whole and is supporting its overall objectives. The key question of course is how this might best be achieved.

3.3 IS Integrating Mechanisms Are Used

Successful information systems demand coordination of effort across functional boundaries. Often modern, large systems demand that different functions cooperate to the extent of superimposing corporate considerations on top of functional requirements. At the minimum this will entail users and IS staff working closely together. To encourage this a range of integrating mechanisms have evolved and the taxonomy discussed in Section 3.2 provides a useful way to analyse these.

Line management control of IS has been exercised in a variety of ways. In the early days of computing the IS department typically reported to a principle user function (commonly finance). This is still common today but larger organisations may have a central IS function reporting directly to the Board or may position IS resources within user organisations, according to the corporate culture.

Cross-organisational teams or committees are widely used to plan and control IS. At the policy level, steering committees are commonly established to bring a company-wide view to application priorities and IS long term plans. At the implementation level, task forces or cross-functional working groups, in various guises, are probably the most commonly found approach to develop systems. New application systems, for example, are commonly developed by the formation of a joint team representing user departments and the IS development department.

Functional coordinators are frequently established with responsibility to coordinate IS and user effort and these can be positioned either in IS or user departments. Where the work load cannot be handled by an individual, or where a high degree of cross functional systems exist, coordinating departments are sometimes established. These are commonly located within the IS function in the form of planning or architectural groups but can also be positioned in a corporate planning department.

Finally, company-wide planning processes can bind IS and users together. These can be short term in the form of a budget planning or 'commitment' process and long term in the form of strategic planning. Such planning processes are usually supported by computer systems and in this sense, as pointed out by Moynihan (Moynihan, 1982), the information systems themselves can act as coordinating mechanisms across the organisation.

3.4 Integrating Mechanisms Still Fail

Although there are many ways in which companies try to integrate IT with the business, evidence of failure is not hard to find. A review of the constraints to the efficient and effective use of IT (Lincoln, 1980) showed that a group of senior IS and general executives representing eighteen large organisations across six countries agreed that their top five key constraints were as follows:

— Obtaining appropriate user involvement
— Agreeing priorities for system development investment
— Predicting implications of organisational change
— Obtaining suitable professional resources
— Taking into account external requirements for information

These conclusions were supported by a subsequent study of the barriers and opportunities of IT (Kearney, 1984), which identified the following major constraints:

— Difficult to cost-justify
— Lack of fiscal incentive
— Need to consolidate requirements
— Dubious or controversial benefits
— Choice of unsuitable equipment
— Insufficient top management support

Both these surveys point to constraints which have little to do with technology but are rather related to the difficulty of coordinating IS, users and top management decisions. This difficulty can often be most clearly seen in the way projects are developed. As stated in Section 3.3 above, development projects frequently use a task force approach and these can work effectively provided that highly competent people with sufficient time are available. However, in many organisations task forces are set up on an *ad hoc* basis and left to find their own way towards integration each time a project is established. While the computer specialists may have their own set of standard approaches and techniques covering, for example, systems requirements definition and subsequent testing, there is often no set methodology in place to define and establish the way in which the various groups involved should work together. All too often the result is delay, confusion and disappointment.

In these circumstances it is not surprising that project management is often identified as a major problem. For example a Price Waterhouse/Computing Opinion Survey (Price Waterhouse, 1987–8) shows that the major issue reported by a panel of 750 DP managers is 'the difficulty of meeting project deadlines' and comments that this issue has remained consistently the highest rated over the previous five years despite many advances in technology and project management techniques. Faced with this, users are tempted to ignore or bypass the IS function as illustrated by a study of the way in which 'competitive edge' systems have evolved (Butler Cox, 1987). This showed that virtually every successful system reviewed stemmed from an idea that had originated outside the systems department and most had not appeared in the planned applications portfolio.

3.5 Early Warning Signs of Failure

Problems in organisations arising from ineffective integration frequently give rise to overt warning signs (Pugh, 1979). Similar warning signs indicating failure to integrate IT can be seen and, indeed, fall into the broad categories identified by Pugh. The most important of these signs are as follows.

3.5.1 Persistent Conflict between Users and the IS Function

Some form of conflict between IS staff and users is very common but the real danger is when this conflict becomes institutionalised and automatic. In these cases the IS department is referred to automatically in a derogatory way (for example 'techies') and casual conversation indicates a uniformly low expectation from IT.

3.5.2 A Proliferation of Ineffective Committees

Here the emphasis is on ineffectiveness; IS steering committees, operating committees, project committees, etc., are formed but fail to function effectively. There are two common indicators. In some organisations ineffective committees will simply be halted. However, the more frequent (and often more difficult to detect) indicator is the gradual slide into ineffectiveness accompanied by the regular attendance of deputies (and deputies of deputies) when it becomes apparent to the senior members that their time is being wasted. This is particularly true of executive steering committees where, because of integration failures lower down the organisation, the top level committee is called upon to deal with relatively trivial topics. This entails a frequency of meeting and investment of executive time which is soon perceived to be unjustified.

3.5.3 Overloading of Top Management

This is frequently seen inside large IS departments where the IS executive is sucked into a steady grind of resolving minor issues. These are usually technical issues which could be resolved at a lower level in a properly functioning department. Similarly, low levels of discretionary sign off at middle management may be a further symptom. It is rarer for the chief executive of an organisation to be burdened in this way, perhaps because so few chief executives feel competent to resolve IT issues. However, as indicated above, this overloading may spill into the work of what is intended to be a top level policy committee and cause it to become ineffective.

3.5.4 Ritual Following of Procedures

IT integration frequently depends upon formal integrating procedures being laid down and followed. However, it is often clear that such procedures are being followed without serious effort or commitment. Perhaps the most obvious example is in the processes associated with the sign-off of systems design by user functions. The delivery of a 50 page systems specification to a user department with the request for sign-off within a day or two is clear evidence that the IS department is not taking the procedure seriously. If the sign-off is then readily given by the user within the requested time it is doubly clear that both parties are simply following ritual.

3.5.5 Excessive Growth of Coordinating Function

Again, this is most commonly seen inside IS functions. If it goes too far it will actively militate against effective integration by providing layers of coordinators preventing direct negotiation with users. A direct symptom, which will help to identify this particular problem, is where the documentation produced as a basis for decision making (e.g. a new system or service) requires a multiplicity of signatures.

3.5.6 Complaints by External Parties

Probably the most common feature experienced by an outside customer, supplier, etc., is the willingness of every department they deal with to blame failings on 'the computer'. Of course, this may come from a genuine dissatisfaction with the service provided by the IS function or from specific current problems. If this is the case then the specific problem will normally be referenced. However, if no specific reason is given or the problems associated with the computer are unreasonable or irrational, then there is a clear lack of understanding and interest on the part of the complainer and consequently a demonstrated lack of effective integration.

3.6 Making Integration Work

Experience has shown that IS integration mechanisms are not easy to establish and need constant attention to function effectively. Before going into detail on the type of mechanism it is useful to establish three general principles which all integration mechanisms should follow.

3.6.1 Set the Level

IT pervades every level of the organisation and an effective organisation will have integration activities for each level. At the operational level, clerical and professional workers must work with IT professionals to resolve problems in their individual use of office or personal computing facilities. At middle management levels, the specification and implementation of departmental systems require IS and functional mangers to work closely together. At the top management level, the integration of IT with the overall aims and goals of the business must be ensured. The level of integration must be accurately selected to ensure the desired effect. Too often, the need for integration is recognised but the processes are at the wrong level and are consequently ineffective. An example is the identification of IT functional requirements by a low level joint study team. Frequently these requirements turn out to be quite irrelevant to the needs and priorities of functional heads.

3.6.2 Choose the Mechanism

Integrating mechanisms must be chosen with care if they are to be effective. Unfortunately expediency often prevails with results which are consequently only partially successful. For example bringing the board of directors together once to review and agree IT strategy for a five year period is common but may have little lasting relevance. In general establishing a working party when the requirement is for an ongoing process will cause the integrating activity to be intermittent and ineffective. Similarly, asking line management to resolve issues which require the broad range of cross functional knowledge is unlikely to produce effective solutions.

3.6.3 Invest the Resources

The best designed integrating mechanism will not function unless adequate effort and skill is devoted to it. The symptoms of failure of integration are often obvious (see Section 3.5 above) but these are frequently ignored or misunderstood and consequently insufficient effort applied. Indeed, such effort is often perceived as wasted and classified as 'staff' or 'indirect' activity. This is exemplified by the failure of joint working parties where two classic mistakes are frequently made. Firstly, properly knowledgeable department members are appointed who have inadequate time available. Secondly, 'warm bodies' are provided who have the time but lack knowledge and experience.

4   INTEGRATION OF IT WITH THE BUSINESS

It is too easy to see the development of the application of IT as a circumscribed process, most of which is carried out within the IS function. While this once may have been true it is now no longer the case and the description of the organisation-wide processes which must contribute to effective use of IT is a critically important basis for ensuring that this technology makes its proper contribution. Figure 1 illustrates the key processes which must be performed successfully if IT is to support the overall objectives of the organisation. This

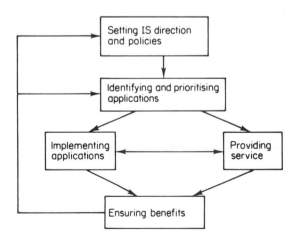

FIGURE 1   Key IS processes

section reviews each of the five key processes, analyses why integration is necessary and indicates what must be done to achieve it.

4.1 Setting IS Direction and Policies

4.1.1 Why Is Integration Necessary?

If effective directions and policies for information systems are to be established and sustained within an organisation there must be a high degree of mutual understanding between those responsible for IS and those responsible for the overall direction of the business. Not only this but the policies governing IS and the organisational framework within which it functions must be consistent with the culture and method of working of the overall organisation. This is frequently not recognised and a supposedly 'ideal' IS policy is established which, because of its foreignness to the business organisation, inevitably fails. Two extreme examples of this are quite common: firstly, when a tightly monolithic IS organisation is given the responsiblity for serving a group of semi-autonomous companies and, secondly, when an organisation which is itself under tight central control attempts to establish a policy for devolving effective control of IS to a low level within the organisation.

4.1.2 Illustration of Failure

An engineering organisation comprised five subsidiary companies and a group services function, including finance and IS, intended to service the requirements of all five subsidiaries. The managing directors of the subsidiary companies became increasingly dissatisfied with the service from the IS central function.

An analysis of the issues showed that the basis for IS management was one of tight central control with the objectives of economies of scale and sharing of scarce resources. For this to perform satisfactorily, common planning processes were required which were regularly reviewed and agreed upon by the managing directors group working as a team. In addition, there needed to be very close linkages and flows of information between the central IS department and the individual companies and that this communication needed to take place at a variety of working levels. Considerable outward looking resource would need to be committed by the individual companies in order to make this happen. Moreover, for the IS function to be able to produce a successful coherent plan and work to it, each of the companies needed to function within the framework of a well organised and smoothly running planning process.

While close integration of the type demanded is feasible and works well in some organisations, the culture of this engineering organisation, which gave considerable autonomy to the subsidiaries, was inconsistent with the fundamental basis on which IS was being managed. Therefore, despite some losses of synergy, each of the five subsidiaries was encouraged to establish local IS functions.

4.1.3 How Can Integration Be Achieved?

The fundamental requirement for achieving successful direction of IS is the effective integration of the IS planning process with the planning process of the organisation at all levels. At the highest level this requires the executive board of the organisation regularly to consider overall policies and plans for IS. However, this can only be effective if IS planning is on an ongoing basis; that is the planning processes in each department, function or business unit must incorporate IS planning as a matter of routine.

Successful interlocking of functional plans requires formal, well understood processes and policies. These may be driven from within the IS department since they are more likely to recognise the need. However, top management support is needed to ensure that these processes and policies are actually followed.

4.1.4 Pointers to Subsequent Chapters

The issues involved in integrating IT with the organisation are addressed in Chapters 2 and 3 of this book. Chapter 2 focuses on the role of top management in the IS planning process. Chapter 3 analyses the policies and strategies required for effective IS management, particularly as they affect multidivisional organisations.

4.2 Identifying and Prioritising Applications

4.2.1 Why Is Integration Necessary?

Perhaps the most commonly expressed concern by senior or functional management within many organisations relates to the relevance and appropriateness of their use of IT. While it is relatively rare for a senior executive to question the need for IT, the view is often expressed that IT is not being used to support the prime requirements of the business. This concern is often justified since to many specialists the opportunities offered are so exciting in themselves that the business implications and benefits are all too easily overlooked. Accordingly the need for integration between IS and the organisation is seen at its sharpest in this task of identifying and prioritising ways in which IT can best be used.

Integration mechanisms must bind together executive management, who will establish business priorities, with IT management, who will work with them to translate these into priorities for the use of IT. This effort requires the coordination of business priorities, technological possibilities, business benefits and IT costs.

4.2.2 Illustration of Failure

A major engineering company had gradually undergone a shift in business orientation so that its main profits arose from the long term servicing of its products as opposed to their original sale. However, most of the computer applications were focused on manufacturing rather than servicing. This became apparent to the chief executive when customer complaints highlighted the inability of his organisation to provide information on the progress of servicing and repair. Only then did he recognise that the change in business direction had not been reflected in the selection and prioritisation of computing applications.

4.2.3 How Can Integration Be Achieved?

Once overall IS directions and policies have been established, specific areas for the use of IT have to be identified and prioritised. The relationship between these two processes is shown in Figure 2 (Rose, 1984).

The analysis of business direction and overall requirements leading to the structuring of fundamental strategies and architectures is shown in the upper part of the diagram. Typically an architecture of itself does not establish a specific applications plan. This is produced by reviewing business priorities and existing systems in order to define specific projects which can then be put in train under the overall guidance provided by the architecture.

An effective applications plan can only be produced by business functions working closely with the IS function. A committee approach, bringing together IS management and senior executives from the functions concerned, is commonly used to achieve this objective. A suitable committee may already be in existence—for example, the Board of Directors of a company—or may need to be especially created. In either case if the committee is to be effective in addressing issues involving an unfamiliar and highly differentiated specialised topic then their work must be managed and focused in an appropriate way.

4.2.4 Pointers to Subsequent Chapters

The selection and prioritisation of computer applications to suit business strategies are dealt with in Chapters 4 and 5. Chapter 4 focuses on the role that top management groups must play in determining these priorities and describes a number of techniques for achieving the appropriate involvement. Chapter 5 describes a specific approach for executive committees which identifies key areas for the application of IT by forging links between critical success factors and critical business processes. Both chapters address the issue which has bedeviled many companies recently, i.e. how to integrate IT strategies with business strategies.

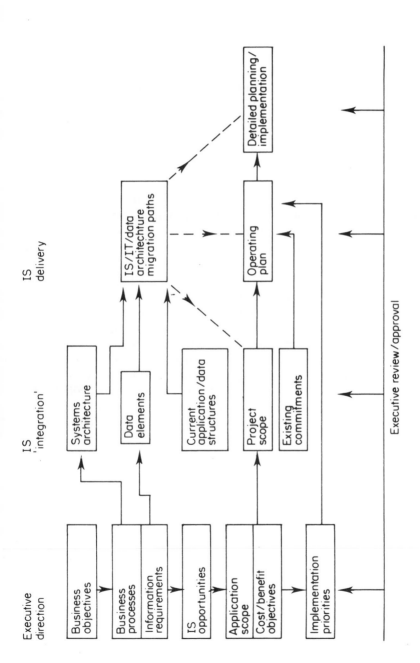

FIGURE 2   Information systems planning and implementation process

4.3 Implementing Applications

4.3.1 Why Is Integration Necessary?

IT is increasingly being used to address aspects of the organisation which are inherently difficult, specialised and complex. The specification of requirements and subsequent implementation is becoming correspondingly more demanding. This requires a range of skills and experience covering both technical and business aspects. Typically a task force approach is used but clearly specified rules and procedures are necessary if the effort required is not to be excessive. The fundamental issues are thus those of integration of specialities, and success will depend on the extent to which the diverse areas of specialised skills and knowledge can be brought together effectively. Many modern applications are concerned with cross-functional, unstructured areas and their analysis requires a high degree of skill differentiation. Considerable integration capability is required to implement these applications effectively and appropriate techniques are needed. For example, the provision of an 'office system' providing personal services, mail, word processing, personal computing, etc., for a wide range of clerical and professional workers has frequently been treated as though it were the same as the provision of any other application. While the project group for a more traditional application can rely for its input on the knowledge of departmental heads, managers are usually quite unable to be specific about the office systems requirements of the people in their department. In this case the integration required is not simply that between non-IS management and IS analysts but between clerical and professional workers on the one hand and technical IS specialists on the other. Thus the requirements definition process needs to go substantially further in canvassing opinion and establishing significant differences in the way in which people work before requirements can be quantified, justified and finally implemented.

4.3.2 Illustration of Failure

A large manufacturing company instituted a 'pilot' system to provide office systems including E-Mail, personal computing, diary, etc., to a large department. The department included many professional staff who travelled frequently so that it was considered to be a particularly appropriate pilot case. A very wide 'menu' of offerings was designed by the computer department on the basis of the widest technical feasibility.

However, the usage of the system fell away very rapidly. It soon became embarrassingly obvious that many of the terminals provided were unused for most or all of the time.

A belated review showed that this was due to the mismatch between the rich menu of services offered—with a corresponding complexity in understanding and use—and the relatively simple services which would have been directly useful for the professionals using the system. The failure lay in the inability of the computer department and the users to match needs and capabilities in designing the system.

4.3.3 How Can Integration Be Achieved?

The frequently used approach to achieve the integration required to implement applications successfully is that of the task force or cross-organisation team. However, merely setting up such a team is insufficient; *ad hoc* teams inventing new procedures each time are unlikely to be effective however skilled the individual team members. There needs to be an established process framework governing the group's way of working which must define such things as relationships with and control by the parent functions, requirements for sign-off of design levels, procedures for resolving contention and commitment procedures. There is an important distinction between Section 4.2, where a unique approach was appropriate to assist an executive team undertake an unfamiliar task, and the present case, where there will be many newly created teams needing established guidance and procedures.

4.3.4 Pointers to Subsequent Chapters

The key issues concerned with the implementation of specific applications are addressed in Chapters 6 and 7. The first of these addresses general problems of developing applications which successfully meet the needs of organisations; that is having identified a specific requirement to use IT this chapter examines and makes recommendations on the management processes required for successful implementation.

Chapter 7 deals with the specific issue of the development of office systems. Here successful integration demands the active involvement of a relatively large number of clerical and/or professional staff if the system provided is accurately to meet their needs. Integration is achieved by a combination of a task force approach together with the use of questionnaires and interviewing techniques specifically designed to ensure that the needs of this situation are met.

4.4 Providing Service

4.4.1 Why Is Integration Necessary?

Ultimately the effectiveness in any organisation of its use of IT depends upon the actual and continued provision of the service to the user functions which is provided by the day to day operation of the computing equipment. As discussed earlier the provision of this service today demands widespread and effective cooperation between many groups of workers.

The key to achieving this high level of integration is measurement. Intuitive assessments are increasingly inadequate; only the establishment of a measured set of processes enables communication to take place effectively. This is required not only among the various groups within the service function but also at the interfaces between the service function and users. As pointed out earlier, service interfaces are more complex and multifarious than used to be the case and the need for measurement as a key tool is even greater.

4.4.2 Illustration of Failure

A large computer utility provided service to several user departments having differing needs. These included:

— An off-site department using the computer service as an integral part of a marketed service to outside customers
— An in-house department with a large number of research and development engineers using computing support intensively
— An in-house department with a fluctuating requirement for computing in support of intermittent short term projects

Forecasting of requirements was done on a different basis from the regular utilisation measurements and there were no formal agreements or service levels.

The desired service levels were substantially different for each department, as were the critical aspects of service. Consequently, there was no time when all users were satisfied and the situation remained in permanent unresolved contention.

4.4.3 How Can Integration Be Achieved?

The modern installation can only offer the service required if it establishes functions and individuals whose role is essentially integrative. In the past these have been provided by the operations function itself and may have accounted for a substantial overhead. There is now an increasing tendency for these activities to be assumed by specialist coordinating groups within user departments. The role of these groups or individuals, wherever they are placed, is to close the gap in communication between user and provider of service by understanding both sides and by managing integrating processes. In order for these processes to be effective they must be supported by measurement systems where the measurements are understood by both IS and users and are based on service level agreements.

Similarly continuity of service cannot be looked at solely from an IS perspective. Only if the needs of the organisation are taken fully into account can an effective recovery capability be established. The IS department and its various users (up to and including executive management) must jointly assess the issues of organisational requirements and continuity costs and take balanced decisions as to how these can be met.

4.4.4 Pointers to Subsequent Chapters

The issues of the provision of service are addressed in Chapters 8 and 9. Chapter 8 describes the management processes and procedures which ensure that effective service is delivered by the operational departments ('the DP centre' as it is frequently described) and in particular focuses on the measurements which are required if this is to be assured.

Chapter 9 addresses the issue of securing IT services and provides a framework which allows senior management to select the level of security investment appropriate to the risks involved to the business of loss of service.

4.5 Ensuring Benefits

4.5.1 Why Is Integration Necessary?

The issues associated with benefits measurement and ensuring value for the money spent on IT have received much attention but much of it has been generalised and non-specific. The question 'Are we getting value for money from our expenditure on IT?' is perhaps the most frequently heard of those raised by senior executives about their computing function. However, in most cases the question is no more than a vague enquiry rather than one focused on specific issues. Moreover, the attention paid to the question is sporadic rather than sustained.

At the lowest level at which this question has significance the concern is often whether what is being currently done with IT could be achieved at a lower cost. This relates only to the efficiency of the IS department and the way in which it works with its users. It raises issues of cost of hardware, numbers of operators, performance and productivity of programmers, etc., which are frequently difficult or impossible to answer unless they refer to a well managed and above all well measured environment.

A more meaningful question, however, would be 'Is our usage of IT giving us a satisfactory return on our investment?' This can be addressed by detailed audits of costs and benefits and significant work has been published in this area (Lincoln, 1986). However, audits are becoming increasingly difficult with modern applications unless a sound background of measurement and quantification has already been established.

The principle (and often unappreciated) difficulty is that the value of IT cannot be assessed if only the closed world of the technology is examined. The issue is that of value to the organisation and for this to be assessed, let alone ensured, an integrated approach must be made.

4.5.2   Illustration of Failure

An insurance company, having spare computer capacity while major new applications were being developed, decided to offer personal computing facilities to the actuarial department. These were taken up enthusiastically and rapidly occupied a large amount of machine time. When the first new major application was developed it was found that there was insufficient power remaining on the CPU to enable the new system to run with an acceptable response time for its users. Although the IS Director was willing to cut back on the machine power available to the actuaries neither he nor they had any measurements of the extent of their usage nor any measurements of business benefits which accrued to them as a result. They could not therefore agree as to priorities or time scales. Senior management became concerned that performance of the new application appeared unacceptable and concluded that the situation was out of control.

4.5.3   How Can Integration Be Achieved?

Integration across IS and user communities to ensure benefits are achieved essentially requires clarification of management responsibilities. Normally benefit accountability is assigned to user line management. However, cross-functional applications can introduce difficulties which in some organisations effectively prevent the implementation of such systems. There are therefore two issues, which must be addressed separately: the achievement of benefits from functional and departmental systems on the one hand and from large, cross-functional systems on the other.

Departmental and functional systems benefits must be dealt with within the normal management process and this must specify clearly the roles and responsibilities of both users and IS staff. There are three broad types of integrating processes which help ensure benefits at different phases of the implementation cycle. Firstly, the system investment process should ensure both that the prime user has defined the expected business benefit and that IS has specified the costs. Secondly, the project management process should tie together the key activities of both IS and users so that costs and time scales are kept under review and all user activities essential to achieve benefits are phased accordingly. User activities will typically include training, documentation, new working practices and reorganisations. Thirdly, an integrated planning and control process can be used to ensure that user operational budgets are adjusted to reflect committed benefits at the appropriate time and related to specific IS costs.

Cross-functional systems use similar integrating mechanisms but often require others in addition. Top level steering committees assist prioritisation of system investments and can take some of the responsibilities of line management. Sub-projects, specifically set up to ensure benefits are defined, targeted and achieved, can be helpful with very large systems. Special audit teams are sometimes used to check that committed benefits were actually achieved. As a general rule the larger and more cross-functional a system is, the more thought and resources are required to ensure that appropriate integration actually occurs. Failure to invest in these resources is perhaps the prime reason why these large projects have such a poor reputation.

4.5.4 Pointers to Subsequent Chapters

The issues concerned with quantifying and communicating to senior management IT costs and benefits are addressed in Chapters 10 and 11. Chapter 10 reviews the problems inherent in cost-justifying specific IT applications, analyses the underlying issues and recommends guidelines for preparing business cases. Chapter 11 looks at the issue of demonstrating to senior management the contribution made by the IS department to achieving corporate objectives and recommends an approach which draws together both quantifiable costs and benefits and user assessments and presents these in a consolidated report.

5 CONCLUSIONS

The pervasive use of IT in developed countries has borne out many of the predictions made in recent years. The impact on many organisations has been substantial but there is still widespread dissatisfaction with the extent to which the perceived potential of IT has been realised.

The principle problems can be traced, in most cases, to management issues. In part these arise from the difficulty of managing the particular esoteric skills needed for IT implementation but the underlying issue is wider and concerns the need for IS departments to interact effectively with the parent organisation.

As the use of IT has become increasingly essential to ongoing business processes, so has the need to coordinate business and IS functions more closely. Following the analysis of Lawrence and Lorsch (Lawrence and Lorsch, 1967) it can be seen that the introduction of IT has been a significant source of increased differentiation in almost every organisation. The differentiation of skills, attitudes and cultures is necessary if IT is to be used effectively but must be accompanied by effective mechanisms to achieve coordination.

This integration can be achieved in a variety of ways and partially effective approaches, such as joint IS–user working groups, are frequently used. However, it is clear that the integrating mechanisms are often inadequate and evidence for this is not hard to find. If integration is to be effective then sufficient resource must be deployed at the right levels and in appropriate ways. The key processes underlying the successful use of IT can be categorised as:

— Setting IS directions and policies
— Identifying and prioritising applications
— Implementing applications
— Providing service
— Ensuring benefits

Integration is necessary in each of these processes if they are to be carried through successfully. In each case, IS must come together with appropriate business groups, ranging from executive management in setting directions and policies to individual users in providing service. Different mechanisms need to be defined and carried through in each case. The remainder of this book is devoted to analysing and defining the specific approaches needed which successfully ensure integration at each stage.

REFERENCES

Aamodt, G.M., and Kimbrough, W.W. (1982) 'Effect of group heterogeneity on quality of task solutions', *Psychological Reports,* **50**, 171–4.
Bell, D. (1973) *The Coming of Post-industrial Society,* Basic Books, New York.
Benjamin, Rockart, Scott-Morton and Wyman (1985) 'Information technology: a strategic opportunity', *Sloan Management Review,* Spring.
Butler Cox Foundation Report (1987) 'Competitive-edge applications: myths and reality', Management Summary Report 61, December.
Butler, D. (1985) 'Information technology and real politik', Address to the International Conference of the Butler Cox Foundation, October.
Clemons and McFarlan (1986) 'Telecom: Hookup or Lose Out', *Harvard Business Review,* March-April.
Colombo, U. and Lanzavecchia, G. (1982) 'The Transition To An Information Society', *Information Society-For Richer, For Poorer,* Editor Bjorn-Andersen et al, North Holland.
Feeny, D.F., Edwards, B.R.,Earl M.J. (1987) 'Computer Organisations and the Information Systems Function' Research study report 87/7, *Oxford Institute for Management Studies,* Templeton College, Oxford.
Galbraith, J.R. (1977) *'Organisation Design',* Addeson-Wesley.
Gibson, C.F. and Hammer, M. (1985) 'Now that the dust has settled, a clear view of the terrain', *Index Indications,* **2** No 5 July.
Kearney Management Consultants (1984) 'The barriers and the opportunities of Information Technology-a Management Perspective', *The Institute of Administrative Management and The Department of Trade and Industry.*
Lawrence, P.R. and Lorsch, J.W. (1967) 'Differentiation and Integration in Complex Organisations', *Administration Science Quarterly,* June.
Lincoln, T.J. (1980) 'Information System Constraints-A Strategic View', *Information Processing 80,* Ed. S.H. Lavington, North Holland Pub. Co.
Lincoln, T.J (1986) 'Do Computer Systems Really Pay-Off?' *Information and Management,* **11**, No 1.

McKinsey and Company Ltd. (1968) *Unlocking the Computers Potential, A Research Report To Management.*

Porter, M. (1986) *Competitive Advantage*, The Free Press, New York.

Moynihan, T. (1982) 'Information Systems as Aids to Achieving Organisational Integration' *Information and Management*, **5**, No 4.5.

Price Waterhouse (1987–8) IT Review.

Pugh, D. (1979) 'Effective Coordination in Organsations', *Advanced Management Journal*, Winter.

Rose, H.L. (1984) 'Information Systems Planning and Implementation Process' *IBM Systems Management Consultancy*, Unpublished Report.

Thompson, J.D. (1967) *Organisations in Action*, McGraw Hill.

Toffer, A. (1976) *Future Shock*, Pan Books.

Weinberg, G.M. (1971) *The Psychology of Computer Programming*, Van Nostran Co, New York.

White, K.B. (1984) 'A preliminary Investigation of Information Team Structures', *Information and Management*, **7**, Nr 6.

Woodruff, C.K. (1980) 'Data Processing People-Are They Really Different?' *Information and Managment*, **3**, No 4

Van de Van A.T.T., Delbecq A.D., Koenig Jr. R. (1976) 'Determination of Coordination Nodes within organisations' *American Sociological Review*, April.

Chapter 2

EXPLOITING INFORMATION SYSTEMS—THE CEO SETS THE TONE

George Bauer

1 ARE INFORMATION SYSTEMS JUST ANOTHER CAPITAL INVESTMENT?

In the mid 1950s, at the dawning of the computer age, there were many exaggerated presentations about the wonders of computers, mostly pointing to what they would be doing in the future. One particular example was noteworthy, however, because it not only sounded outlandish but was said to have already happened. The talk was given at a large technical meeting in the United States and was entitled 'Can a computer create a freight car?' Engineers in the audience vaguely remembered undergraduate days spent studying thermodynamics, and some even remembered discussions about the second law of thermodynamics suggesting that matter could not be created or destroyed. But regardless of thermodynamics, creating a railroad car with a computer sounded like a pretty far fetched idea, so the audience listened with great interest.

The gist of the presentation was that apparently railroads have a certain number of freight cars that they use to haul products. Sometimes these cars belong to the railroads, and sometimes the cars belong to other companies that lease them to railroads. The problem a railroad has is how to maximise the use of both leased and owned cars. Evidently a computer had been purchased by a particular railroad to help in their complicated chore of keeping track of where all the cars were at any point in time, where they needed to be and how best to get them to their next location. The title of the talk struck home when the speaker contended that because they now knew more about their cars, sooner, they had more of their own cars available for hauling freight and hence had literally created new available rolling stock.

While the engineers in the meeting were still trying to reconcile the second law of thermodynamics with the railroad cars, the speaker went on to say that they were doing the payroll and accounting on the same computer. But the *coup de grace* came when he said the very same computer was the centre piece of their

Managing Information Systems for Profit.   Edited by T. J. Lincoln

effort with a certain government agency to make the case for higher freight rates. One was struck by the fact that although both the railroad cars and the computer were capital investments, there was a clear distinction between the railroad car, and the computer that 'created' the railroad car. It had not only to do with the power of the device to do logical operations, but particularly its ability to translate data into useful information.

The thought this example evoked in 1955 and indeed lingers today is the question of how one plans and organises in an enterprise, to make the best use of this power. Since planning and organising an institution is almost the job description of its chief executive officer (CEO), surely this must be one of his major preoccupations. There is little doubt today that the sheer amount of a company's investment in computing is sizable in its own right, and would normally command the attention of a very high level executive. However, this quality of being able to influence decisions about other capital investments and even operations, through its by-product, information, puts the computer in an unusual if not unique position. If one thinks about the railroad example, a freight car has a single purpose or function. Certainly there are box cars, chemical cars, coal cars, etc., but one thinks in terms of using that capital investment in a fairly known, predictable way. The method of making decisions about those capital investments is straightforward. Buildings can be treated in much the same way, and even variable function machine tools, although having several options, are also straightforward. But there is something a bit different about the computer capital investment. It 'did' different kinds of things in the case of the railroad. It seemed to have a certain integrating character.

It would appear that the nature of information technology is such that it cannot be treated as just another capital investment, but must be seen as an integral part of business planning and operations. Whether as a productivity tool to human effort (accounting/payroll) or as a way of getting fresh insights into reality through information (creating railroad cars), special attention must be paid to it in the business process. But there are some even more profound issues that make a focus on information technology of particular interest to a CEO. One is its potential to open up new ways of doing business or competing and another is the effect it can have on the very way an enterprise is organised. Little wonder then that more and more the CEO is looking carefully at information technology and concluding that it is more than just another capital investment and needs to be managed in a more sophisticated way. A recent business opinion survey conducted by Price Waterhouse (PW Information Technology Review, 1986–7) makes the point dramatically. It says: 'IS has become an accepted newcomer to the boardroom. It is not something that can be bought. It must be managed'.

Much has been written about the management role in business or in any institution for that matter. In the classical sense it is usually summarised in three magic words: Plan–Execute–Control. There is a certain universal sense in which this is a description of any management role, whether a first-line manager or the most senior executive. One difference is the dimension and scope of each of these words. As one travels up the conventional organisational pyramid, the emphasis at the lower levels is heavily on execution, while the higher one gets in an organisation, the more planning and control become the key factors.

At the top of a business, the CEO has the role of doing very broad planning and handing down and negotiating objectives with operating units or functions, and doing very broad control (*The Economist*, June 1986). Execution is largely a role of engaging in the objectives process, creating the right environment within which planning can take place and sending the right signals to the organisation.

It is the thesis of this chapter that the role of the CEO is not only to engage in certain top level planning and control work himself, but to create the planning and control mechanisms within which his managers do their planning and controlling, particularly with regard to IS. This chapter will explore ways in which the power of computing can be exploited in an organisation and how a chief executive officer can assure that he is getting the maximum return from his investment. The chapter focuses in turn on the role the CEO has in planning, executing and controlling his IS investment.

2 THE CEO ROLE IN PLANNING IS

If the above is true, one of the key roles of the CEO is to create a planning system that not only accommodates traditional business planning but also this unusual animal called information systems. This is his way of assuring the IS plans relate to and support the business plan. He must create a planning system that forces this.

Many CEOs become schizophrenic at this point. Since they have usually come up through a specific discipline, they quickly become 'content oriented' in their specific discipline when dealing with planning. There is a great temptation with senior management to quite naturally gravitate their thinking about IS planning to something they know best. Thus they become deeply involved in that area with which they are most familiar. It is not unusual for them to spend much of their planning time in the bowels of their speciality. The former salesman will tend to spend a great deal of time delving into potential marketing aids. The former industrial engineer will want to review in detail the IS strategy of the manufacturing department and the former accountant will spend a great deal of time probing the control aspects of the finance systems.

One of the fundamental roles of the CEO, however, is to assure that a planning system and particularly an IS planning system exists which assures that lower level management will properly do their job of planning. The CEO role is not a detailed technical one of creating plans. It is largely one of assuring that the right creative business minds and creative technical minds have come together, have communicated and have developed executable plans as a result.

A picture may be helpful in describing what a typical business and IS planning process might look like. Figure 1 shows a general outline of such a process as successfully practised by many large and medium sized companies today.

The key thing to note here is that the process is highly interactive and interdependent. It happens at two different levels. The first four steps are strategic in nature, usually looking forward three to five years. The last two steps are tactical and deal with the specific allocation of resources. The process usually happens at two different times: the strategic phase often in the spring of the year and the tactical phase in the fall of the year looking to the next twelve months. Following are typical stages in this planning process.

2.1 Step 1—Setting Enterprise Goals and Objectives

This is the task of assessing the environment of the future, making a set of assumptions about what will happen and then deciding where the enterprise wants to be in that future. Goals or mission may be thought of as qualitative and directional in nature. Objectives are often thought of as quantitative or translating goals/mission into hard targets. An example may be helpful. Consider the recent case of a money management arm of a large financial services firm in the United Kingdom. The future environment was one of deregulation of the securities markets, and a wider ownership of stocks and bonds. This could lead to a set of assumptions about the size of the unit trust (mutual fund) market, including institutions and individuals. The goal of this money management firm may either be to become a substantial factor in the broad market or a major factor in a niche market. This is a qualitative judgement. In this case the firm chose to be a major factor in the utility unit trust niche market.

With some analysis,a decision can be made about what part of the market is reasonable for the firm to capture. This is a quantitative decision.

Thus the money management firm set a goal of being a major factor in the $500,000,000 utility unit trust market as the securities market deregulated and had an objective of $100,000,000 under management in five years (20% of this $500,000,000 total utility unit trusts) with a gross revenue of $500,000 or 1/2% of funds under management.

The CEO of the institution has the role of assuring that the process for assessing the environmental assumptions and creating goals and objective is present. He must also initiate action and make decisions on what they will be for the firm. In the example of the money management firm above, he may choose to go for 20% of the utility unit trust market because that is the critical mass necessary to retain good people to manage a unit trust. This is the kind of intuitive judgement the CEO brings to the business planning process. Thus

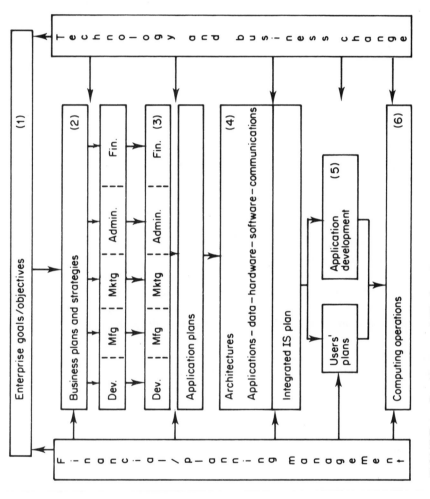

FIGURE 1   Business and IT planning

the CEO creates a planning system and lends his experience and judgement at the very outset.

It may seem strange that the CEO role in planning information systems begins with this kind of a summary of his business planning role. Although this initial step in the planning process may use IS as a tool to do the necessary analytic work, the more important point is that the stage is set for the next level of management to do its strategic planning, particularly its IS planning. With this process visible to the lower levels of the organisation, they in turn can see specific direction and become more serious about their part of the effort. This visibility is the beginning of assurance that the IS investment will indeed support the business.

2.2 Step 2—Setting Functional Objectives and Strategies

The next step in the process is assuring that the overall objectives of the company are translated into functional objectives. These in turn need strategies to support them. Strategies are simply ways of meeting objectives. Thus a revenue objective of $500,000 in the case of the investment company translates into certain sales volumes, and the marketing function must in turn create strategies for advertising, sales aids, etc., to accomplish these volumes. This work is normally done in each of the line functions and some of the staff functions including the IS function. It focuses on the makeup of the future environment to take advantage of emerging functional opportunities. Associated with this planning is a set of assumptions on which the functional strategies are built. These become the base assumptions, and changes are appropriately made to the strategies when assumptions change.

As these functional strategies are being developed, they will generally create IS requirements. The extent to which they do will depend in large measure on the knowledge and experience of the functional strategist. However to get the maximum benefit for present information systems investment and insight on future IS possibilities it is essential that the IS group be involved with the functional strategies at this point. The IS person must have a significant knowledge of today's technology and developing technology. If properly done this joint effort should not only ensure a better articulation of the functional IS requirements but should stimulate the functional strategist to think more creatively about his options. In many cases this process has literally opened up new ways of doing business as the business mind catches a glimpse of what is possible today or in the future with computing. In the case of the investment company, for example, the tying in of terminals in a broker's office to a central system, allowing quotes and sales proposals on-line for individual clients could well be the key to capturing $100,000,000 of the utility unit trust business.

Another example of marketing–IS interaction was the Management Services Director of one very large insurance company in the United Kingdom beginning to promote the idea of a portable personal computer for its direct sales agents long before a viable, commercially available product was on the market. Recent announcements have now confirmed his foresight and much ground work has already been laid. Not only is a device now available and the data to supply it been developed, the company's sales management has embraced a new way of doing business. The key role of the CEO is to construct a planning system that forces the functional strategist to take note of IS as both a support to and creation of strategic thrusts.

Thus a subset of the functional strategies becomes the functional IS requirements. These must be stated clearly and must capture the fruits of the interactive process between businessman and technologist. IBM, for example, in its own internal IS planning has called this statement an 'identifiable module' of IS support. Based on the old adage 'If you can't describe it, it may not exist', this statement becomes essential. The test is that it should be thorough enough so that any executive who calls for it could read it, understand it, and assure it was included in the corporate IS strategic plan. As a matter of fact, nothing enhances the quality of these modules quite as much as a CEO periodically asking to see one.

There is one other additional element of the 'identifiable module' of IS support for a business plan and that is a statement of value. At strategic plan time, it is very difficult to develop a conventional business case with a comprehensive cost/benefit analysis. Actually, too much quantification at this point can inhibit creativity. The emphasis at this stage is on how we can use present or future IS, or data, to implement strategies which meet objectives. The word 'value' is important because it connotes something broader than 'benefit', and does not get confused at this point with rigid cost/benefit numbers. Dotting the 'i's' and crossing the 't's' cannot be forgotten, but comes at a later stage. Enough is simply not known at early stages to do a thorough analysis, but the 'user' can be pressed for how a system will help them, qualitatively.

2.3 Step 3—Developing IS Functional Plans

As the interaction of functional strategist and IS analyst progresses, the general IS application programmes which respond to the functional requirements take shape. These may either generate new data or use data that already exists. They may have communication dependencies. They may use existing investment or they may require new investment. They may require skills that do not exist. Step 3 is the translation of functional requirements into terms that can be understood and dealt with by the IS community. This requires great conceptual skill, especially at this early stage, and demands senior people. Hopefully much of it can be done in parallel with Step 2, if the right interaction is taking place between the analyst and the function. This work is often done by a separate group in the IS organisation, reporting directly to the Director called the requirements and strategy group. It should carry the power and the proxy of the IS Senior Management in carrying out this work.

In the case of the investment company, Step 3 becomes putting 'meat on the bones' of the IS requirements that support the functional strategies. Not only must administrative systems be developed to process unit trust orders but data bases and communication networks are needed to support the terminals in brokers' offices. This network not only allows brokers to access information in selling unit trusts but could potentially accommodate the broker ultimately placing orders. The skill needed in this step is not only developing a strategy for the use of technology that meets the needs spelled out in the functional plan but a strategy that allows flexibility to accommodate as much change as possible. Thus in the case of the investment company, today's batch network and order entry applications design should cater for the possibility of on-line order entry along with inquiry with the associated communications techniques sometime in the future.

The CEO through his IS management must urge that the most flexible kind of IS strategies as Step 3 be developed. He does this by insisting that his IS analysts know as much as possible about his functional counterparts' problems. He must also insist that the functional counterpart has signed off on the IS support so there is commitment on the part of the function that the IS support is adequate and that the cost will be accepted.

It is at this point that the statement of value in the identifiable module of IS support should be a planning requirement. As the IS strategy takes shape to support the function, the function should begin to fine tune its value. In the case of the investment company, as the administration systems take on flesh, it may have a functional objective of improving administrative productivity and statements of value should be consciously focused on, as Step 3 concludes.

2.4 Step 4—Developing the Integrated IS Strategic Plan

This step becomes one of integrating the applications needed to support the functions into a coherent IS plan. The combination of the functional applications downward in Figure 1 becomes the corporate IS strategic plan, just as the upward integration of the functional business strategic plans becomes the corporate business strategic plan. This process requires great knowledge and experience. It is the critical stage of the process and where most organisations are weakest. The business applications need to be translated into four main architectures which give the general shape of the four main elements of the IS plan. They are, in their order of construction:

1. The data architecture
2. The applications architecture

3. The hardware/software architecture
4. The communications architecture

The extent and complexity of these will be commensurate with the size and complexity of the business supported. However they, like the identifiable modules of IS support, should be inspectable by the CEO or his representative. More often than not, after the initial strategies are set up, they will only have to be modified year on year based on new technology or new requirements.

In our investment company example the marketing and administrative applications must be integrated with finance and other functional applications to develop a combined architecture. This architecture is very much like the traditional use of that word. Just as the architecture of a house defines how rooms are placed and relate to each other, so the applications architecture gives shape to the individual applications and shows how they relate to each other. By the same token, the data architecture is much like the foundation of the house, serving various rooms and supporting new additions. Just as once a foundation is set, it is difficult to change, so the data architecture must be as comprehensive as possible to accommodate change.

Just as the architectural detailed drawings of a house spell out size of walls and strength of floors to support the functions of a house, so the hardware, software and communication strategies become the structure within which the IS work takes place. It must be an integral part of the planning process.

The main role of the CEO is to assure that the same kinds of disciplines and processes so necessary to build a house are imbedded in his IS planning process. It is common for many CEOs to be intimidated by their technical management at this stage. Although the jargon can be a superficial barrier, this process, like so many others that need to be managed, usually yields to a commonsense approach to questioning.

As one moves through the mechanical and technical processes of planning, it is often easy to forget one of the most important IS strategies—human resources. An assessment of future skills needed, both technical and managerial, and associated strategies to get these skills are essential to accomplishing the technical strategies. The issue of rotating personnel in and out of the computing department for better user understanding and management training must be tackled in the strategic IS plan.

2.5 Step 5—Tactical Application and User Planning

While Step 4 concludes the strategic planning process, Step 5, tactical planning, is just around the corner. Most companies begin their operating plan, or following year's budget, in the fall of the year. This plan becomes the translation of the first year of the strategic plan into hard projects and resources. The main focus is on development projects and computer capacity, with the balance between maintenance of old applications and development of new ones a critical factor. Major issues of priorities usually surface at this point in the planning process. The CEO should assure that a proper escalation procedure exists so that the option exists for him to get involved if his senior functional executives have a conflict of requirements versus development resource. His key consideration should be that strategic directions are not completely sacrificed at the altar of near-term expediency.

It is important that the operating plan focus on adequate resource in the using function. The concepts of data and systems ownership should be key corporation concerns. That responsibility and associated resource are essential to carrying out the user role. The user, if an integral part of the IS strategic plan process, should see the IS operating plan process as a commitment to his strategy.

2.6 Step 6—Developing the Tactical Computing Plan

As a part of the operating plan, the computing facility is perhaps the most important. However, if the process has worked well to the last step, it should go relatively smoothly. Computer capacity planning becomes the combination of all the previous application work. The main CEO role is to assure that the facility is effectively used and that corporate policies are in place to give direction to its structure. It is the implementation of the strategic hardware/software architecture articulated in Step 4.

There are two remaining parts of Figure 1 that need explanation. The block to the left in Figure 1 represents the necessary glue that holds the entire process together. Since the IS planning process should be an integral part of business planning, the IS planning process should be the responsibility of whoever the CEO charges with that business planning role. There is a certain amount of written structure associated with a planning system. In addition, administration of that structure is a sizable task. A calendar needs to be created and administered. Decisions have to be made at many points and interaction of many parts of the organisation are necessary. Thus the glue necessary to keep the entire process together is a comprehensive job. These disciplines are usually associated with finance or a separate planning function. It will often include an analytic unit that does some planning content work for the CEO, particularly in the objectives setting area. But no matter where the planning function exists, it should get the attention of the CEO as it develops the framework of the planning process. He is the owner.

The block on the right side of Figure 1 makes the point that one thing about the future is certain; there will be changes. These will be both technological and business changes, and must be accommodated. Thus the strategic and operating plan documents are not books that gather dust on the shelf. They must be updated at various levels based on the significance of the change. There is a body of thought that says planning is a waste of time because changes will make plans invalid. That is right as far as it goes. But the basis for business or IS planning is not that we can predict the future infallibly or that it will not change. The rational for planning is that we know the assumptions on which our present plans are based. When these change, we have a base from which to move intelligently. The CEO must assure that his planning process, particularly for IS, has this self-correcting mechanism built in.

The above notwithstanding, a word needs to be said about not becoming too bureaucratic in the structure of the planning process, both IS and business planning. There are those who talk disparagingly about the structural approach and this clearly is a danger. In a recent study (Butler Cox Foundation 1985) some findings indicate that an analytic, deterministic approach does not result in double IS plans. And that certainly is a potential outcome. It would seem that the fact that a structure exists is not the problem; the problem is that it may be the only thing that does exist, with no content. This structural dimension of planning is essential, but only as a skeleton. Without the muscles, nerves and brain, it is as inert as the skeleton that resides in the zoology lab at any school. But by the same token, without the skeleton, not much happens with a human being.

3   THE CEO ROLE IN EXECUTING THE PLANNING SYSTEM

If it is true that one of the key roles of the CEO is the creation of an effective planning process, then certainly another key role is to assure the effective execution of that planning process. The job here is one of assuring that adequate staff work is done, that there are effective mechanisms for allowing the right technical minds and business minds to interact and that the CEO is engaged in the process at key points. Perhaps the first most important point at which the CEO must enter the execution picture is at objective setting time.

3.1 Manage the Objectives Debate

No matter how one begins the business/IS strategy process, the CEO will inevitably be drawn into the objectives process, formally or informally. It has often been said that setting objectives is 'the easiest thing in the world, or the hardest thing in the world, depending on how serious one is'. One of the key roles of the CEO is of course to set objectives for his institution. They must be realistic and achievable, but more importantly must be accepted by the various parts of the organisations as reasonable targets toward which to shoot. If the objectives are not reasonable, the strategies, or 'ways of achieving the objectives', will be equally unreasonable. It is important that adequate analytic staff work has been done that describes a particular opportunity. But more important is the negotiation and iteration that takes place on the objectives between the senior manager and his divisions or functions so that the latter feel a sense of ownership. This process of negotiation of objectives is extremely important not only for the organisation but also for the IS strategic plan. It is not only the way the CEO forces imaginative business strategies, it is a way of forcing the organisation to make the best use of existing or new information technology. After objectives have been agreed, the typical future picture looks like Figure 2. The present products and/or services tend to drop off over time, and get further and further away from the objectives.

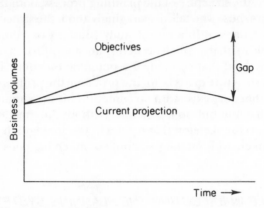

FIGURE 2   The planners' dilemma

This phenomenon is often called 'planners' droop' and is the beginning of the creation of strategies, both business and IS. This process does two things for IS. First it calls on the IS function to create systems that contribute to narrowing the 'gap' between objectives and projections. Secondly, it assures that at the end of the day IS resource is prioritised to assist the business rather than build technical monuments.

The CEO must engage in and assure the objectives debate is carried out at each level and execute the final decisions on the targets the organisation will go for. If done properly, the ownership of these objectives and the associated strategies or 'ways of meeting these objectives' should filter down through the organisation, and forces the execution of effective IS strategies at every level.

3.2 Focus on the Business Equation

Generally objectives are set in most organisations at a very high level. For example either in terms of return on investment or net profit after tax. These then get translated into divisional or functional objectives as they filter down to lower levels. One of the real inhibitors in most organisations to the comprehensive use of IS resource is not enough emphasis on each part of the business equation. That equation is classically expressed as follows:

$$PROFIT = REVENUE - COST - EXPENSE$$

The basic objective of course is to increase profit by increasing sales/revenue, decreasing cost or decreasing expenses and preferably all three. By starting at this basic level, a CEO can cause the focus of IS to play on the fundamental elements of the business. One of the problems of technical people is they often have trouble identifying with the things that motivate senior management. One of the best ways for the CEO to assure that his IS resource is supporting the business is to assure that throughout the organisation all of the elements of the business equation are being looked at in the execution of planning for information systems. Once objectives are set in one or the other of the parameters of this equation, they become fair game for the IS strategist.

Traditionally the 'expense' element of the business equation has been the prime focus of information systems. The beginning applications were in the accounting area, where the clerical processes were mechanised and expense reduced by replacing one expense component—people—, by another expense element—machines. Computing is run in many companies as an 'expense' or 'cost' centre, quite independent of the main thrust of the business. Coming at the most effective use of IS from this direction often inhibits its use to a straight dollar-for-dollar replacement in the expense element of the equation. There is nothing wrong with this phenomena but the CEO should be encouraging the use of technology in broader ways than these traditional ones. A way to do this is to focus on the sales/revenue and cost elements of the equation. Much has been written about the use of computing in reducing the cost of manufacturing a product. However, with the movement of over half of the companies in Western world countries to 'service sellers', the cost of these 'products' become proper targets for IS. Providing railroad cars to the right place at the right time could be seen as the service the railroad performs and computer plays a vital part in reducing the 'cost of product' element of the railroad business equation.

By the same token, new order entry systems of many companies are obviously aimed at more than the expense element of their business equation. Their major growth in revenue volumes is due in large measure to the focus they put on the sales element of the equation. By allowing customers ease of order entry often by direct on line access and by the associated competitive advantage, the sales element of their business equation goes up dramatically. It is quite possible that at least initially the expense element may have gone up as a percentage of revenue, but ultimately that became the thing that enabled sales to go forward. This is precisely the kind of thinking the CEO wants to encourage as the planning process is executed across the organisation.

3.3 Ensure Department Boundaries Do Not Dominate

The CEO must constantly be aware of the inherent conflicts and 'turf' issues in his organisation, and consciously deal with these elements as he implements his planning process. The first reality is that functional managers do not tend to look across organisational lines. Thus the CEO must first perceive cross-organisational possibilities, and then press the planning process to deal with these possibilities, either in the context of the regular planning process or in special issue-oriented groups, sometimes known as 'task forces'. It has often been suggested that the most effective way to develop and implement IS plans and strategies may not be with the traditional planning tools alone. The suggestion is that a far more important component of the process may be the recognition of the fundamental human characteristics of 'turf' control.

Perhaps the most important management system issue in the planning of IS is the danger that the natural boundaries between functions in an organisation will be a hindrance to the best use of IS. Most managers, like the senior executives who tend to want to tinker with the systems in their area of expertise, have come up in business through a particular discipline, be it sales, manufacturing, finance, engineering, etc. It is quite difficult to think in terms of processes that may go across functional or traditional organisational lines. One of the important things the CEO must do—perhaps his most important IS role (because only he can promote it)—is to assure that cross-functional looks have been taken at business processes to assure that IS possibilities have not been overlooked. In a real sense this is where the lateral thinking of his systems analysts give him clues. Because the IS function gets to know most of the functions of business in quite an intimate way, they often have insights into new ways of viewing the business processes that are not apparent to others. Thus the CEO can use the IS analysts to stimulate him on potential cross-functional ideas that he can then explore in the strategic planning exercise.

Perhaps an illustration of how one company dealt with a cross-functional strategic issue would be helpful.

As methods of selling product shift, the traditional boundaries between sales, administration and distribution are beginning to blur in many industries. The growth of markets brings new demands on the process of marketing in its broadest sense which is more and more coming to include not only selling but administration and physical distribution as well. And often the IS support becomes an integral part of that process. The chief executive must recognise this and create an environment, both planning and human, that allows creative thinking to be done. The following example describes how IBM dealt with a cross-functional issue, that is typical of the computer industry, as well as many other industries.

The need for a new approach to marketing certain products began to emerge in the early 1980s as volumes of low cost products became an increasing part of total sales. Firstly, the sheer volume of products such as terminals and personal computers was straining the then current administrative processes of ordering, scheduling, releasing, etc. Secondly, the profit margins on these new high volume products were such that the traditional costs of marketing were prohibitive and a more efficient interface with the customer was appropriate. And lastly, the bulk nature of the physical distribution process needed to be accelerated. A build-to-order mentality needed to be replaced by a 'just-in-time' delivery from stock mentality. Through the strategic planning process, this emerging phenomenon came into focus. Initially the planning in each of the sales, administration and distribution areas began to overlap and it became clear that a different approach was needed. This led management to call for an aggregation of plans across functions. What would not have been done, had individual functions continued down their traditional paths, was forced by the senior management. Their role was not to invent the system, but rather to press the appropriate elements of the organisation together in a new way in order to create a new method of doing things. The human clue to this amalgamation was the creation of a new kind of marketing thrust that allowed an entrepreneurial spirit for a narrow, but definable part of the business.

In this case a strategy for 'high volume/low cost products' was brought forward. The functions of sales, administration, physical distribution and information systems forged a new approach for marketing in its broadest sense. It basically allowed a customer, either through its sales person or direct interaction with the warehouse, to order such a product, individually or in bulk, and assure delivery consistent with the customer needs. The approach is comprehensive and includes dealers as well. This new approach required a move towards standardisation which in turn rippled back into the development and engineering strategies and in turn reduced product costs. As so often is the case, these kinds of new approaches have many by-products.

The associated logistics have brought about a major restructuring of the various processes associated with the distribution of a product and they became embedded in the various operating plans of the interested functions. One of the major changes facilitating this new approach as well as shaping it was the IS systems that support the processes. They are in fact the gating factor and early involvement was essential to the effort.

The main point of this example is simply this. The legitimate role of senior management or the CEO was to:

1. Perceive changing conditions in the business.
2. Set in place a planning system that not only forced functions to look at their traditional roles but new ones as well. It also forced a cross functional look at processes.
3. Insist on a hand-in-glove relationship with information systems, not only to facilitate new business strategies but also to shape them.

3.4 Ensure Planning Group Dynamics

Perhaps the most important stage in executing the IS planning process is the interaction of step 2 and step 3 of Figure 1; that is developing the functional strategies and the IS plans that support them. As in the case of a task force looking across departmental or functional boundaries, the CEO must foster mechanisms or methodologies that force the businessman and technologist together within a disciplined or structured framework.

One approach to achieving this is known as 'executive information planning' (EIP). These sessions often last several days, and usually are conducted at off-site locations. They operate best when stripped of 'hierarchical' influence, and strive for peer to peer relationships among the businessmen, and between the businessmen and the technologists. The group usually operates best with a facilitator, a person who focuses primarily on process and moves the group through an agreed agenda. This is ideally a third party who has no role in the subjects being discussed. He should be no one who poses a threat to any of the EIP participants and is skilful in leading interactive sessions. Often a third party resource person is helpful in these sessions. His role is quite different from that of the facilitator. He listens carefully and helps clarify business issues, knows IS and hence can help identify technical issues. This resource person must also be no threat to the participants and often plays the part of coach, offering intellectual leadership if the sessions begin to flounder.

A closely related approach focuses on critical success factors. This approach begins the session with an articulation of those things that must go right if the organisation is to succeed. This approach has the effect of isolating what is important, prioritising these factors and seeking ways IS can support the accomplishment of these factors.

A third approach is to begin with the constraints, either within the organisation or within the present technology, that keeps the businessman from making his objectives. The approach not only forces out IS strategies that may not have been conceived until then, but also has the effect of generating a list of action programs that deal with tactical problems. These 'constraints reviews' often highlight management systems issues and 'turf issues' that must be dealt with before technical issues can be attended to.

One of the key roles the CEO plays in the execution of the planning process is assuring these kind of group dynamic sessions are going on. Many CEOs are concerned with the size of their computing bill, as well they should be. They are plagued with the question of whether they are getting value for money in this important area. One of the best ways to have a comfortable feeling about the IS investment is to feel comfortable that the planning system has been well executed, with the users who pay the bills firmly exercising their leadership role.

But the job is not over! The gnawing question still remains: 'How does the

CEO know when the planned value hits the bottom line?' The answer can be summarised in three words ... inspect, inspect and inspect!

3.5 The CEO Role in Controlling the IS Plan

No discussion of the CEO's role would be complete without mention of his control or inspection role. There is an old adage that seems to be true: 'People tend to do what you inspect ... rather than what you expect!'

And experience has shown it clearly applies to information systems. Many existing financial control mechanisms in the fabric of any business focus on IS, such as capital acquisition procedures and normal accounting control, but these do not get at the broad level of control apropos to the CEO. The control the CEO exercises over IS is achieved via the following:

1. Inspection of strategic plans
2. Inspection of operating plans
3. Setting corporate IS policy
4. Ensuring value from IS investments

Each of these control mechanisms are discussed further below.

3.5.1 CEO Inspection of Strategic Plans

As indicated earlier, the strategic plans are usually done in the spring of the year and are completed towards the end of the second quarter. The business units or functional groups generally present their plans to senior management for approval at that time. These plans are largely visions of the future which state the business goals and objectives, certain comments about the future environment in terms of assumptions, and the strategies—that is very broadly how the objectives will be met. The role of the CEO will be to review these in some detail and, with assistance from his staff, test them for reasonableness. While the bulk of the executive time is normally spent on the business strategies themselves, it is important at this time to call for an inspection of the 'identifiable module' of IS support which the planning process has called for. The focus should be first on the process used to develop the content of this module. Did the right people participate in its construction? Is it included in the business unit or functional IS support plan and has it been signed off by the proper parties? And perhaps most important, what is the value of the proposed IS investment? The planning process should call for a statement of value to be included in the support module and this can now be inspected. It is important to recognise that at strategic plan time, quantification of cost and value must necessarily be very broad and imprecise. The objective of the strategic plan is to get as much creative thinking as possible into ways of using

IS to support the business strategies. It is not to do a thorough cost/benefit analysis.

At this point the CEO can probe the extent to which there is evidence that cross-organisational thinking has been done. Normally he would look to his planning or finance staff to help identify such opportunities. As mentioned earlier the IS function, with the proper leadership, can often bring insights about 'processes' which go across organisational lines and how they might be improved. Some CEOs go so far as commissioning a separate piece of planning work which takes a 'process' look across the whole business and has as its objective how these processes could be improved both with and without information technology. The main objective of this inspection is to assure that no possibilities for the use of the present IS investment or new investment have been overlooked because of traditional organisational lines.

And finally after the process of developing the IS strategies has been inspected, and the knowledge and experience of the CEO has been brought to bear, the remaining work to be done is a review of the IS strategic plan itself. That plan is a translation of the IS strategies expressed in the various business plans, into an integrated IS strategy that will accommodate the future. As mentioned earlier this plan contains a series of architectures describing the future course of data bases, computing applications, as well as hardware, software and networks. One does not need an indepth knowledge of technology to probe these major areas. They are broad roadmaps, and should be tested for their ability to meet broad user requirements. A key question of course is: 'Have the operating functions signed off on the IS plan?' This would include a sign-off on the projected portion of the cost each operating unit would be charged for.

3.5.2 CEO Inspection of Operating Plans

The inspection role continues with a review of the business operating plans and associated budgets, usually in the fall of the year. The main focus of these business plans are the tactical programs and associated resources to accomplish the next year's objectives and ultimately the strategic objectives.

Thus the operating plan must be inspected from an IS point of view, to assure that investments are being made and programs implemented that keep the business on the strategic track. Just as in the strategic plan there should be an identifiable module spelling out the broad IS support needed, so in the operating plan an identifiable module should be inspected. That module must state what the IS investment is and how that investment moves the function along its strategic path. Not all IS investments will be strictly for business-as-usual. A review of the difference between long and short range accomplishments should be looked at for a proper balance, particularly in application maintenance versus application development. Most CEOs of dynamic industries like to see over 50% of their applications resource going to development.

Perhaps one of the most important things the CEO should assure at operating plan time is that when an investment is made in IS, the associated quantified benefits in using departments are actually captured in the department budgets.

In the operating plan, a key focus is on 'doability'. Just as in the strategic plan, one is more interested in creative ideas and broadly what are the opportunities for IS, so in the operating plan one must be almost ruthless in the demand for doability, particularly of the applications development plan. To inspect this dimension of the operating plan, the three key factors in applications development failure must be looked at. The first is an adequate definition of user requirements, the second is technical skills in the IS department and the third is a development project–management system. If inspection shows these three issues are adequately attended to, the development plan can usually go forward and will be successful. With regard to IS investments for the IS department itself the same rigorous quantitative and qualitative scrutiny should be applied.

3.5.3 Setting Corporate IS Policy

One of the instruments of control the CEO uses is corporate IS policy. There needs to be a corporate umbrella under which the IS planning in the various organisations can be done. These policies are normally thought of as part of the 'powers reserved' in multidivisional or multinational businesses. The main aim of these IS policies, or standards/guidelines as they are often called, is to ensure that the best interests of the corporation are protected. Each should be tested against that criterion and found legitimate. The publication of these policies sends signals to the rest of the organisation about how the CEO views IS and the way he wants IS implemented. Many CEOs are sensing that they need flexibility in managing multiple divisions or multiple functions, and they need to lay down some standards to control their IS environment. Some major areas susceptible to this kind of policy thinking can be summarised in the following categories:

1. Computer environment standards—a guideline spelling out what hardware and software environments are appropriate for subunits of an organisation, for example to preserve the flexibility of combining or splitting product lines or organisational entities.
2. Network environment standards—a guideline spelling out what communication facilities and protocols are appropriate for subunits of an organisation, for example to facilitate communications across units in terms of data, electronic mail, voice, image, video, etc.

3. Data management standards—a guideline spelling out definition of data and roles/responsibilities for ownership of data, for example to preserve the data in each operating unit as a corporate resource.
4. End user computing standard—a guideline for handling the decentralisation of computing power, for example to preserve the proper use of IS at each level of the hierarchy while allowing the maximum use of operational data.
5. Security standards—guidelines to assure adequate protection of data assets within the corporate entity as well as customer information consistently across business units.

These corporate policies become legitimate factors to inspect as the CEO reviews both the strategic and operating plan.

3.5.4 *Ensuring Value from IS Investments*

Another control instrument the CEO uses is the procedure for assuring that the benefits from IS investments are captured. He must ensure that a control process exists to test cost and value at each of the stages in the life cycle of an IS project. A schematic of such a process may be summarised as in Figure 3. The process starts with a description of the IS support needed by a user. This is coupled with a statement of value and becomes an integral part of the business plan. Then as the IS project moves through the IS management system, the project control procedure must call for progressively more specific statements of cost and value. As the project definition clarifies, more precise estimates of IS cost can be projected. And as the output of the system takes shape the user becomes more able to estimate value, both quantitative and qualitative. These further refinements should become part of the decision process for moving from each phase to the subsequent phase of the project management system. As the final phases of implementation are reached and the major investments take place, the quantitative value should be imbedded in the user departmental plans. And if no quantitative value is available, a statement of qualitative value should be in the user operating plan, so the CEO can again assure himself that the value justifies the investment. Another step is often taken six months after system implementation, to audit the results once again, to test costs against projection and to test the value of the system against the original projections. This post-audit is another indicator of how well the process is working.

As the CEO reviews plans and as he gets involved in IS matters through various inspection mechanisms, he should test for himself the existence and operations of what many call this 'interlock system'. If the savings generated by information systems are not captured in the operating plan, they probably will not happen.

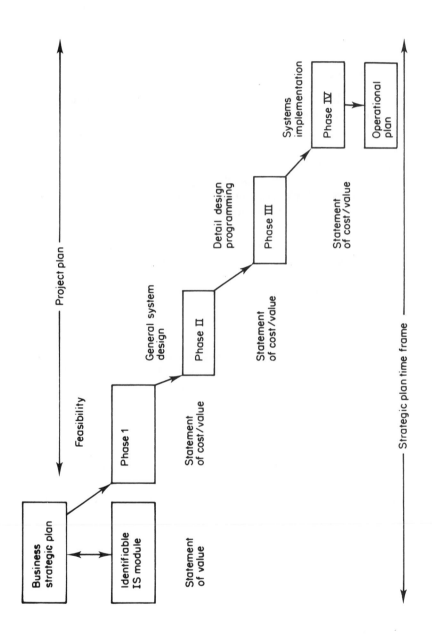

FIGURE 3   Cost/value appraisal

4 SUMMARY—THE CEO'S CHECKLIST

As a way of summarising the CEO's role, both in terms of planning as well as the instruments of control, the following checklist is offered. While not comprehensive, it represents what experience has shown to be some of the main points which, when adequately focused on, make for successful IS plans.

4.1 Strategic Plan

1. Do the business strategic plans have an 'identifiable module' on IS support required to accomplish the business units strategies and are they accommodated in the IS plan? Look at one or two each plan period and see if they make sense. Do they have statements of value associated with the major requirements?
2. What is the evidence that the IS group has stimulated the functions or business units to think creatively about the use of technology in their plans for accomplishing their objectives?
3. Does the IS plan accommodate the users requirements—have the users 'signed off on the plan'? Do they 'own' the plan?
4. Does the IS strategic plan conform to the corporation policies on IS in the areas of:
   (a) Common technical environment
   (b) Networks
   (c) Data management
   (d) Data security
5. Is there evidence of 'cross functional' thinking going on?
6. Are there any business issues that have been identified as a result of focusing on IS support that have not been concluded?

4.2 Operating Plan

1. Is the operating plan a legitimate first year of the strategic plan?
2. Is there an interlock mechanism that assures that tangible value/benefits are captured in the operating budgets of the using departments?
3. Are the application development plans doable in terms of requirements, skills and project management discipline?
4. Does the IS operating plan conform with the corporation policy on IS in areas of:
   (a) Common technical environment
   (b) Networks
   (c) Data management
   (d) Data security

4.3 Is IS Worth It?

After all the foregoing effort is expended, the CEO might well ask, 'Is IS worth it?' There is much in the management literature today that deals with the potential of IS. It ranges all the way from gaining the competitive edge to creating entirely new markets. A recent charge from a finance director to his IS management team at a final session of a week-long intensive planning session says it all. 'We look to you fellows to protect our flanks; to be sure you are working so closely with our business functions that we won't be scooped by a competitor with new technology, or miss a market opportunity because we were asleep at the IS switch.'

There seems little question that IS warrants a stronger top management involvement. It may well be that the frontier of IS is not in how many more circuits we can stack on a microchip but in how we can more effectively manage what we already have. Reflecting back to the 1955 question 'Can a computer create a railroad car?', one is still fascinated by the question of how one manages the power of a computer in an organisation. There appear to be no magic answers; only magic words! And these are *plan, execute* and *control.*

REFERENCES

'Developing and Implementing a Systems Strategy,' Butler Cox Foundation, October 1985.

PW Information Technology Review, Price Waterhouse of UK, 1986–7

Chapter 3
EFFECTIVE IS POLICIES AND STRATEGIES IN MULTI-DIVISIONAL ORGANISATIONS

Brian Edwards

1 INTRODUCTION

1.1 Power and Authority

This chapter is about power and authority, as applied to the direction of information systems activities in all but the simplest businesses. In any consideration of power and authority there are two domains:

(a) The rationally and objectively argued issues, where we assume the players to be broadly altruistic, seeking the greatest good of the organisation
(b) The subjective and emotional areas where personal ambition, rivalries, pecking orders, job satisfaction and stress dominate

This chapter addresses the first domain, for two reasons:

(a) Because this does not purport to be a book about management psychology.
(b) More importantly, because if the objective structures and systems are comprehensive and satisfactory, the destructive potential of the subjective side is constrained. The creative potential, the voltage generated by subjective feelings, can be effectively channelled.

'Power and authority' in business can be described in terms of *topics*, that is those things about which managers ought to have discretion, and in terms of *bounds*, that is the financial and other limits on discretion.

This chapter will develop the idea that power and authority, in relation to IS management and direction, can be applied distinctly to two areas. These are STRATEGY, which identifies *what* information technology (IT) is to be applied towards, and POLICY, which describes the framework of principles and rules which describe *how* IT is to be planned and managed.

Managing Information Systems for Profit. Edited by T. J. Lincoln
© 1990 John Wiley & Sons Ltd

1.2 Why Is This Chapter Being Written?

It is written because in some years of consulting work I have come upon many cases where organisations have become almost paralysed through ambiguities and conflicts in this area. There is a perpetual tussle between forces tending to centralisation and others seeking decentralisation, and there is often a belief that a satisfactory resolution can only be found in the victory of one or other of those extremes.

The business environment to which this chapter relates is a multi-divisional one. The immediate image summoned up by that is the conglomerate type of commercial enterprise, where several business units operate with some degree of autonomy, possibly in varied industry sectors. But it is equally applicable to tightly integrated businesses, with functionally differentiated divisions, to municipal authorities, to some government departments and to large businesses which are segmented regionally.

All such organisations face a continuing management dilemma: how far is it appropriate for the divisions to go their own way; how far should they be coerced or constrained by the centre? Devolution is generally thought to produce benefits in terms of entrepreneurialism and initiative. Centralisation on the other hand aims to generate economies of scale in operations, to achieve critical mass in certain resources, to promulgate a coherent and healthy group culture and to preserve organisational flexibility through consistent practices and systems. This dilemma affects many aspects of group management, but none more than IS, because of the scale of the investment, the long pervading effects of key decisions and the extent of cross-functional business processes.

I am not here referring to the centralisation and decentralisation of computing, but of authority. In fact, compromise positions can be described and justified. Simply by showing this to be so managements have been given greater confidence in themselves and their frequently pragmatic arrangements.

1.3 Towards Productive Compromise

The arguments in favour of the compromise position commended for many (but not all) organisations will be developed in the following way. Firstly the dilemmas facing organisations are illustrated by real cases of conflict, and sometimes of mutual suspicion. Then the different kinds of authority needing to be distributed or reserved are explored in increasing detail.

The discussion in this chapter is based on extensive consulting work in many government and private businesses, and also on formal research. This took the form of a field study in which I was involved (Feeny, Edwards and Earl, 1987).

In this chapter it is made clear where the research explicitly supports the arguments and assertions.

2 SOME REAL CASES—TOP MANAGEMENT DILEMMAS

A feature common to all the following case studies is that the dilemmas were articulated within senior management circles and escalated ultimately to group board or chief executive officer (CEO) level. In no case had there been a consultative or decision making process (for IS) at top level before that escalation. In some cases the need for such processes was recognised through the debates generated.

It is not suggested that the solution adopted in each of the following is held up as an ideal; the purpose, rather, is to illustrate the diversity of approach.

2.1 A Large Petrochemical Group

This had operated for years in a stable market by running a highly integrated and centrally controlled operation. With the increasing volatility of oil industry economics this made less sense. The business was redefined as a number of divisions, each of which was set relatively free to be entrepreneurial and innovative within specified trading and product boundaries.

The 'relative' freedom included the right to build and operate IS resources, and some divisions did so. The dilemma was: where did that leave the central IS resource, hundreds strong, which had hitherto enjoyed a position of monopoly supplier to the group? Should it continue to exist? If 'yes', should its remit and organisation adapt; and if so how?

The solution adopted included the following dispositions:

(a) A group was established at corporate level to articulate and proclaim group policy about specified aspects of systems and technology principles and practices.
(b) The 'central IS resource' was redefined as a profit centre organisation, offering benefits to internal clients in terms of specific skills and assets.
(c) Both these institutions were placed in the portfolio of a corporate director, who established a high level committee to review and authorise their dispositions and investments.

2.2 A Large Municipal Authority

This was at an advantage in having a treasurer and an IS chief who were wholly convinced of the business case for extensive implementation of office systems in the City Council's departments.

The powers in the land were, however, the chief officers of the departments, and the Council committees and sub-committees which direct their priorities. The dilemma was: how could the need for departmental direction and prioritisation of office systems be reconciled with adequate technical convergence? How could the Council assure itself that the potential of office systems in the varied portfolio of Council services and management approaches got systematically reviewed?

The emergent process divided the issues into two sorts:

(a) Definition and selection of the most appropriate technical vehicles and vendors for providing office capability—this was placed with the existing corporate management services organisation.
(b) Deciding upon the functional requirements and priorities of each business area or department (Housing, Education, Environmental Health, etc.) within the department, but under the overall authority of the committee of chief officers and key committees of elected members.

2.3 Fast Moving Consumer Goods

This represents an important industry sector, but one which is coming under increasing pressure owing to the growing power of retailers and the static nature of many markets, in volume terms at least.

The origins of DP in one branded food company were typical, based on creating a central IS stronghold as a service to the operating units. That IS stronghold began to be seen, whether fairly or not, as remote, arrogant, expensive and irrelevant to the units' real business problems and opportunities. What could be done? The dilemma was how to develop flexibility and responsiveness while not writing off the investment.

Once again, there were seen to be two kinds of issue, and the solution involved recognising the difference between:

(a) The functional needs of the divisions (which were genuinely different both in nature and in priority)
(b) The technical environment embracing both a redefinition of the roles and authority of the central IS strongholds, and a statement of direction for key technical components

2.4 A Technology Based Group

This had been composed by the merging of a number of previously independent companies. Continuing go-it-alone strategies in IS matters began to exasperate group management, to the point where the group commissioned the construction of a set of group common systems. These were aimed primarily at the production information and inventory control application areas, including MRP.

To build a common system is one thing; to implement it across a series of business units which still operate as fiercely independent baronies is another. Do the common systems stand a chance, and if so what modifications to group habits are necessary to enhance that chance? The dilemma can be summed up as cultural incompatibility.

At the time of writing a solution does not appear to be close. A functional systems base which might possibly be objectively unimpeachable lacks champions in divisions and sites. The difficulties of migrating from diverse local systems to the common system have not been appreciated. There is no basis of authority and mandate within the business management structure to provide the management pressure or voltage necessary.

2.5 A Large Quasi-Public Sector Business

This is investing heavily in an extensive IS development which is aimed primarily at making the company more reactive and responsive to its customer set. This development will be implemented across a number of regionally defined business units.

What are the prerequisites for success in implementing the common system in all of the regions? How will less enthusiastic regions be induced to conform? What should the regions do about IS application potential which appears to lie outside the intentions of the common system? The dilemma focuses on what autonomy the business really intends the regions to possess.

Major joint reviews were undertaken in which the following issues were formally addressed so that both the specific common system and other systems ventures will be pursued with clear authority:

(a) The business benefits of the key common system, and what the business units needed to do obtain and to confirm them
(b) The group-wide technical provision including the concentration of computing into fewer major, more cost effective data centres
(c) The divisions' degrees of freedom to pursue systems initiatives independently, and the means of selecting and mandating future common provisions

The above is a tiny sample of the cases in which I have been involved, where the issues have been control, mission, influence, decision making, investment, priorities, veto, consensus; or in short: *power*. People feel instinctively that IS ought to be susceptible to the same business processes that direct other technology based support, with apparent acceptability. (For example many of the groups operate fully charged-out research divisions successfully.) It does not seem to be so: why not? One reason is probably the fact that IS impacts, in a novel way, so many of the human and cultural aspects of an organisation's work and habits that it is different from other technological developments. The customer–contractor relationship which can support a divisionally sponsored research project in the group research division cannot cope with the intimate needs of an organic systems venture.

3 STRATEGY AND POLICY

In this chapter these two words will be used in somewhat specific ways in order to make some points about managing systems in complex organisations. It is not necessary for the world, nor even for the reader, to use the words in this way for those points to remain valid, but some influential people in the business are beginning to do so.

Any search for dictionary definitions quickly shows that these words have been used almost interchangeably, which is why it is impossible to be prescriptive. But one can make a personal selection, and two definitions which come closest to the present intentions are:

strategy   A method, plan or stratagem to achieve some goal
policy   The principles upon which any measure or course of action is based

(Both from New Webster's *Dictionary of the English Language*)

The words STRATEGY and STRATEGIC have been grossly overused both in business generally and in discussions about IS. 'Strategic' frequently is used to mean simply 'important'; 'the strategy' sometimes means some plans which have no obvious justification save a very high level source in the organisation, or very expensive consultancy, as their origin! In this chapter we will use 'IS strategy' to mean *what is to be done* with and through IS services. This will be explored and exemplified in the following Section 4.

The other word to be used in a special way is 'policy', which for the purpose of this discussion is distinguished from 'strategy'. This word has been less abused in business. However for present purposes it is the distinction which matters. Policy will be discussed further in Section 5.

4 IS STRATEGY—OR DO WE MEAN STRATEGIES?

The term 'strategy' was introduced earlier. We need to be clear about what the strategy is about, what it is for and what makes for a good strategy.

4.1 Charting the IS Contribution

A useful approach to the discussion is to start with the diagram in Figure 1. This is a simple chart which allows us to explore where an organisation is, and where it would like to be, in terms of IS contribution.

A position on the vertical axis indicates the contribution which IS makes to the *basic business operations*; taking orders, instructing store movements, billing customers, paying people and so on. The highest points on this axis are probably occupied by the clearing banks and the scheduled airlines. Other financial services businesses are quite high; low technology metal bashing is often very low on this scale. Retailers are quite scattered, but some are moving up fast through both store systems and distribution systems.

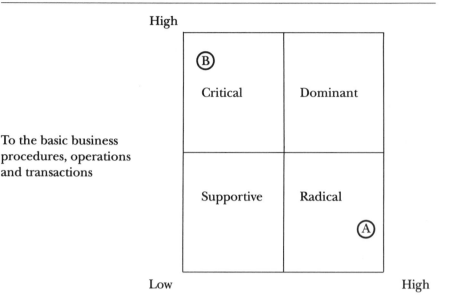

To the basic business
procedures, operations
and transactions

... To the business image; the *next* products
or services; market adaptability; active or
defensive competitive positioning; binding
suppliers, agents or customers

FIGURE 1   *The contribution of information systems*

The horizontal axis indicates the contribution which IS makes to the
organisation in rather different areas. These are more to do with survival
and dominance in the marketplace: the *next* products or services being
developed; image to the customer; competitive positioning, in either an active
or a defensive sense. 'Competitive edge' is an overused but compact term to
describe these kinds of objective. In Britain there is an outstanding example
of this in the retailing of one travel operator's inclusive tours: Thomson's TOP
system (Feeny, 1988).

It could be possible for an organisation to have a combined position
anywhere on the diagram. The fact that current operational IS systems have
only a modest contribution to transactions does not preclude an organisation
from conceiving of a major breakthrough in competitive edge terms—so it
could be low right (A). Similarly another organisation might be dependent on
IS to the limit in transactional terms, but might have no differentiation from
its competitors at all, and so be top left (B).

4.2 The Naming of Parts

It is useful to identify and name certain domains in the above chart:

SUPPORTIVE   IS is performing usefully in the organisation, but is not seen as a key factor either operationally or competitively.

CRITICAL   IS is so embedded in the business operations that an outage causes a major crisis which would rapidly be brought to the attention of very senior management.

RADICAL   In this area IS is no longer a way of doing the business differently; it is a way of doing a *different business.*

DOMINANT   IS is both the key vehicle for delivering or controlling the products and services of the business, and also the means through which the business extends and consolidates its market position and financial performance.

Consultants are notorious for reducing any aspect of Life, Truth and the Universe to a 2×2 matrix! Sometimes boundaries exist arbitrarily for naming purposes. In this case the domains are truly distinctive; the boundaries are discovered when an organisation is moving from one domain to another, either by accident or design. It experiences strain or even crisis as management approaches which are suitable in one domain are found to be inappropriate in another.

4.3 Management Issues

Some 'management approaches' which need to be adapted or even transformed involve:

(a) The kind of *leadership* which the IS resource requires under the different circumstances
(b) The correct *placement in the organisation* for IS
(c) *How much money* the organisation should be thinking of spending on IS
(d) How to assess the *effectiveness* of that spend in relation to the business objectives
(e) The view taken of *competitors'* IS practices and developments
(f) The possible business effect of a *computer disaster*, and the response to that

4.4 Components of IS Strategy

It is salutary for any organisation to consider where it now lies, and where it would like to lie, in that pattern. Making those judgements and putting plans in hand to make the necessary changes are what an IS strategy is about, namely:

WHERE   the organisation intends to get to, in terms of systems support to the business or systems integration into it.

WHEN   various target positions need to be achieved if they are to be effective.

PROFITS   attributable to achieving the target positions—or indeed the penalties of failing to do so.

RESOURCE   implications; not only in terms of money for technology, but also of skill and human resources. In doing that the users' investments should be considered, as they can exceed that incurred in the more obvious technology areas.

RISKS   associated with the strategy—that is the risks to achieving benefit, the risks of overrunning in time or cost. (Only if risks are clearly charted is it possible to work out how to manage them and to lay contingency plans.)

It used to be said that IS strategy should respond to the business strategy, and that a prerequisite to good IS strategy formulation is effective feeding from the business planning processes. That model is insufficient now if we consider IS ambitions of the competitive edge sort. That is because the IS capability to do some function, or to do it at a drastically lower cost, may now be a *determinant of* business strategy, an enabler of new products or services. Consequently the interplay between business and IS planning needs to be continuous.

4.5 An IS Strategy Aimed at a Radical Objective

A recent example in the UK of a simple but truly radical application of IT illustrates a number of the previous themes. It concerns the retail grocery trade. A changing pattern of trading (towards superstores) was making the smaller high street supermarkets unprofitable. Two chains, Tesco and Finefare, actively explored alternative uses for these stores.

One use would have been as deep discounting 'box stores', where limited lines are sold with minimal store costs. This sector was however already well penetrated by profitable competitors.

The search for differentiation identified a key constraint in that type of operation, namely that the number of lines that could be run in a store was limited by the number of prices that the checkout operators can remember. That is because low operating costs are only possible where the goods are not individually price marked and where checkout can be rapid and productive.

Now the number of prices that can be remembered is around 250, which when multiplied up by flavour options leads to around 700 line items. An electronic point-of-sale (EPOS) system with bar-code scanning does not have that constraint (there are limits, but they are in the tens or hundreds of thousands range).

If, then, sufficient merchandise lines had been packed so as to be scannable and to offer a full range, a store could operate:

(a) With a richer assortment
(b) On low store costs
(c) With enhanced customer service
(d) With the opportunity of good sales data

provided that EPOS kit were available at an acceptable price. It was, and projects were launched. The results were the then new Victor Value chain from Tesco and the updated Shoppers' Paradise chain from Finefare. Both were very successful, as the first grocery chains that had implemented EPOS as an indispensable and integrated component of their retailing and merchandising strategy in the UK. This was reported in the financial pages of the serious and popular press at the time.

Note that it is no longer possible to isolate the expense and benefits of the IT component of the investment separately. It is an implicit part of the total relaunching package, along with store refurbishments, new graphics and logos, new own-brand lines, new uniforms and all the rest. Without the technology however this new store profile would not have been possible.

A further interesting point about the example is that the scale of the IS investment was not huge and the amount of systems development was minimised by using available material where possible. The elapsed time from concept to first stores live was very modest: a system of radical significance does not necessarily require a mega-project.

Returning to Figure 1, it should be noted that positions in the grid are not stable. That is to say that a given application might in maturity regress from a right-hand side position. It was suggested that this case illustrates a 'radical' application. In time, the rest of the trade may catch up. Consequently, the set of systems could become simply 'critical' or they might become the foundation and springboard (to mix the metaphors) of a continually innovatory process for developing the business and systems integrally. This is what has been dubbed 'dominant'.

The reason for expanding on this case is that it is all illustrative of IS strategy— it is about what systems can and should do for and with the business. Clearly it can only sensibly be developed and articulated at business unit or divisional level, unless the business opportunity is manifestly a group-wide one, requiring a common systems approach.

IS strategy is therefore about what, from a business perspective, is needed by way of system services and applications. Sometimes a distinction is made between 'IS strategy' and 'IT strategy'. IT strategy is about the ways and means through which technology in total is mobilised to deliver the IS strategy. It may not necessarily be developed at the same business level as IS strategy.

5 THE LIMITATIONS OF IS STRATEGIES

Further exploration of the components and right orientation of strategies could absorb a whole chapter but our present concern is the response of the multi-divisional organisation. It would not in fact be possible to characterise say the British GEC or Texas Instruments or American Express at corporate level in terms of that analysis of possession of IS strategy. The businesses within those groups are so disparate that each of them could have a distinct position now, and an ambition for the future which is possibly different from its brothers. That is to say, in my terms and usage, each business or division is likely to have a distinct *I/S strategy*.

So far we have considered what an IS strategy is, and how fundamental it can be if an organisation plans to imbed IS and IT in its very brains and sinews. Chapter 2 in this book discusses the planning process through which the strategy can emerge both to reflect the Chief Executive Officer's business requirements and to maintain technical integrity.

We need now to consider what is the position of the top businessman when he is no longer Chief Executive Officer (CEO) but Head of Division, Divisional Managing Director, Chief Officer (in the municipal sense) or Permanent Secretary (in the British Civil Service sense).

Many aspects of the IS planning that the Divisional Manager becomes involved with require precisely the same processes as those the CEO uses, notably those involved with evaluating IS potential (see Figure 2), assenting to justified investment cases, adjudicating priorities, and reshaping the business in response to the challenge of IS opportunity. How then does he differ?

The difference is that, as in much else of what he does, the Divisional Manager operates within the framework of group policy. Other policies relate to such things as accounting and financial planning, personnel, corporate advertising and logos, property and estates, and procurement. In those other policy areas the policies can range from group preempting all the work of definition for divisions to totally devolving it to them.

Most common is the arrangement where the topic is delegated to businesses, but where either rules or guidelines shape the way the businesses do it, for example by defining contents and structure for individual business's plans.

Exactly the same applies in IS, but it is surprising how often these *how to order it* features become confused with *what to do*. At the risk of being repetitious: the former are what we have called POLICY and the latter are about STRATEGY.

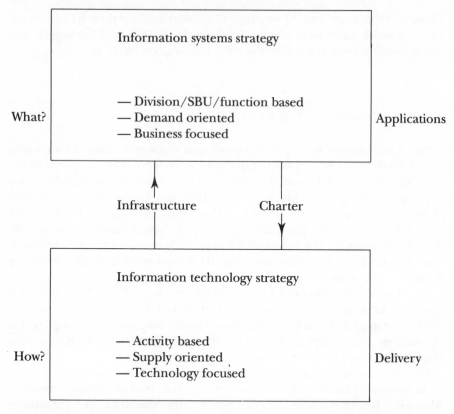

FIGURE 2 *Information systems and information technology strategies delineated (Earl, 1986/88)*

6 IS POLICIES DEFINED AND DEFENDED

Why have policies in a multi-divisional organisation at all? The answers are not exclusive to IS; they are partly active and creative, and partly protective. Active reasons include:

(a) Propagating methods from the most effective members (divisions, business units, etc.) to those others to whom they are relevant
(b) Developing a depth and breadth of skills in the group which the businesses individually could not aspire to
(c) Setting financial rules which are designed to facilitate initiative
(d) Exploiting every possible area of potential group synergy

Protective reasons include:

(a) Ensuring proper evaluation of risks and of quality
(b) Preserving coherence in group operations
(c) Preserving organisational flexibility
(d) Setting financial rules which are designed to compare things equitably

6.1 Enabling and Restraining Policies

Later, in Sections 6.2, and 6.3, there is a discussion of IS policy topics. Every multi-divisional group should understand its position in relation to each topic, as one of:

(a) 'We do not feel justified in having a policy about that and so we have decided not to develop one.'
(b) 'We ought to have a policy about it but haven't yet established it.'
(c) 'We have a policy and it is so-and-so.'

Section 6.2 lists and discusses ENABLING POLICIES. These are policies which, if articulated, aim to promote, foster and speed the deployment of effective information systems and services. Section 6.3 deals with RESTRAINING POLICIES, which aim to control the IS activities of each business either for its own good or for the greater good of the group. Both these lists have been built up after dozens of encounters with multi-divisional organisations, examples of which formed Sections 2.1 to 2.5.

The origination and validation of these sets of policies are themselves interesting. The lists were first generated in response to a client's challenge; having been persuaded of the validity of the strategy/policy distinction, he wanted to see a comprehensive list. Later there was an opportunity to validate the lists in field research. The lists are presented in decreasing order of frequency in our sample.

If we consider that the active exploration of IS potential is important for divisions individually, and for the group collectively, enabling policies are obviously of first importance, and they are accordingly discussed first.

6.2 Enabling Policies

6.2.1 Group Resourced Services

There are several kinds of group IS resource which can be made available to divisions including:

(a) People, e.g. consultants
(b) Technical, e.g. national network

(c) Research and market intelligence about computers, software, outside consultants

(d) Full range IS service department; in other words a self-sufficient data centre including technical support and development services

(e) Central/shared R & D

A 'full range IS service department' may be present simply as a take-it-or-leave-it service, or it may be made the only authorised source of IS development and operation, or it may be dispensed with.

6.2.2 Negotiation of Volume Discounts, Privileged Terms

In a buyers' market *or* a sellers' market, the leverage obtainable through group procurement is considerable. Group procurement should not be confused with group standardisation.

6.2.3 Shaping Suppliers' Approaches

(This is to managing marketing, support and servicing across the enterprise.) 'Shaping suppliers' approaches' means inducing suppliers to respond to the group's organisational intentions and to employ communications channels that foster the group's integrity. It is not helpful if a computer supplier tries to exploit anarchic local ventures *or* massive rationalisation if these are not consistent with the way the business is trying to run.

6.2.4 Charge-out Rules

It may be surprising to find these asserted to be an *enabling* policy issue, but in fact the only reason for going to the bureaucratic trouble of charging out anything to businesses should be to influence behaviour. For example, to charge out pro-rata for mainframe usage promotes prudent consumption; to modify this by allowing a first year holiday promotes innovation and changeover from old to new. Charge-out may exist between group resource and business units, and/or from units to users.

6.2.5 Need, and Terms of Reference, for a Group I/S Controller or 'Guru'

This position is increasingly being created in multi-divisional groups, to be the developer and guardian of the group IS policy. It is frequently distinct from the position of the manager of group IS resources. The key policy issue is sometimes held to be the extent of his mandate. This is unreal; the issue is really what is the extent of *group management's* writ in IS matters.

6.2.6 Provision of Common Systems to Business Units

'Systems' here includes 'services', such as Office Systems or Information Centre services. The *policy* issue is not about what applications of technology should be developed in common but about what criteria should be used in selecting them. These should have a great deal to do with the intentions of group management towards the business units.

Virtually every proposition for a common system will meet resistance from business units, for a mixture of subjective and objective, and valid and invalid reasons. These militate against its prospects for successful implementation. Consequently the venture requires:

(a) Justification of an unassailable order
(b) A powerful management system that will ensure adequately flexible response by group, and ultimate compliance by business units

6.2.7 Reviews of IS Potential in Business Units

The policy states who carries these out—when, how and with what external help (group or outside).

The group may be more zealous than some of the divisional management to ensure that IS opportunity is kept under *active* and *regular* review, and may organise help for this.

6.2.8 Asset Sharing

For example:

(a) 1 MVS test site
(b) Loadsharing
(c) Equipment swapping
(d) 1 disaster fall-back site

Where common machine and software architectures are agreed, it can be a usefully economical approach to create shareable resources. But the justification and funding of these can present problems.

6.2.9 Legal and Tendering Procedures; Complex Bid Management

For many divisions a radical system venture may involve unprecedented relationships and decision processes. It aids and lubricates the processes if there is an understood and accepted rule book, and if any group procurement organisation fully understands the distinct problems of IS procurements.

In the generation of requests for price quotation (RFPs), and bid and benchmark evaluation, radical systems ventures will be stretching the conceptual and technical capabilities of business units. A group may decide that expertise in this area can usefully be disseminated—or provided as a group service.

6.2.10 IS Manpower and Skills Planning

In the three plus decades of history of the IS professions this has been a continuing problem. Approached on a group basis, some of the problems can be reduced.

6.2.11 Organising Unit Missioning for Production of Corporate Common Systems

'Unit missioning' is where one division mounts a development project on behalf of several or all divisions, in contrast to the use of a central or external development resource. This feature does not need to be considered unless there are expected to be group common systems.

6.2.12 Retention of Outside Consultants

Professional and suppliers' consultants can provide a valuable service, but it is helpful if a coherent policy exists about engaging them, and about assuring their conclusions.

6.2.13 Benefit Reclaim and Postaudit Processes

'Benefit reclaim' is shorthand for the business processes that ensure that asserted system benefits are actually reflected in both qualitative and quantitative business plans and controls—and hence are actually achieved. 'Postaudit' is concerned with assessing the effectiveness of installed services, confirming or challenging their business benefits and recommending improvements.

6.2.14 Group Negotiated Technology Agreement

It surprises some people to find this topic listed as an enabling one. But where Trades Union cooperation is essential, comprehensive arrangements are to be preferred to piecemeal ones, and can become most effective lubricants.

6.2.15 Other Enabling Policies

These emerged as suggestions or were not included in the survey. These were:

(a) A forum, voluntary or mandated, for divisional IS executives
(b) Project management for IS implementation
(c) Intercompany electronic data interchange (EDI)
(d) A systems component in career planning for business General Managers
(e) Umbrella policy about IS management issues and organisation within business units
(f) Choosing the placement of application systems among mainframes, distributed systems and intelligent workstations

6.3 Restraining Policies

'Restraining policies' sounds like a negative concept. Possibly 'converging policies' would have been a better title, but the other has now had considerable currency. The essential point is that these policies exist for positive and beneficial purposes. Note that some headings sound similar to those in the enabling list. This is because the 'downside' of having rules is that there must be procedures through which they are administered.

Tidiness is not a significant business objective, unless it contributes materially to results. So in IS terms the restraining policies can only be justified if they possess positive virtues when seen in business results. Energetic clutter can be more effective than orderly but moribund disciplines.

6.3.1 Compatibility Requirements

(a) Network architecture
(b) Machine and software portfolio
(c) Data interchange with corporate systems

'Compatibility' is different from 'group IS standards' (see 6.3.6). Compatibility provides a required degree of interconnecting capability or of organisational flexibility in reassigning operational units among business. 'IS standards' are more important for assuring the auditability of what has been built and for allowing career moves of people across the whole group rather than just within a division.

6.3.2 Degrees of Freedom for Business Units to Procure and Operate I/S Equipment and Services

This relates not only to buying and running computers but also to employing IS professionals or contractors, developing systems, and building a technical support capability. If group management decide that there should be *no* such freedom, they need to be careful in justifying it and in policing the situation!

Included here is the rulebook for IS procurement sign-off, which must be clear about what differences there are (if any) from other non-IS procurement rules. Also in this group is the whole issue of budgeting for capital and revenue expense.

6.3.3 Mandating Process for Common Systems

The manner of constraining business units to accepting and operating common systems is a key issue, and policy must accept and reflect business culture. Common systems may be mandated, or businesses may be offered financial incentives to use them, or common systems may simply be made available, with no more than guideline status.

6.3.4 Extent of Provision

For:

(a) Disaster recovery
(b) Privacy and security
(c) Quality and systems audit

The issues here are the policy about investment to cover these items, the justification for that investment and the means of ensuring compliance. The brevity of this paragraph by no means reflects the importance of these three issues.

6.3.5 Conformance to Any Industry Standards or Guidelines

This is here presented as a defensive policy—we must not get shut out of any emerging consensus. A more proactive policy could well be justified in some industries, actually taking a lead in developing and negotiating standards, or taking a dominant position in standards authorities such as the Article Numbering Association for retailers in Britain.

6.3.6 Group IS Standards

For example, documentation, data dictionary, languages, etc. The objective of these standards is to allow the group to ensure the general integrity and security of its information/data resources. By enhancing the communicability of information about systems, standards also maximise the opportunity of sharing systems among businesses.

6.3.7 Conformance to Group Job Specifications and Levels in IS

This can permit or obstruct career flexibility throughout the group for its IS professionals, depending on how far it is observed in business units. Career planning and personal progression need a commonly understood language and set of definitions if they are to be fair and effective.

6.3.8 Degrees of Freedom for IS Units in Respect of Outside Revenue Earning Activities

There are attractions in offering services for sale, but they usually involve possible diversion of skills from internal application. A policy here is vital.

6.3.9 Charge-out and Benefit Reclaim Procedures

Charge-out *procedures* are restraining, in that they require conformance to bureaucratic or computer based procedures for planning and control, in order to implement the hopefully positive charge-out *rules*.

6.3.10 Staffing Levels

That is headcount benchmark. The group may or may not wish to influence the people—intensive aspects of the units' IS ventures in quantitative terms.

6.3.11 Ergonomic Standards

For example, for VDU operators. This is an issue which applies uniformly across all business units, and the group can validly decree what level of assurance is expected.

6.4 Authority for Policy

Field research showed that most of the policies in both groups were present to some degree in most of the subject companies. The approaches to enforcing policies were:

'Advisory' 20%
'Mandatory' 20%
'Not mandatory but very powerful' 60%

Conformance was achieved in the limit by:

Board arbitration 40%
Financial sanctions/finance community 40%
Others 20%

The single most surprising feature of the above rankings was the moderate showing of three policy topics about staffing, skills, careers and headcounts for IS staff. This is surprising because we hear so much about the chronic problems that DP managers face in respect of skills and resources, and group standards or initatives might have an ameliorating effect.

Only 40% of IS executives volunteered present or past skill and resource issues as failures, weaknesses or things to be improved. We believe this suggests that, though by no means licked, the skills and resource problem is now less dominant as a concern. It may be that it is simply accepted as a fact of life, an environmental condition which has to be managed around.

6.5 Selecting Policy Topics

It was stated earlier that the lists of policy topics is somewhat daunting. They are less so if we recognise that the relevance of any one topic is strongly affected by the nature of the multi-divisional organisation.

Many of the policy topics will be seen to be key issues, and others of peripheral interest only, when any particular multi-divisional group is considered. But a review of the applicability of all the items gives confidence that one has been thorough.

Consider, for example, the type of multi-divisional group which is composed of regional divisions which offer identical services to the customer set in each of their regions. The presumption will be very much towards homogeneity and consistency, and so those topics which are concerned with issues like common systems and the policy about distributing the computing work will dominate the planner's thoughts.

In one complex retail chain nine policy topics (five enabling and four restraining) were selected for most immediate attention. This illustrates an important feature; any organisation reviewing the lists will find its own priorities.

The retail chain appeared to need most immediate attention to the following:

(a) Group provided services
(b) Provision of common systems and 'unit missioning' to build them
(c) IS manpower and skills planning, and asset sharing
(d) Charge-out rules
(e) Benefits reclaim and postaudit
(f) Degrees of freedom to run IS in the units
(g) Compatibility requirements
(h) Industry standards and guidelines
(i) Group sign-off on IS procurements

These conclusions, and a number of other specific recommendations about distribution of decisions and resources, were not arrived at principally through discussions with IS people. Rather, the executives interviewed were chosen to represent the operational and planning parts of the business. This emphasises that the approaches to IS policy formulation are essentially determined by business culture and the ways in which that may be changing.

7 ORGANISING IS IN MULTI-DIVISIONAL ORGANISATIONS

This section is concerned with the general deployment of IS resources to corporate and business/divisional entities in the organisation, not with structures within an IS department. It comes late in the chapter by design, because organisation planning should not be undertaken until many of the policy choices have been made—choices, that is, about what topics the group needs to have a policy for and what that policy might be, at least in outline.

7.1 Unqualified Centralisation and Decentralisation

In two extreme cases, organisation of IS support need be no different from that suitable in a unitary business. These are:

(a) The business which determines to retain central control of resources, planning, service delivery, etc., in spite of possessing some elements of multi-divisionalism. This is 'centralised'.
(b) The business which runs its divisions at arms length, and operates as a remote holding company. Hence each division will be on its own, just as if it were a free-standing plc, in respect of IS organisation. From a group perspective this is a totally 'decentralised' option.

Between these two extremes there will be many intermediate positions, but all of these should recognise that there are some IS issues which rightly belong to divisions and others which must remain 'powers reserved' for groups. Divisional issues will in particular focus on what IS should be doing for the division's changing business needs. Group powers reserved will deal primarily with the definition of policy as described in the foregoing, and with the articulation and monitoring of it at divisional level. (It must be remembered that there is a strategy dimension here too because there will be a need for corporate IS applications and services.)

7.2 Adaptations of Centralised and Decentralised

These extreme forms of centralisation and decentralisation are less common than other intermediate forms, and yet organisational choice is still presented as 'either–or'! In the research already alluded to (Feeny, Edwards and Earl 1987), the frequency of five distinct forms and the apparent trends observable then (1987) were explored. The need to modify the perceived arbitrariness and remoteness of a classic centralised arrangement has led to two kinds of adaptation:

(a) Making the IS resource respond more like a business and show greater customer sensitivity
(b) Power sharing through the sort of devolution of strategies already described, modified by policies or powers reserved

The five organisational models are, briefly:

(a) Centralised—corporate service: the classical group data centre, with mandate, providing all services to the group companies
(b) Centralised—internal bureau: as above (1) but running in a 'businesslike' way as a profit centre
(c) Centralised—business venture: as above (2) but having an additional mission and revenue target for outside work
(d) Federal: some corporate powers reserved and some corporate services, but much activity and authority devolved
(e) Decentralised: no controls over divisions' IS beyond standard planning and control requirements, e.g. for capital sanction

It was found that the number of instances of each model as the *predominant* form in each case was as shown in Figure 3.

The combination of some centrally reserved powers with other locally delegated ones sounds very like a federal system, in national politics, which is why it was so named. It appears to be very much the preferred way of doing things, but it is *not* universally valid. As the table shows, an increase in decentralised cases is expected. This reflects an increase in the number of businesses which are moving towards truly decentralised business operations, as hoped-for synergies have proved either illusory or too difficult to achieve.

7.3 Designing the Federal IS Organisation

The federal IS organisations must therefore allow for:

(a) Model organisations for the 'states', i.e. the divisions' IS organisations
(b) A model organisation for a residual headquarters IS function, including centrally provided services and the articulation of corporate systems strategy
(c) A model organisation for the 'federal power' which will develop, promulgate and monitor IS policy throughout the group

	1983	1987	Outlook
Centralised corporate service	5	2	1
Internal bureau	3	1	0
External bureau	1	2	0
Federal	3	8	9
Decentralised	2	1	4

FIGURE 3   *The right hand column indicates the researchers' judgement of the fate of each form, as the* **predominant** *model in the firms studied, a few years into the future. The evident trends in the first two columns have been confirmed by others' work at Templeton College, so far unpublished*

Discussions about the last role often get hung up on the question of how much specific power the IS policy person should have. I do not believe that it is at all helpful to define any 'powers' at all. If the holder cannot operate successfully by exhortation, persuasion, inspiration and politics, there is little hope.

To show why explicit powers are unhelpful, consider the situation if the holder does have specific powers—e.g. to veto unapproved computer procurements. A divisional manager whose plans are non-concurred on this account will reasonably appeal straight to senior group management. This is exactly the same situation, however, as would result if the federal IS person, having failed to persuade a division, felt that the deviation was disruptive enough to provoke his/her own appeal to senior group management. But the second approach (no *personal* authority) avoids much unnecessary bureaucracy, and the need to propose and ratify an arbitrary rule book. All that is required is a mechanism to ensure that procurements do receive review.

The ideal approach to IS policy is one which recognises the role of key line management in endorsing and mandating it through the line organisation. This is justified and accepted only where the policy topics are seen as ones which genuinely warrant line management attention. This further avoids the sterile quest for specific powers for the person who is steward of IS policies—the 'guru' mentioned in the lists of policy topics.

Further exploration of the organisational issues must be postponed. The key point is that the compromise here offered is very responsible. The objectives should be to exploit compromise in a way which maximises the strengths and eliminates the weaknesses of more extreme models.

Some businesses have arrived at a federal structure by natural evolution, and have been relieved to discover that their position is both recognised as responsible and possessed of a name!

8 FACTORS DETERMINING SUCCESS

Field research identified how effectively various parts of the studied organisations had managed to integrate IS into the business, at the business unit level, and what features characterised the high achievers. They could be described as high, medium or low in this characteristic of integration; some factors were all shared by all the high set, and were all absent in the low set.

Some of these factors bear specifically on the issue of managing things in the complex organisation, and they follow, in summary. There is more detail in the research reports.

(a) Business management in the divisions perceived that future IT exploitation was of strategic importance, and were able to describe applications and service intentions which illustrated this.

(b) That was possibly brought about because they all had an ongoing process of executive education in the topic. The vehicles for this varied among the companies studied; the resolution to do it did not.

(c) An IS executive was appointed within each division or business unit, and was seen as a key player in the management team or Board of that unit.

(d) There was some IS development resource positioned in the business unit, fully primed in the culture and methods of the unit, and able to respond to changes in unit priorities.

(e) There was a clearly identifiable top-down planning process for IS applications and services, within the division or business unit. This was evidenced both by respondents' self-assessment on a six point scale of caricatures and by their description of the process.

(f) The introduction or piloting of new technology took place at the business unit level under business unit control, even though funding and technical support were sometimes corporate provisions.

(g) Charge-out for IS services is kept simple (user allocation at a high level) and sophisticated pricing methods are avoided.

9 CONCLUSIONS

The early parts of this chapter explained why there are real difficulties—contradictions and dilemmas—facing IS management in complex organisations. Later parts developed the argument that certain approaches, while not simplifying a necessarily complex scene, will help to give direction and confidence.

'Direction and confidence' are needed by several communities:

(a) Those trying to run a complex portfolio of businesses dynamically yet efficiently
(b) Those trying to run effective business units within that umbrella in a competitive fashion
(c) Those supporting both communities of business people with dynamic IS provision, and advertising developing IT potential and capability to them

Key features which seem able to move these things forward include understanding the nature and importance of STRATEGY as the determinant of what is put together—IS strategy for what must be done and IT strategy for how (technically) to do it. This is coupled with understanding POLICY as the determinant of how IS and IT are to be managed, funded, justified and directed across the organisation.

Policy will be better understood as the organisation proceeds to select what topics to have a policy about, and of what the policies should actually be. Then it is more obvious how to develop the overall control framework, frequently a federal one, which provides the right degrees of 'freedom under the law'.

The discussion in Section 8 suggests that where effective integration is an objective—and where is it not?—there are some preferred ways of doing things.

IT *can* be managed productively in complex organisations, but it is a mistake to imagine either that it is simple or that it can be done without involving the senior business management. At the beginning of the chapter a number of genuine case studies was presented. In every case where there has been an effective improvement in the situation such business management has been involved, sometimes as the initiator of a change activity, but always in endorsement and promulgation of it. In the notable failing case, the failure follows from a refusal of corporate management to accept its duty to bang heads together in subordinate divisions and a belief that the implementation of an all-pervasive common system is merely a technical issue.

REFERENCES

Earl, M.J (1988) 'Information systems and information technology strategies delineated', in *Management Strategies for Information Technology* p. 63, Figure 3.8, Prentice-Hall.

Feeny, D.F. (1988) 'Creating and sustaining competitive advantage with IT', in *Information Management—The Strategic Dimension* (Ed. M. J. Earl), pp. 99–117, Clarendon Press, Oxford.

Feeny, D. F., Edwards, B. R., and Earl, M J (1987) 'Complex organisations and the information systems function—a research study', Oxford Institute of Information Management Research and Discussion Paper, RDP 87/7, Templeton College, Oxford.

Chapter 4

LINKING IS STRATEGIES TO BUSINESS OBJECTIVES

Michael Clark and David Shorrock

1 THE RELEVANCE OF INFORMATION TECHNOLOGY TO BUSINESS STRATEGY

A great deal has been said and written in recent years about the need for business executives to regard information systems and technology as an integral part of their corporate strategy—a good example is the Butler Cox report 'Value for money' published at the end of 1986 (Butler Cox, 1986).

The argument runs briefly as follows:

1. Businesses have grown increasingly dependent on information technology (IT) to the extent that organisations of any size and complexity could not function without it. This process started when basic transaction-processing and record-keeping functions were computerised and accelerated dramatically for many firms with the advent of communications-based systems. These often require that one firm has the ability to communicate with another's computer systems, and this capability can even be a condition of doing business with large and powerful customers.
2. IT brings with it a potential for competitive uniqueness and leverage when used imaginatively, particularly in the management of channels and provision of better customer service, which is increasingly being exploited.
3. All this has led to a proliferation of IT equipment and systems which has been particularly marked in information-intensive industries such as financial services and travel but which no industry has altogether escaped. The cost of all this, which has for some organisations been largely uncontrolled for long periods, has led to top management's increasing concern with cost-effectiveness (the subject of another chapter of this book).
4. It is this combination of operational dependency, strategic potential and cost which makes IT too important a subject to be left to specialists. Senior line managers must somehow become aware of the business implications of what is going on in the IT field, relate them to their own business goals and

priorities, and give appropriate and timely direction to those responsible for managing the technical and operational aspects of IT on their behalf.

2 INVOLVING TOP MANAGEMENT

Though top managers in every field of business do not lack reminders of the importance of involving themselves in these matters, finding an effective way for them to do so is not easy. Time pressures, combined with an understandable fear of technology, mean that far too many executives simply duck the issue. They typically rely on the appointment (often from outside) of an MIS (management information systems) Director who appears well qualified to fill the managerial gap, forgetting that no matter how able the appointee, there is no way that the right direction can be set for IT without intimate knowledge of the business context. Previous knowledge of other businesses can be not only irrelevant but totally misleading.

It is a grave mistake to believe that managing an IS function is all about understanding things like hardware price–performance, what is available in the latest software packages or how to get the best deal from a telecommunications supplier. All these things may of course be important when it comes to choosing and designing an IT delivery vehicle but at the truly strategic level—i.e. the level at which one decides what IT is to do to support the enterprise—it is irrelevant. Any document purporting to be a strategic statement about information systems which is entirely written in terms of hardware characteristics, network topology, development methods, costs, operating characteristics and other technical issues is simply begging the question 'why?' and must be supported by an adequate business justification before it can have any validity. It is the authors' contention that in the large majority of cases doing the strategic thinking necessary for the development of such justification can only be done effectively if it includes as a major element some kind of group process. The combined experience and judgement of the management group responsible for business strategy needs to be brought together in a controlled way. No matter how well established and expert the corporate planning department may be, and no matter what new technologies may bring in the way of automated methods for integration of planning, analysis and systems design, there will always be a need for business leaders to put their heads together whenever new strategic initiatives or revisions have to be made.

The most appropriate techniques for doing this, and some of the practical and behavioural issues involved, are the subject of the rest of this chapter. The techniques described have been developed with managers' rather than technical experts' needs in mind and are intended to make efficient use of management time, avoiding technical jargon whilst enabling direction to be given with the clarity and unambiguity needed if misunderstandings between IS and general management are to be avoided. The behavioural issues are every bit as important as choice of technique; the task of directing a group planning process should only be undertaken when there is a good understanding of the problems inherent in controlling an interacting group of people, whatever their status or purpose.

3 THE PLANNING ENVIRONMENT

Michael Earl, in his paper 'Formulation of information systems strategies—a practical framework' (Earl, 1986) makes a useful distinction between the terms 'IS strategy' and 'IT strategy'. He suggests that the former is best used to define what should be done with technology and the latter to define how it is done. IS strategies are therefore business focused and aim to identify the systems support priorities and plans relevant to a particular business unit; IT strategies on the other hand are technology focused and aim to show how a given set of requirements is to be met. IT strategies can moreover embrace the needs of a number of business units, each with their own separate IS strategies and in the case of corporations comprising multiple divisions or businesses which share a common IT facility.

Earl goes on to propose, based on research into the planning experiences of a number of companies, that there are three basic approaches to the development of a relevant portfolio of IS applications—in other words an IS strategy according to his definition. Briefly these approaches are as follows:

1. The analytical or 'top-down' approach which derives IS requirements from a systematic study of corporate goals, strategies, critical success factors, problems, etc., obtained by discussion or interview with managers of an appropriately high level within the business.
2. The evaluative or 'bottom-up' approach which subjects an existing portfolio of applications to examination by users and IT experts to see whether component systems meet criteria expressed in such terms as obsolescence, technical excellence, etc. This evaluation is then used as the basis for a plan of system revision and replacement.
3. The creative or 'inside-out' approach which seeks to harness IT to business opportunity through the generation of new ideas such as are unlikely to arise from use of either of the first two methods. The way to generate such ideas is either by individual inspiration or via some kind of creative 'think tank' but in either case follow-up work on feasibility is necessary.

The relevance of each of these methods depends on the maturity of the organisation doing the planning and the type of industry it is in. Some industries (banking being an obvious example) have long used IT as the basic delivery vehicle for their services; there is therefore in such sectors a large IT infrastructure already in place whose existence will have considerable influence on the choice of planning method. A successful bank would, for example, already be at the stage where a 'bottom-up' review, though it may not seem particularly strategic, could well be the best place to start at a given moment in time. On the other hand, given the current competitiveness of the financial sector, the 'inside-out' approach might seem the best if the object of the planning exercise were to find ways of using IT as a support tool for new business ventures. In this latter case the availability of an existing portfolio of applications (a characteristic of a 'mature' sector) would be particularly useful for two reasons: firstly, because it represents an accumulation of IT skill and experience which could facilitate a rapid response to new ideas; secondly, because research (Earl and Runge, 1987) has shown that a large proportion of 'new' strategic applications are in fact existing internal ones which have simply been made available to customers and other outside agencies.

The 'top-down' approach would seem generally more appropriate for organisations in less well-developed industry sectors (consumer products would be an example) where the need is more likely to be to prioritise within a broad range of possible options.

The more mature the organisation the more likely it is to want to move away from 'top-down' towards either 'bottom-up' or 'inside-out', depending on whether the planning emphasis is on retrenchment or expansion.

However the experience of the authors suggests that all methods are equally valid and any one company is best advised to make judicious use of all three at different moments in time as circumstances and priorities change.

4 THE RELEVANCE OF GROUP TECHNIQUES

How then does one go about implementing any of these approaches?

Where essentially new strategic IT directions need to be taken (as in both 'top-down' and 'inside-out') the situation is very fluid. The range of possibilities is wide, past experience is either limited or possibly even misleading; functional and other biases need to be allowed for and a concerted act of managerial will is usually required if success is to be achieved.

On the other hand the 'bottom-up' approach, depending as it does on criteria which are completely objective such as system age (Buss, 1981) or which approach objectivity (because they rely on expert views of existing systems), lends itself to a much more structured approach. A number of organisations have developed tools (IBM, 1988) based on questionnaires designed to evaluate the strengths and weaknesses of existing systems. Their aim is to help reduce the potential area of disagreement about what future system priorities should be; they can undoubtedly be a useful means of achieving this aim in the right circumstances.

The greater the uncertainty and range of possibilities (and therefore the potential for disagreement) the more the need for group involvement and the less the usefulness of these 'objective' approaches. However the introduction of group dynamics considerations into strategic planning processes makes them much more difficult to manage. Consequently it is not uncommon to find structured approaches being used in situations for which they are really inappropriate, simply in order to appear to be 'doing something' whether the output is useful or not.

This chapter focuses on the situations which are difficult to manage, namely those which are essentially 'top-down' or 'inside-out'.

5 A CONCEPTUAL FRAMEWORK FOR GROUP PLANNING

Before describing specific group planning techniques, it would be useful to review the fundamental stages involved in any planning activity.

Given that the initial commitment to an organised process has been made by the group and a clear objective has been defined, the first stage is to achieve a common level of understanding of just where they are starting from (a process we will refer to later as UNDERSTAND THE ENVIRONMENT). In other words, can we distil from the mass of preconceptions and bits of partial experience and knowledge within the group a set of agreed starting parameters on which to base subsequent discussion about where we need to go next? This activity can take many forms—agreement on a set of shared problems could be one approach, and analysis of what the competitive priorities of the business are could be another, as we will see in the next section of this chapter.

The second stage is broadly speaking to select a set of priority issues or actions for the group, chosen according to some agreed selection criteria (a stage we will refer to as SELECT OBJECTIVES). The selection criteria used can and should in some way reflect the fundamental aims and objectives of the group. In the commercial sector profit potential can often be used as the main overriding criterion, but more subtle and indirect criteria come into play the further the group is removed from the 'sharp end' of business, for example in areas such as public service or research.

Once a clear set of priorities has emerged the third stage is to plan the follow-up actions required in order to implement them (which we will refer to as the DEVELOP PLAN stage). This involves allocation of responsibilities for high priority items, deciding what, if anything, to do with lower priority ones and establishing appropriate check points at which progress can be reviewed either by the group or its sponsor during the fourth (EXECUTE PLAN) stage.

Specific techniques encompassing these stages will be dealt with later in this chapter.

6 'TOP-DOWN' PLANNING TECHNIQUES

It has been a common experience in recent years for the authors to be called into situations where the management of a business unit was looking for help in defining a broad and fairly basic range of support systems. A number of techniques has been evolved to assist this process and one, based on Rockart's critical success factors concept (Rockart, 1979), is described elsewhere in this book.

Another more specifically IS orientated technique used extensively in IBM UK is known as executive information planning (EIP). This is in some senses a successor to and derivative of the often-quoted business systems planning (IBM, 1981) which was in vogue in the 1970s. Though the basic concepts of BSP still survive (and have in fact been given a new lease of life with the advent of automated information engineering techniques) it was in practice found too cumbersome a process from the point of view of senior managers impatient for results. Its requirement for teams of interviewers, note takers, flowcharts and data definitions, and its tendency to take rather a static view of organisations, rendered it more or less obsolete in its original form by the early 1980s. The emerging requirement as seen by most BSP consultants was for a shorter and more responsive process which substituted the synergy of the small group for the unwieldiness of the interview-based approach.

EIP (IBM, 1980) emerged out of this requirement in the late 1970s and has been in constant use ever since. In common with all techniques driven by individual consultants there are variations in style and emphasis but as a basic minimum all planning exercises based on EIP principles have the following in common, and are illustrated in Figure 1:

1. A briefing meeting lasting 2 to 3 hours and involving the senior executives of the business unit concerned (usually some 6 to 8 people). The EIP method is described by the consultant and final commitment to the exercise is made.

    A simple model of the business is drawn up. This does no more than define, in brief verb–noun statements such as 'manufacture product', 'distribute product', 'manage raw materials', etc., the fundamental business processes carried out by the organisation. This process model both defines the scope of the study and the basic structure of the ensuing planning meeting.

2. A 2 to 3 day planning meeting attended by the management team and senior representatives (usually two) of the IS department. At this meeting the management team, with the consultant acting as facilitator, go through the following steps:

    (a) Agree the major information-related problems experienced in managing each of the business processes defined at the briefing meeting—a list showing cause and effect relationships is drawn up by the consultant and displayed. (By this stage the process of 'understanding the environment' described in the previous section should be complete.)

    (b) Define in business terms a set of information system requirements

Sequence of activities	Set up meeting(s)	Briefing meeting	Planning meeting	Follow-up phase	Follow-up meeting
People involved	- Chief executive - Planning consultant	- Senior management team - Senior IS manager(s) - Planning consultant	- As for briefing	- 'Solutions' team assisted as appropriate by - Line managers - External information sources (Consultants, manufacturers, software houses, etc.)	- As for planning meeting
Outputs	- Commitment to EIP process	- Understanding of EIP process and objectives - Model of business	- Prioritised statement of requirements - Action plan for investigation into requirements' implications	- Options - Recommendations	- Decisions - Action plan for implementation
Duration	- Typically 1-3 hours	- 2 hours	- 3 days	- 6-8 weeks	- ½-1 day

FIGURE 1

which, if implemented, would provide solutions to the problems identified.

(c) Agree the likely financial benefit to the organisation of meeting each of these requirements (assuming for the moment that this could be done at zero cost).

(d) Prioritise the list of requirements, using financial and other appropriate criteria. (This is the second, 'select objectives', stage of the process.)

(e) Agree a plan of follow-up action to be carried out by a designated 'solutions team' and allocate responsibility for it, usually to a senior IS manager present. (This is the third, 'develop plan', stage).

3. A follow-up phase, with terms of reference defined at the planning meeting, designed to address all the questions to which the management team need answers before they will be ready to make decisions on implementation of the defined requirements. The questions will always be specific to individual circumstances, but will inevitably cover such issues as costs, time scales, risks, implications for existing systems, options available, etc.

A specific time period (usually 6 to 8 weeks) is allocated to this follow-up process, which constitutes the first part of the 'execute plan' stage.

4. A meeting of the management group at which the results of the follow-up investigations are presented and implementation decisions made by weighing the benefits of each system solution (provided by the management team at the planning meeting) against the costs and other implications (assessed by the solutions team during the follow-up phase).

The chief virtues of the EIP process are its simplicity of structure, its formalised follow-up process and the synergistic effect of group activity involving both line and IS executives. Its links to the strategy of the business are most obviously made during the problem definition stage, where there is a deliberate focus on problems which inhibit the achievement of defined corporate and functional objectives. The potential limitations of the EIP process are:

1. In situations where business strategy has not been previously well thought-out or communicated within the management team the problem definition phase of EIP cannot be fully effective; much time can be wasted either in arguing about what the organisation's strategy and objectives ought to be or in discussing relatively low-level operational problems which avoid the issue. (In other words the 'understand the environment' stage of the planning process has not been properly completed.) If there is a risk of this happening the study needs to be preceded by some sort of strategy definition activity (possibly a CSF workshop). This is not usually too difficult; it just takes more time.

2. EIP is not deliberately aimed at changing or developing the management

team's perception of what their strategy ought to be.
3. EIP's focus is on management problems and associated information needs rather than on technology; this is one of its major strengths in practice provided the requirement definition phase is properly followed up. A consequence of this is that it does not, unless one adds elements of education to the process, enlarge managers' existing understanding of the potential relevance of IT to their chosen strategy.

Provided these points are borne in mind EIP can be an extremely effective means of focusing the managerial mind on information systems and their benefit potential, and engendering a new atmosphere of cooperation and commitment in an area which is so often plagued by misunderstanding and misdirected effort.

7 'INSIDE-OUT' PLANNING TECHNIQUES

Any planning tool intended as an implementation of the 'inside-out' approach to IS strategy formulation has to be based on the assumption that a major business objective is to establish, consolidate or regain a position of competitive advantage in the market place through use of IT. It must therefore include an analysis of the competitive situation, derive strategic implications therefrom and match IT potential to the competitive opportunities (and threats) which this analysis reveals.

Top-down techniques such as EIP include an element of this, in that any review of corporate problems in an industrial or commercial organisation can scarcely avoid issues which relate directly or indirectly to the firm's competitive position. Equally, a review taken from a bottom-up perspective should always take as one of its criteria the degree of competitive advantage (in the form of significantly lower costs, speed of response to market changes, product or service uniqueness, etc.) conferred by the firm's current computer systems. If these compare badly with competitor firms' systems the review will at least have have pointed out where competitive edge is lacking.

But if the focus of planning is to be on searching for new uses of IT with the specific aim of beating the competition a uniquely 'inside-out' tool is required. IBM's own technique for meeting this requirement has been developed under the name strategic application search (SAS). It is, like EIP, a series of linked activities involving a briefing, preparation, a structured planning meeting and follow-up, but with important differences which reflect its different purpose. Its essential elements, illustrated in Figure 2, are:

1. A briefing meeting for up to a dozen key line and IS executives to:
   (a) Explain the SAS process.
   (b) Bring the management team to a common level of understanding of

Sequence of activities	Set up meeting(s)	Briefing meeting	Market analysis	Workshop	Follow-up phase	Follow-up meeting
People involved	- Chief executive - Planning consultant	- Senior management team - Senior IS manager(s) - Planning consultant	- Senior managers in syndicates	- As for briefing	- Designated line and IS executives	- As for workshop
Outputs	- Commitment to SAS process - Proposals on syndicate membership and 'market analysis' assignments	- Understanding of SAS process and objectives - Commitment to work on 'market analysis' assignment	- Analysis of competitive position and company threats and opportunities	- Statement of competitive strategy - Prioritised statement of supporting IS projects - Action plan for project feasibility investigation	- Conclusions on project feasibility and value - Recommendations	- Decisions - Action plan for implementation
Duration	- Typically 2-4 hours	- 3-4 hours	- 3-4 weeks elapsed time	- 2 days	- 6-8 weeks	- ½-1 day

FIGURE 2

competitive forces and the value chain concepts as defined by Michael Porter (Porter and Millar, 1985, and Porter, 1985).

(c) Describe some of the ways in which IT is used to obtain competitive advantage in various industry sectors.

(d) Allocate preparation tasks (previously agreed with the chief executive) to 2-or 3-person teams chosen from the group.

2. A 'market analysis' phase in which the selected team members, using Porter's competitive forces model, research specific elements of their competitive environment to determine likely future trends and evaluate their own corporate strengths and weaknesses, threats and opportunities.

3. A 2-day workshop during which:

(a) The results of the market analysis carried out by each team are presented.

(b) The competitive threats and opportunities are discussed and prioritised. (Only now has the 'understand the environment' part of the planning process been completed—a consequence of the fact that SAS lays great stress on understanding both the competitive and the technological environment, which takes time and effort.)

(c) The main elements of corporate competitive strategy are agreed in the light of the threats and opportunities exposed by the market analysis.

(d) The team is restructured into small groups and each is given the task of investigating a specific approach to using IT in support of the chosen strategy. The different approaches are in essence:

— Automation of individual information—intensive activities (to reduce cost or save time, for example Stalk, 1988)

— Creation of electronic links (internal or external) to optimise trade-offs between different value-chain activities (by moving information-processing work from one point to another in the chain, for example)

— Use of existing information in new ways to add value (by repackaging it and making it available to customers as an additional service, for example)

These three recommended approaches are not necessarily mutually exclusive; they can and do often lead to very similar conclusions about IT usage. The point is that they require the syndicate teams each to start from a different position, thus ensuring that a broad range of ideas is brought up for consideration.

(e) The ideas generated by this process are presented in plenary and prioritised in accordance with their perceived strategic impact (i.e. stage two in our conceptual planning framework, 'select objectives', is completed).

(f) A plan of follow-up action (stage three, 'develop plan') is agreed. This is very similar to that produced in an EIP planning session and has similar implications for the fourth, 'execute plan', stage. The difference is that there is added emphasis in SAS on evaluating the feasibility and risk associated with implementing the ideas brought up during the planning meeting, and assessing the value and sustainability of the competitive advantage likely to be obtained from them.

In summary, both EIP and SAS hold to well-established planning techniques which stress the need for preparation, structure and a clear understanding of the purpose of each stage of the process. They are equally valid exercises but neither can be regarded as a substitute for the other because their purpose is different; careful consideration of just what outputs are required and of the state of maturity of the organisation wanting to do the planning are needed before deciding on the appropriateness of either.

8 WHAT CAN GO WRONG?

No matter how good the basic structure of a planning process it is nevertheless common in business life for plans to fail. The reasons for this are many and varied, as will be seen later in this chapter, and no absolute guarantee of success can ever be given no matter how well chosen the process, how carefully it is managed or how deep the level of commitment amongst those involved.

In the experience of the authors the risk of failure can however be minimised by:

1. A realisation that the initiation of a plan, such as is achieved by either of the techniques just described, is only the start of a process; the road to successful implementation may be a long and arduous one.
2. A readiness to accept the disciplines inherent in the planning process to the extent that they become institutionalised. A well-run EIP or SAS can serve as an example of how subsequent planning activity should be controlled in order to maintain relevance and impetus.

The rest of this chapter is devoted to a discussion of the principles underlying all planning activity involving groups of people. They are therefore equally relevant to the senior executives who must of necessity be involved in 'top-down' and 'inside-out' planning sessions and to IS managers and their staff to whom much of the follow-up work will in practice be delegated.

There are many examples of schemes or plans that have failed, ranging from the epoch-making down to the personal level of experience of those days when absolutely nothing goes right! In between the path, particularly in information systems, is strewn with projects that have failed—failed to meet deadlines, overrun budgets and ended up satisfying no one. There is, of course, always a long list of reasons and excuses given to support failure. Figure 3

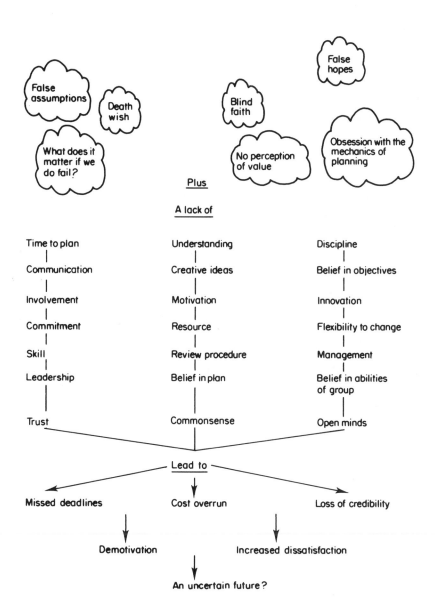

FIGURE 3   Why plans fail

summarises some of those that have emerged frequently from the groups that have passed through the hands of the authors. The order is of no significance. Whilst many of the items are self-explanatory, it may help to pick out some for further comment.

1. 'Lack of time to plan'. The more there is a need to plan the less time groups seem willing to devote to it. This leads to many of the other reasons for failure including lack of understanding and commitment coupled with a low or superficial level of thinking.
2. 'No perception of value'. Often a group looks at a project in isolation without a clear perception of its value to the enterprise and the financial impact on enterprise performance if the project is delayed.
3. 'Obsession with the mechanics of planning'. Many groups evolve or have imposed upon them a rigid hierarchical planning process with standard forms that have to be completed by specific dates. This uniformity of output may give senior management a warm feeling and may be appropriate in some organisations—however it can easily stifle innovation and creative thinking—again forcing thinking down to a superficial level. This is incidentally one of the dangers of the kind of 'bottom-up' planning methods referred to above.
4. 'Lack of belief in objectives'. In a case where objectives, such as revenue targets, were imposed and where the business environment was changing rapidly, one quote was 'the easy way out is to agree to every objective and rig the plan to show the achievement of these objectives in the hope that peace and quiet can be bought, free from management interference, for the next few months whilst changes in the business environment cover our tracks'.
5. 'Blind faith'. An 'it will be all right on the night' attitude coupled with a lack of personal commitment.
6. 'Lack of understanding'. It is quicker and less bother to assume that 'everyone knows what I am talking about'. No attempt is made to ensure a common level of understanding within the group. This is especially common when working under severe time constraints.
7. 'Lack of discipline'. A new plan is a delicate flower and needs nurturing when back in the cold light of the office following a planning session— a piled-up in-tray can destroy it aided by a lack of individual and group disciplines.

9 GUIDELINES FOR SUCCESSFUL PLANNING

Despite the analysis above there is no doubt that a large number of plans almost succeed, after a fashion, in the end: some by native wit, ingenuity, cunning and hard work to overcome the unforseen obstacles, some by the application of the hard sell to get the goal shifted (the 'you do not really want what you are asking for—do you?' approach) and some by the method least likely to produce ulcers—the development of a group motivated by clear objectives and rewards backed by a planning process which suits their particular style.

Before proceeding with the guidelines, it is helpful to consider a definition of planning which influences the development of the logistics, rules and disciplines later in this chapter:

PLANNING IS THE PROCESS OF DECIDING WHAT TO DO IN THE FUTURE

A number of key points emerge from this definition of planning:

1. A PROCESS is involved to keep the plan refreshed at suitable intervals, thus reflecting significant changes in the environment. It is essential that the group in a planning session feels comfortable with the process it develops.
2. DECISIONS must be taken by the group on the basis of arguments which everyone in the group understands and which have been expressed freely in open forum. Unanimous support for a decision is desirable and should be achievable in most sessions. It should be noted here that an individual bent on destroying a planning session can do so if all rules governing the normal conduct of a session are blindly followed.

   Commonsense *can* overcome the filibuster
3. 'WHAT TO DO'—perhaps more importantly 'What *not* to do'. Most people, particularly in information systems, are working under pressure with a backlog of work hanging over them and threatening to bury them at any moment. The last thing needed is more work—particularly if the request is prefaced with 'It will only take you a moment' or 'You remember that favour I did for you . . . '. Inevitably all requests like this arrive over the telephone when everyone is working flat out to meet a deadline. The easiest way to get rid of the caller, unfortunately, is to say 'yes'. He is satisfied, gives an incomplete description of what he needs and rings off. A scribbled note is made of the request which is either lost or subsequently misinterpreted. The length of the immediate interrupt has been minimised but only at the expense of wasted effort and aggravation at some point in the future. On the other hand, to say 'no' initiates a selling pitch by the caller who has had plenty of time to think through his arguments before telephoning. This forces an immediate response which can of course be short, sharp, aggressive and to the point but which, preferably, if eventual total isolation is to be avoided, should be based on sweet reason founded on a sound grasp of the priorities attached to the current and planned workload. In this way, there is a chance of making the best decision for the individual, the group and the enterprise.
4. The FUTURE as far as planning is concerned may be twenty years ahead for

a strategic plan or one day ahead if worrying about how to get through the following 24 hours. The important factor is to vary the planning horizon in order to create a series of different perspectives of the work the group is doing to ensure that the short term objectives of the group do not conflict with the longer term goals of the enterprise. For example, supplement regular tactical planning sessions with a long term strategy session at least once a year.

Following this definition of planning, the conceptual structure referred to earlier in this chapter and common to all planning sessions as run by the authors will now be examined in more detail. The difference between individual sessions arises from the differing analytical techniques employed at each stage and not from variations in the basic structure.

Figure 4 shows the structure and its stages split between the plan development and plan execution phases. The first element of the planning cycle, UNDERSTAND THE ENVIRONMENT, presents the greatest challenge to any individual or group and results in the identification of a list of possible relevant objectives at which to aim. It is the foundation on which the plan is built.

Questions of concern at this point are:

1. How to bring the whole group up to a common level of understanding?
2. How to cut through walls of prejudice to identify individual strengths and weaknesses?
3. How to achieve a fresh and stimulating perspective of the roles of the members of the group in their relationships both inside and outside the group?
4. How to motivate the group to ensure that the quality of the output exceeds the sum of the individual contributions?
5. How to raise the level of perception of the individual?
6. How to achieve commitment?
7. How to attain the necessary level of understanding as efficiently as possible?

As mentioned earlier, suggested techniques to address these questions are discussed later in this chapter.

The next element in the planning cycle, SELECT OBJECTIVES, takes the range of possible objectives identified in 'understand the environment' and prioritises them according to criteria agreed by the group. Thus selection could be made on the basis, for example, of the maximum return on investment, availability of appropriate resources, most critical business processes or 'he who shouts loudest'—the group decides.

The DEVELOP PLAN element analyses the activities needed to achieve the selected objectives with responsibility for each activity accepted by an individual

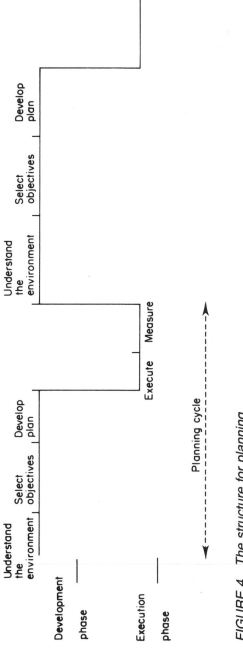

FIGURE 4   The structure for planning

member of the group together with a completion date. A suggested layout for the document is shown in Figure 5.

A more complex document than this is not normally needed as the output from an initial group planning session and indeed can reduce its effectiveness. More detailed plans giving manpower and skill requirements and start times, for example, will be produced by those responsible for individual activities for input into later planning review meetings and will conform with enterprise standards for planning documentation where these exist. At a group planning session the emphasis is on quality of output based on quality of thinking.

Objective:

Activity sequence number	Description of activity	Who	By when

FIGURE 5   Suggested layout for planning document

The final two elements of the planning cycle form the EXECUTION PHASE. The execution of the activities in the plan is followed by measurement of the results. These actual results are then compared with forecast and the reasons for any divergence analysed. This comparison of actual and forecast results and subsequent analysis forms a very important part of the input to the first element 'understand the environment' of the next planning cycle. As a result of the experience gained on the first cycle, understanding of the environment can be enhanced provided the necessary time and resource is set aside for the analysis—frequently this does not happen, resulting in an avoidable risk of failure to meet agreed objectives.

In summary, the structure for planning is very simple and logical. For it to be a success depends not just on the quality of the documentation or on the quality of execution but primarily on the understanding of the environment by a committed, motivated group. How can this be achieved?

10 LOGISTICS OF A PLANNING SESSION

This section looks at the practical aspects of setting up and running a group planning session through the examination of five important elements contributing to success:

1. Participants
2. Facilitator
3. Sponsor
4. Environment
5. Rules and discipline

10.1 The Participants

The participants should be members of a group who would expect to work together in the area being addressed. They do not necessarily come from the same department and could, for example, be managers from a range of user departments working with information systems department managers to solve problems associated with a particular application development.

Where the management team of a department is involved in a planning session, do not leave anyone out on the excuse of 'someone has to look after the shop!'. Even if they do not appear to be directly involved with the issues to be discussed, their views and perception as outsiders can be very valuable— never forget that one of the benefits of a planning session lies in its value as a team building exercise. It is easy to construct the very barriers within a department that the planning session should be removing. The same policy should be applied to those who have recently joined the management team, especially from outside the enterprise. A simple, apparently naive, question can sometimes break through entrenched positions and point the discussions in a new and productive direction.

An important point to bear in mind when selecting participants is that every one of them will be a member of the team implementing and reviewing the output from the planning session. There must be no passengers and, above all, no part-timers. The complete group must attend the entire session. A planning session is difficult enough to run productively without the disturbance of changing participants.

On the question of the number of participants, the ideal is between six and eight. With larger numbers it becomes very difficult to hear everyone's views and to keep all participants involved in the discussions. The result is a loss of quality and a drop in motivation—boredom sets in very easily!

10.2 The Facilitator

The facilitator drives the planning sessions through from the initial setup meetings at which the objectives, team composition and administration details and responsibilities are agreed with the sponsor, through the session itself to a series of postsession reviews with the team and its sponsor.

To maximise the chance of success, the facilitator must come from outside the group involved in the planning session, either from another department in the enterprise or from outside the enterprise altogether. This detachment of the facilitator from the group in the planning session is essential if productive control is to be maintained. An experienced facilitator is at a premium and can make all the difference between success and failure. Any group can run into difficulties during a session—and most do! Perhaps the discussion has lost its way or a conflict of priorities has produced an impasse. An experienced facilitator can guide the group to get it running again without their becoming dependent on him—important since it is the group's plan and not the facilitator's and it is they who will be implementing it.

10.3 The Sponsor

It is advisable for all planning sessions to have a senior executive as a sponsor. In the case of EIP and SAS workshops this will be the chief executive of the business unit and he will himself be present throughout; but at lower level planning meetings the sponsor should be the executive to whom the senior manager in the planning session reports.

The role of the sponsor is to:

1. Review and agree the objectives of the session with the facilitator
2. Agree to the team composition
3. Agree to the session being held and the costs involved
4. Attend the presentation at the end of the planning session to review output if he has not himself been a participant

The involvement of a senior executive as sponsor has a very important bearing on the commitment of the team to the planning session itself. The participants are aware of senior management attention and expectations and because the work they will be doing during the session and the conclusions they draw from it are regarded by the enterprise as important enough to warrant the sponsor attending the final presentation, the challenge motivates the team to a higher quality of achievement.

The presentation of the plan to the sponsor at the end of the planning session, rather than a few days or weeks later, also improves the chance of the plan being accepted and the investment in the cost of the session being seen as worth while. However well the presentation material is put together, the edge will go off the supporting arguments as the level of adrenaline drops sharply on returning to the office.

10.4 The Environment

Time taken selecting a venue for a planning session is time well spent. The quality of the output is, without doubt, directly affected by the environment. Points that should be considered when making the selection are:

1. Choose an off-site location. Resist the temptation of convenience and cheapness to use a conference room in the group's work location. Interruptions will inevitably occur and coffee and lunch breaks will become extended as participants are unable to resist checking on what is happening in their absence. This is particularly the situation when the planning session hits a tough problem.
2. Make the session residential at an hotel or management centre in pleasant quiet surroundings. The ability to relax during session breaks is very important and the fact that the group is staying together for the duration of the session promotes team building and increases the profitable use of the time available for discussion.
3. The conference room should be generous in size to accommodate the group sitting, if possible, in comfortable armchairs arranged in a horseshoe with at least two spare chairs. If, as is often the case, armchairs are not available then a U-shaped arrangement of conference tables is a good alternative. It is important that the layout of the room is such that eyeball to eyeball contact is possible between all members of the group with equal facility. The horseshoe arrangement ensures this and comfortable easy chairs help to prevent aching backs becoming a factor affecting the quality of discussion. The provision of two spare chairs enables the position of individual members to change during the session if they wish. Unless a considerable volume of papers is required for reference by the participants during the session, conference tables are not neccessary.

The recommended room layout is shown in Figure 6. The provision of a soft drinks table at the back of the room is an important feature since it gives the opportunity for individuals to stretch their legs and ease some of the tension they may be feeling in the group environment by walking to the table at times of their own choosing without breaking into the discussions. Figure 7 gives a checklist of items for the conference room.

The final point on this section concerns the lunch break. If the concentration of the members of the group is to be maintained in the afternoon, it is recommended that lunch is a light self-service buffet with no alcohol served. This will give time during the break for rest and relaxation as well as for eating.

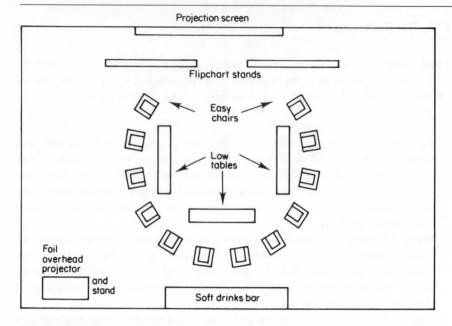

FIGURE 6   Preferred conference room layout

10.5 Rules and Discipline

The application of a few simple rules and commonsense discipline is essential if the planning session is to be productive. The introduction to each session should include a discussion of rules and discipline and a summary should be put up on a flipchart on the wall of the conference room as a continual reminder to the members of the group.

The eight basic rules can be expressed as follows:

1. THINK
   (a) Try to step outside the situation and look at it from a different perspective.
   (b) Do you really understand the question?
   (c) Do not take anything for granted.
   (d) Question your assumptions.
   (e) Is personal prejudice or ignorance a barrier?

2. THINK BINARY
   (a) Think as simply as possible.
   (b) Do we know or don't we?
   (c) Have we done it or haven't we?
   (d) Break a problem down into basic elements.

Easy chairs with solid upholstered arms
and
Low tables
or
Conference tables and chairs with a U-shape
Soft drinks table—replenished twice daily
Projection screen
Overhead foil projector
Spare bulb for projector
Extension cable for projector
Blank foils
Selection of foil pens—water soluble
Two flipchart stands
flipchart paper—check it fits the stands
flipchart marker pens—selection of colours
Pads of removable self-stick notes—one per participant
Pads of lined paper—one per participant
Pencils
Erasers
Pencil sharpeners
Ballpoint pens
Material for attaching flipcharts to walls without damage

FIGURE 7   Conference room checklist

3. BE UNANIMOUS
   (a) Obtain the agreement of all individuals in the group on all key issues. It
       may be that the one person holding out against the rest may be correct.
       Apply the Think and Think Binary rules to reexamine all the arguments
       on both sides.
   (b) Be aware of obtaining unanimity at the expense of clarity by generalising
       statements to the degree that they mean all things to all people.

4. DON'T DUCK IT
   (a) Most groups have some particularly difficult and challenging problems
       to face and, under pressure of time, it is very easy to avoid tackling them.
       Yet in many cases,they may involve fundamental assumptions related to
       many of the other activities of the group
   (b) If there are skeletons in the cupboard, take them out regularly, shake
       the dust off and have a look at them. The decision may be to put them
       back, but at least it will have been a group decision.

5. DON'T INTERRUPT
   (a) The most difficult of all disciplines!
   (b) Interruptions waste time and are counterproductive by irritating the speaker. Maybe the speaker is a well-known idiot on the subject under discussion but he is more likely to discover it for himself if he is allowed to finish. A deathly silence can work wonders!

6. LISTEN
   (a) Don't just avoid interrupting, concentrate on what is being said with an open mind.

7. STICK TO THE POINT
   (a) If a point is worth discussing, discuss it and finish with it. With a difficult thorny topic it is very easy to move the discussion away into areas in which the group feels more comfortable. Again, if it is worth discussing, stick with it.

8. ONE MEETING
   (a) Don't allow side discussions to take place. All discussion must involve the whole group.
   (b) If any member of the group leaves the room, stop the discussion until the group is complete again.

11 SUMMARY

This chapter has examined three approaches to the development of an IS strategy—'top-down', 'bottom-up' and 'inside-out'. It has suggested that the appropriateness of each of these techniques depends principally on the state of IT maturity of the organisation and on the overall objective of an individual planning exercise. Two of the techniques developed by IBM and used in workshops run for a wide range of businesses have been described, with emphasis placed on the need for structure, careful preparation and follow-up. The importance of the disciplines of group dynamics in successful management of planning workshops has been stressed and the authors have drawn on their experience to suggest that lack of awareness of these disciplines is a major cause of the failure of so many planning exercises. They have proposed guidelines for successful planning and given detailed advice on how to set up and run a planning session.

REFERENCES

Butler Cox Report Series (1986) 'Information technology: value for money', December.
Cash, M.D.J. (1981) 'Penny-wise approach to data processing', *Harvard Business Review*, July/August.

Earl, M.J. (1986) 'Formulation of information systems (IS) strategies—a practical framework', Oxford Institute of Information Management.

Earl, M.J., and Runge, D.A. (1987) 'Using telecommunications-based information systems for competitive advantage', Discussion Paper, Oxford Institute of Information Management.

IBM (1980) 'Gearing up for the future with executive information planning', IBM UK Form 24-8201 (Shand, G., *et al.*).

IBM (1981) 'Business systems planning—information systems guide', IBM Publication GE20-0527.

IBM (1988) 'IS investment strategies: making a difference on the bottom line', IBM Publication G520-6497-00.

Porter, M.E. (1985) *Competitive Advantage*, Free Press, New York.

Porter, M.E. and Millar, V.E. (1985) 'How information gives you competitive advantage', *Harvard Business Review*, July/August.

Rockart, J.F. (1979) 'Chief executives define their own data needs', *Harvard Business Review*, March/April.

Stalk, G., Jr. (1988) 'Time—the next source of competitive advantage', *Harvard Business Review*, July/August.

Chapter 5

PLANNING FOR PROFIT

Bryan Ward

1 INTRODUCTION

1.1 Good News and Bad News

In many organisations, especially at the most senior levels of management, the role and use of IT is regarded with mixed feelings.

On the positive side it is acknowledged that appropriate IT applications and services can change the way in which companies operate. For example a Finance Director of a multinational company recently commented: 'With more sophisticated technology-based administrative and office systems linked by global communication networks we are experiencing a signi cant speeding up of business activity, resulting from a communication capability of the highest quality, both within the organisation and with customers and suppliers. This has significantly enhanced our level of customer service. These technology-based systems are also changing the very way in which we do our jobs.'

Others acknowledge that with suitable planning IT can deliver competitive advantage, reduce costs, avoid expense and improve the quality of decision making. In addition IT can also make a major contribution to the profits of the organisation by, for example, facilitating the earlier launch of new products.

Yet major doubts on the real effectiveness and management of IT remain, as the following quotes illustrate:

> 'we spend a fortune on data processing. I find it difficult to see the big improvements that data processing has contributed to this organisation in the last 5 years.' General Manager, Insurance

> 'the budgeting systems developed by the computer department are too clever and complicated for the people in my department to use.' Finance Director, Local Government

> 'they (Data Processing) charge a fortune and we have little option but to use what they provide.' Director, Retail Industry

Managing Information Systems for Profit.   Edited by T. J. Lincoln
© 1990 John Wiley & Sons Ltd

'I am convinced that information technology can help us break new ground; but it takes so long for a good idea to be developed into a definable project. In addition my directors find it very difficult to quantify the potential benefits likely to be obtained.' Chairman, Leading Multinational

Why do these doubts exist after 25 years experience of using computers and how can they be answered?

1.2 Current Concerns About IT

The above quotations are symptoms that something is significantly wrong in the way IT is planned and controlled. Detailed studies have focused attention on the following major areas of concern:

(a) Expenditure
   — What is our total IT spend?
   — How 'effective' is our IT spend?
   — Is our spend in line with our competitors?
   — What increase in IT spend should we anticipate?
(b) Benefits/value
   — Do our IT applications fit our business needs?
   — Are we getting a satisfactory Return-on-Investment?
   — Can we judge IT in the same way as other projects?
(c) Business plans/controls
   — Can major IT projects really be 'owned', managed and controlled by senior executives?
   — How can we link our IT strategy to our business strategy?
   — Can IT really be used as a 'competitive weapon'?

The consequence of these concerns raised by senior executives is that they are increasingly reluctant to invest further in IT until sound answers are provided.

1.3 Managing IT as a Strategic Resource

In many situations IT has acquired strategic status gradually, and invisibly. Top management have approved IT projects in the past, such as on-line order entry, material management, major transaction processing systems, etc., without fully realising the impact on the business. IT has thus evolved from a supportive role to one which is vital to the very existence of the enterprise. Too often, this only becomes apparent when next year's DP budget comes with words like '... and this money has to be approved, or else ...'.

In contrast, some companies have managed the introduction of IT as a strategic resource. They have said, 'Here is our business strategy. Here is our competitive strategy.' Then they have worked with their IT functional management and said, 'Is there a role for IT in supporting our major strategies?' If there is, then IT becomes a necessary component of a much larger, strategic investment.

The difference between these 'styles' of managing IT can often be easily seen by asking Chief Executive Officers (CEOs) how they view their IT expenditure. Responses vary between:

(a) An 'eagle' which materially assists the enterprise to 'soar' towards the achievement of both long and short term business goals and objectives.
(b) An 'albatross' weighing down the enterprise by seldom contributing to the real requirements of the business and making a major 'contribution' to the overheads.

1.4 Selection of Profitable Applications

For an enterprise to perceive IT as an 'eagle' the Board must have clearly defined roles, responsibilities and ownership in relation to the strategic management and use of IT. To move to, and sustain, 'eagle' status it is necessary for the Board to regularly review:

(a) The fundamental business goals and objectives which IT should support (de Gues, 1988)
(b) The IT-based applications and services which are likely to yield the best returns (profit) in support of the business goals and objectives
(c) The resources—people, money, etc.—which should be allocated to the development, implementation and sustained use of the IT-based applications and services

But the strategic allocation of resources is often fraught with anxieties. Naturally, there is contention among the management team for the often limited resources available. Ultimately the CEO must arbitrate and decide, but how can the CEO increase the probability of getting it right? How can consensus be achieved within the team?

A structured approach to deal with these issues has been evolved within IBM over the last eight years (Hardaker and Ward, 1987). This approach, known as 'Process Quality Management', (PQM), is designed to assist the management team reach consensus on the most critical business activities; i.e. those whose performance will have the biggest impact on the success or failure of the enterprise. It has been found that agreement on these activities sets a solid foundation for the determination of IT priorities. Thus concerns expressed in Section 1.2 above can be addressed in a more structured fashion and a planned approach to the maximisation of profit from IT-based applications can be formulated.

This chapter describes PQM, summarises the experiences gained from using it in a wide variety of situations and provides practical guidelines to those who wish to use the Methodology.

2 THE 'PROCESS QUALITY MANAGEMENT' (PQM) METHODOLOGY: OVERVIEW

2.1 Objectives

The fundamental philosophy of PQM is that IT-based applications and services are an integral part of the strategic options of the enterprise as a whole. PQM is essentially a top down, business led approach.

The objectives of PQM are to enable the management team to:

(a) Identify the key requirements for improving the overall business performance of the enterprise
(b) Conduct an audit on the current investment in IT-based applications and services
(c) Identify the principal opportunities and priorities for future investments in IT-based applications and services
(d) Review the relevance of current Quality Improvement Projects (if a Quality Programme exists)

Underpinning the objectives of the Methodology is the requirement that the management team jointly agrees its business needs before discussing IT priorities and future funding.

2.2 The Basis of the PQM Methodology

The roots of PQM lie in IBM's Business Systems Planning Methodology (IBM GE20-0527) which provides a top-down analysis of the information requirements of the business. In addition PQM uses the concept of Critical Success Factors (Boynton and Zmud, 1984; Daniel, 1961; Gulden, 1986; Leidecker and Bruno, 1984; Rockart, 1979; Shank, Boynton and Zmud, 1985) to encourage management teams to focus their attention on the critical issues of the business, and then to base the IT strategy on these.

Initially, PQM's focus was oriented towards identifying the strategic IT opportunities to support business requirements. The use of the Methodology involved the entire 'top team' of an enterprise and required two days of their time. Subsequently the PQM Methodology was developed to analyse business process quality as part of a major quality drive within IBM.

From 1983 onwards PQM has also been used for both business and IT focused planning sessions with senior management teams and has additionally been used with senior management to analyse major 'culture change' projects. Finally PQM has been recently enhanced to encompass a wide spectrum of additional activities (see Notes 3 and 4).

2.3 The PQM Methodology—What's Different?

There are a number of approaches offered by consultancy houses throughout the world, which enable management teams to identify their business priorities. These approaches, while having similar broad objectives, all tend to emphasise different aspects. PQM places particular stress on the following:

(a) It focuses on team consensus and agreement, highlights major issues and then provides the motivation and framework for the team to take action.
(b) The time required for the planning session is short—two days. But of course there is a great deal of follow-up work to do.
(c) The output from the planning session is very concise and action orientated.

A PQM workshop will first define a team's reason for existence—the Mission (in the case of the Board this will define the reason for existence of the enterprise itself). The team will then develop the limited number of items which must be addressed if the Mission is to be accomplished. These are the Critical Success Factors (CSFs). They then establish the key Business Processes required to manage each of the CSFs and subsequently identify which are the Most Critical Processes (MCP), i.e. those in need of urgent management attention. A review of how IT currently supports these Processes is then conducted.

2.4 The PQM Process

An overview of the PQM Process is shown in Figure 1.

2.5 Participants in PQM Studies

2.5.1 The Sponsor

The study Sponsor (frequently referred to as the 'ranking manager') should be the person holding the Mission, the leader of the particular management team. The Sponsor should be clear about the steps to be covered during the planning session, the approximate timing of each phase and his/her role during the meeting. The Sponsor chairs the planning session, at which his/her entire management team must be present.

In certain circumstances there is not always universal agreement at the outset of a study that the Mission owner is the 'ranking manager'. This can occur with teams drawn from many parts of an enterprise to manage a project, constitute

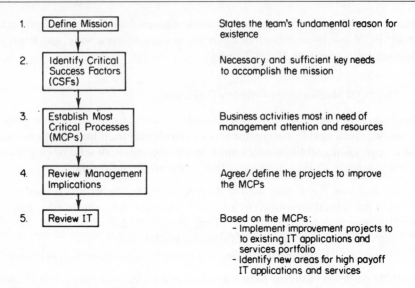

1. Define Mission
States the team's fundamental reason for existence

2. Identify Critical Success Factors (CSFs)
Necessary and sufficient key needs to accomplish the mission

3. Establish Most Critical Processes (MCPs)
Business activities most in need of management attention and resources

4. Review Management Implications
Agree/define the projects to improve the MCPs

5. Review IT
Based on the MCPs:
- Implement improvement projects to to existing IT applications and services portfolio
- Identify new areas for high payoff IT applications and services

FIGURE 1   PQM overview

a taskforce or be responsible for one or more (cross-functional) Business Processes. In the majority of cases the use of PQM has created consensus on leadership, but added vigilance is required by the Facilitator at the beginning of the planning session where this situation exists.

The Sponsor should consider carefully whether challenges to the status quo are going to be personally acceptable. PQM rests on participation and vigorous debate which may not be consistent with the Sponsor's style, corporate culture or national characteristics.

2.5.2 The Facilitator

A Facilitator is required to assist the Sponsor and his/her team to use PQM. In the case of management teams of more than six it is recommended that two Facilitators are present. The role of the Facilitator encompasses setting up the planning session with the Sponsor, running the Methodology during the planning meeting and ensuring that follow up occurs.

While the Facilitators are normally external to the enterprise, trained internal personnel—frequently drawn from Training and Development Groups—have run in-house sessions successfully. Experience shows that internal Facilitators must not run the PQM Methodology for the team(s) to which they report.

2.5.3 The Team

PQM is frequently used by the 'top team' (the Board, the Executive, the

Management Committee, etc.) to establish their vital business needs and then assess the implications for IT. Within large enterprises the 'top team' may be that responsible for directing and managing the entire organisation or that responsible for a major operating unit.

Other teams can benefit from using PQM; for example teams responsible for the implementation of major projects, policy formulation and business process management.

While the optimum approach is to use the Methodology with the 'top team' and then cascade its use down the organisation, major benefits can, and do, accrue to individual teams using PQM to focus on their fundamental requirements and priorities.

Experience has shown that the Methodology can be used across a broad spectrum of industries, and assists management teams whose remits have covered a wide variety of tasks. Details regarding the scope and use of the PQM Methodology are provided in Notes 1 to 4.

2.6 Follow-through

At the conclusion of a PQM planning session the leader of the team frequently asks, 'well how do you think we have done?' The answer is always qualified by the fact that the real judgement on how the team have 'done' can only begin to be assessed some six months hence. So while the planning session may itself have been successful, the reality of the situation is more akin to the 'Long March' of the Communists in China when Mao Tse Tung later observed 'the longest journey begin with a single step'.

Rigorous application of PQM enables business teams to identify their most critical issues and the ways in which IT can contribute to their solution. Appropriate follow-through is essential. In the best examples a 'sea change' may well have taken place. The management team have decided on both their business and associated IT priorities and areas of focus. The team has collectively determined its most profitable IT applications and will ensure they are implemented. They have a collective will to deliver the 'profit plan'.

Section 3 contains a detailed description of the way in which the 'classic' PQM Methodology is applied, together with tips, hints and examples to maximise the benefit of its use to management teams and their Facilitators. Section 4 goes on to illustrate alternative ways PQM can be deployed.

3 PLANNING FOR PROFITABLE IT INVESTMENT

This section describes the 'classic' use of the PQM Methodology which enables a management team to:

(a) Determine its business priorities

(b) Establish the IT-based application and services required to support the business priorities

(c) Plan the implementation of the required improvement projects

The reasons why management teams wish to achieve these objectives are many and varied. The nature of the business may change as acquisitions are made or major new products launched. A subsidiary may be re-missioned to encompass new responsibilities. Major market place changes may introduce new opportunities or threats. A joint venture may be established and required to 'get its act together'. A new leader may wish to build his team and communicate his hopes, desires and aspirations.

In many planning sessions PQM is used with the principal intention of establishing the priorities for the use of IT. In other circumstances PQM is used when there is a general feeling of unease regarding, say, the progress—or lack of it—with a major project. Whatever the rationale for using the methodology the end result will be team commitment and consensus on where resources must be deployed to meet business priorities. For those studies embracing IT requirements, the focus will be on improving the existing portfolio of applications and services, and developing and implementing new ones to support business plans.

Figure 2 shows the detailed steps which are the basis of the 'classic' use of PQM which first defines the team's business criticalities and then uses this information as the basis for the development of the IT Strategy. This section contains details of the major items to be addressed at each step. The number given to each of the steps in Figure 2 corresponds to its sub-section number within this section.

3.1 Conduct the Briefing

Rule 1: Do not embark on a PQM planning session without the Facilitator completing an adequate briefing with the Sponsor.

3.1.1 Preamble

Before embarking on the detailed setup work for the planning session it is vital that the Facilitator briefs the Sponsor on the aims and objectives of PQM. The Sponsor can then decide whether it is an appropriate mechanism for focusing on the perceived problems of the team. If it is, then the preparation work for the planning session should proceed.

3.1.2 Meeting Setup

Normally 2 hours is required for the briefing meeting. The principal tasks to be undertaken by the Sponsor and the Facilitator are to:

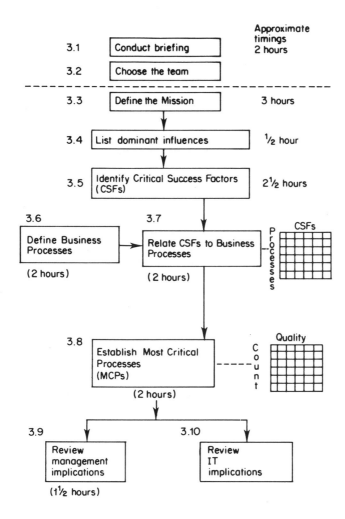

FIGURE 2 The PQM methodology. NOTE: Steps 3.3 to 3.6 are completed on day one of the meeting. Steps 3.7 to 3.9 are completed on day two of the meeting. Step 3.10 is addressed after the meeting as input is required from the IT group for its completion

(a) Draft the Mission Statement which the Sponsor 'owns' (unless a Mission Statement already exists).
(b) Produce an outline set of Business Processes likely to be appropriate for the draft Mission.
(c) Book an off-site location for the meeting. This location may be at a geographically remote site within the enterprise itself.

(d) Prepare and issue a briefing note for all participants (see Appendix 1).

3.1.3 Prior Analysis

Experience shows that it is essential to do the following at the briefing stage:

(a) Develop a schematic of the major groups with whom the Sponsor and his team relate to/interact with, both inside and outside the enterprise, i.e. the 'Key Relationships'.
(b) Decide whether it is appropriate to brief all directors (or managers) who will be attending the meeting.
(c) Evaluate any previous planning work that has been undertaken by the team with consultants, planners, etc., which could provide useful input to the PQM. Where relevant this material should be incorporated into the planning session documentation to avoid possible duplication of work and potential confusion.
(d) Ensure that the Sponsor is aware that the planning session is just the first step. The really hard work lies in the months (sometimes years) ahead when improvement projects are identified, developed and implemented.

3.2 Choose the Team

Rule 2: All relevant managers must be present at the planning session. Do not run it if any key player in the team is missing.

Experience strongly suggests that every member of the Sponsor's immediate management team should be involved—nobody missing, no passengers. Most management teams have about ten people and that number is 'containable' in a standard planning session. As the number of participants increase so do the problems of maintaining 'control'. The largest PQM session run to date has been with nineteen people.

If even one member of the team cannot attend, postpone the study until all can attend. PQM requires 'buy-in' by all, not only to create the agreed output but also to get team commitment to it. Too often if a key player is missing there is disruption and confusion during follow-up sessions. Avoid this situation at all costs.

Equally, exclude all hitchhikers. This is hard, concentrated work for the management team itself. Leave the aides and personal assistants etc to look after the store.

Everyone in the 'team' must have a direct interest in progressing the Mission. This has led, on a number of occasions, to managers from 'service functions' (e.g. IT or Personnel) participating in the planning session.

The type and nature of teams who have participated in PQM planning sessions are discussed in Notes 2 and 3.

3.3 Define the Mission

Rule 3: The Mission must be defined and agreed by the team before proceeding to the next stage of the study—otherwise all that follows will be wasted effort.

3.3.1 What Is a Mission?

The English language is rich in words like mission, goals, objectives, aims, etc., and their usage and meaning are far from standardised. The word 'Mission' is used in PQM very simply to mean the reason why the particular management team exists; what they are collectively being paid to do.

The Mission Statement is the vision and guiding light for the team, and all those managed/influenced by them. Accordingly the Mission is usually communicated to all relevant internal groups and where appropriate to customers, suppliers and trading partners (and see Demb *et al.*, 1989).

3.3.2 Defining the Mission

The Mission Statement will not require further definition work if an appropriate one already exists for the enterprise, or if, in the case of larger national/international/multinational enterprises, standard Mission Statements exist for territories, business units, etc.

The definition of the Mission commences with the Sponsor tabling for discussion the draft Mission Statement circulated with the briefing note. The team should then discuss this and through debate develop a Mission Statement with which they all concur.

The following principles should be observed when developing the Mission Statement:

(a) It should be short—not more than 3 or 4 brief, terse statements.
(b) It must be capable of consistent interpretation.
(c) It should be clear, visible and unambiguous.
(d) It should contain the following elements:
    * 'to do something ...
    * for ...
    * such that ... ends are achieved'
    (although the sequence is variable).

There may also be fundamental elements which lie behind all Mission Statements for an enterprise. These are itemised separately as 'core values' or 'basic beliefs'. These form the background against which all Mission Statements are performed and include such items as:

(a) 'Quality and safety are dominant principles in all we do.'

(b) 'People are our most important asset.'
(c) 'Service to the customer.'
(d) 'Respect for the individual.'

In some instances teams also develop a short 'Glossary of Terms', to clarify further the deeper meaning of a few key words in the Mission Statement (and see David, 1989).

3.3.3 Who Owns the Mission?

PQM takes the view that the Mission effectively belongs to one person, the 'ranking manager' or supremo of the team participating in the study. This may be the CEO of a multinational company, a Divisional VP, a plant manager, a project manager, a sales branch office manager, etc. But the buck stops at that person's desk. He or she owns the Mission. The team is created to achieve it.

3.3.4 Is the Mission Understood?

It is amazing how many management teams do not really know what their Mission is. Sometimes this is because of a rapid turnover of members of the team, sometimes it is because the environment has changed sufficiently to make the old Mission irrelevant and sometimes it is because a Mission Statement has never been prepared.

International/multinational companies can present particular problems. Here the Mission Statement must be in very explicit English, or capable of 'tight' translation into other languages if it is to be promulgated on a global basis.

3.3.5 Examples of Mission Statements

(a) An international business—the Board
  'Meet customers performance requirements worldwide as the supplier of choice of materials and systems based on the targeted applications of materials science.'
(b) Manufacturing plant—Director and Reporting Managers
  'To supply products and services that are competitive in terms of Function, Cost, Quality and Delivery and ensure customer satisfaction.'
(c) Personnel function—Director and Reporting Managers
  'To support the organisation's management in those of its responsibilities that involve people and, where assigned, the community by providing an environment which allows our company in the UK to attract, motivate, educate, develop and retain people to:
  * meet business goals
  * fulfil our basic beliefs.'

Further insight into the use of PQM Methodology can be be obtained by referring to Appendix 2, 'Running a PQM Planning Study'.

3.4 List the Dominant Influences

Rule 4: Ensure that each member of the team makes his/her contribution to the Dominant Influences so that the real issues impacting the Mission are tabled.

The agreement of the Mission means that the team now knows why they 'exist' and they should now consider the Dominant Influences on the Mission. The purpose here is to list everything and anything the team believes could impact Mission achievement. These will include those items that may adversely effect the ability of the team to achieve its Mission and those items of strength which can be exploited further. This is the moment for full and frank comment, and the establishment of the 'realpolitik' within the teams operations. 'Brainstorming' is used to develop the Dominant Influences (see Appendix 2).

When developing the Dominant Influences, the team will refer to the Mission, the 'Key Relationships' diagram (if it was developed at the briefing session—see Section 3.1) and a 'Mission Relationships' diagram, as shown in Figure 3. The team should consider the future environment in which the Mission will be performed, as well as recording the past 'lessons of history'. A typical list of Dominant Influences will contain thirty to sixty items.

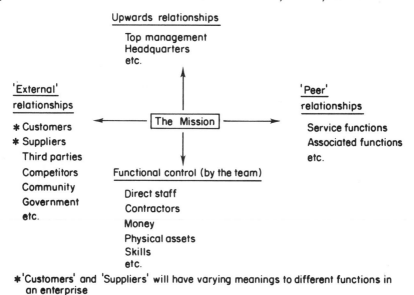

FIGURE 3   Mission relationships

Examples of Dominant Influences are:

Customer profitability	Trade barriers
Legislation	Production capability
Future demand	European Economic
Environmental issues	Community—1992
Cost cutting	Employee confidence
In-company communication	Business teams
Management style	Distribution costs
Customer service	Management information
Weather	Training
Present culture	Competitors

The identification of Dominant Influences is an essential step before identifying Critical Success Factors. While many of the Dominant Influences will eventually contribute to the formulation of CSFs they will not all do so since some will typically be background concerns and not criticalities.

3.5 Identify the Critical Success Factors (CSFs)

Rule 5: A limited number of CSFs must be agreed on by the team as being the individually necessary, and jointly sufficient, list of essentials that must be achieved if the Mission is to be fulfilled.

3.5.1 What are CSFs?

Critical success factors thus are, for any business, the limited number of areas in which results, if they are satisfactory, will ensure successful competitive performance for the organisation. They are the few key areas where 'things must go right' for the business to flourish. If results in these areas are not adequate, the organisation's efforts in the period will be less than desired (Rockart, 1979).

The Dominant Influences, listed during the brainstorming session, and other items noted during team debate, are a rich source of material for agreeing the CSFs. Often they are grouped into a number of 'clusters' from which the CSFs are developed.

3.5.2 How Many CSFs Can a Team Manage?

Experience from many studies has established that the ideal number of CSFs is five or six and that there must be no more than eight CSFs. These numbers are based on the number of management tasks that a team can focus on continuously. Frequently management teams handling a crisis situation will have a maximum of only four CSFs.

3.5.3 The Essential Nature of CSFs

Each CSF description should be devoted to a single issue. This means the word 'AND' is effectively forbidden if two quite separate themes are addressed. Teams are often tempted to combine CSFs as a way of reducing the total number. This must be avoided.

There will normally be a mixture of tactical and strategic CSFs. If they are all strategic, the business might founder in the short term while everybody concentrates on the blue skies ahead. Equally, if all CSFs are tactical, the business might burn out like a super-nova. The ratio of tactical to strategic depends on a number of factors including the nature of the team using PQM. A preponderance of tactical CSFs from the management team of a Regional Sales Office would be expected, whereas Corporate Headquarters will normally have an almost entirely strategic list.

CSFs must be agreed by the entire team. Accordingly, it is appropriate that they begin with words such as 'We must...' or 'We need...'.

3.5.4 Examples of CSFs

Some general examples of CSFs drawn from a variety of planning sessions are given below:

(a) We must have effective partnerships with all our key customers.
(b) We need to increase our external visibility
(c) We must understand the basis on which customers judge our performance
(d) We must ensure the successful implant of this 'culture change' project into a major European subsidiary by end 1988.
(e) We must secure an adequate supply of parts which meet our stringent Quality Standards.

3.5.5 The 'Necessary' and 'Sufficient' Rule

Each CSF under discussion should be constantly tested for 'necessity' and 'sufficiency' against the Mission. When the team agrees 'Yes, if we get that, that, that, that and that right, we will do it!', the CSF list is 'complete'. A useful test of completeness is to check whether the team agrees that if their CSFs are not managed forward then they will certainly fail with their Mission. This tends to concentrate the mind.

It is also desirable to test the wording of the CSFs against the Mission. If a team's Mission includes 'to become the worldwide supplier of choice', there is little value in recording as a CSF, 'We must become the worldwide supplier of choice'. What we must know is if there are any criticalities to becoming 'the worldwide supplier of choice'. In other words the team members must not 'play back' the Mission as a series of CSFs.

3.5.6 CSFs—Final Checks

Once 'consensus' on the CSFs has been reached experience shows that the management team should be reminded that:

(a) All CSFs are 'equal'. They may be managed to completion in differing time scales but unless they are all addressed then the Mission will fail.
(b) The CSFs are those that the team has developed for todays Mission, in today's environment. A major change in either the scope of the Mission or the environment in which it is being undertaken should trigger a CSF review.
(c) The CSFs should be reviewed by the team, at least on an annual basis.

At this stage the team knows what they have to do (the Mission) and they have agreed the necessary and sufficient items that need to be achieved to do it (the Critical Success Factors). However CSFs as typically defined are not directly manageable and accordingly the analysis must proceed towards Business Processes which provide the framework for management.

3.6 Define the Business Processes

Rule 6: Each Business Process must have an owner, and the owner must be a member of the management team that agreed the CSFs.

3.6.1 What Are Business Processes?

Business Processes can be viewed as a linked series of activities, transcending functional organisation boundaries, which are required if the business is to function efficiently. Examples might be those activities required to bring a product to the market, to manage the demand and supply inventory or to manage billing and accounts receivable. There is a clear difference between Business Processes and CSFs. Business Processes are concerned with activities and flows of information, whereas CSFs are key areas for management focus.

Initially teams usually define processes in a fairly bland, wishy-washy way. 'Invoicing', for example, or 'Maintenance', or 'Sales', or 'Customer Service'. These are not helpful descriptions and PQM recommends a rigorous approach to the definition of Business Processes which specifies that:

(a) The language structure of each Business Process description should follow a VERB plus NOUN sequence.
(b) Each Business Process should have an owner; one owner—the person responsible for carrying out the process.
(c) The owner should be a member of the management team that agreed the CSFs.

(d) No owner should have more than three or four Business Processes to manage.

For example, 'Introduce New Offerings' describes a process. It has the verb of action—'Introduce'—so something should be being done, and it has the noun portion—'New Offerings'. It can have an owner and its quality or performance can be measured. It is also cross-functional, critical to the business, and every colleague on the management team should be deeply concerned about its success.

3.6.2 Process Descriptions

It is vital to understand that such verbs as 'control', 'reduce', 'optimise', do not describe Business Processes. Rather, they describe the wanted results of Process Management. For example, 'Optimise Stocks' describes a desire rather than a Process and the team should be looking for the major processes by which they succeed in 'Optimising Stocks', e.g. setting and reviewing stock holding levels, establishing policies for slow moving or obsolete stock. A valuable test is to ask which member of the team would like to be owner of the Process under discussion. With Processes such as 'Reduce Headcount', 'Optimise Administration Costs', 'Improve Morale' there tend to be few serious volunteers.

In the same vein PQM recommends against the use of adjectives or adverbs in process descriptions. Terminology such as:

Do COMPREHENSIVE Customer Satisfaction Surveys
Define Skill Requirements EFFECTIVELY
Negotiate HIGH IS Service Levels
Enter Customer Orders ACCURATELY
Educate Vendors EFFICIENTLY

are describing desired results and are CSFs rather than processes.

3.6.3 Ownership

The team focuses on those Business Processes required to fulfil their Mission. Some of these will be owned and managed by the team directly; others will be owned by other teams. If a team relies on a Business Process owned elsewhere, it will typically institute a controlling or negotiating process described by such verbs as 'negotiate', 'escalate' etc., and assign ownership of these within the team.

3.6.4 Developing Business Processes

A number of techniques can be used to derive the list of major processes.

When the Briefing (Section 3.1) has been comprehensive a suggested list of Business Processes, circulated by the Sponsor in the briefing note, can be tabled and discussed.

Where this has not been done the Facilitator gives four or five examples of processes for the group to use as a starting point. Appendix 3 provides examples of IT Processes and Appendix 4 illustrates a general set of Business Processes.

The team should have copies of the Mission Statement, the Dominant Influences and the CSFs available for reference at all times. All of these can help to stimulate agreement on the Business Processes.

In some instances the enterprise has already implemented Business Process Management techniques. In these cases a Business Process Directory for the entire enterprise exists, and those processes which the team 'own' can be extracted from it. In these circumstances the processes applicable to the Sponsor and his team will be distributed as part of the Briefing Note (Section 3.1). Whilst a review of the Mission/CSFs/Dominant Influences may create some additional processes, or Sub-processes, to be managed by the team, the bulk of the work is done.

Experience shows that a team normally has between 30 and 40 exclusive Business Processes which it 'owns'. It is important to confirm that the ownership of all Processes has been assigned with the team.

Having defined the Business Processes owned by the team it is now important to begin to focus on the key processes. This starts by relating the CSFs to the Business Processes.

3.7 Relate CSFs to Business Processes

Rule 7: Take each CSF in turn and consider which Business Processes are required to manage it, adding new Business Processes if needed.

3.7.1 Relate CSFs to Processes

To fulfil the Mission the 'management' of the CSFs is vital. But, as has been discussed in Section 3.5, the CSFs are not, in themselves, directly manageable. It is the Business Processes that define what a management team 'Do'. It is the Business Processes that can be owned, defined, measured and managed.

It is therefore necessary to 'relate' the CSFs to the Business Processes to provide an overall view of the importance of each Business Process to the management of the CSFs. This step is best done by constructing a matrix of CSFs versus Business Processes.

3.7.2 Building the Matrix

PQM relies heavily at this stage on the wisdom, experience, knowledge and opinions of the management team.

The team builds the matrix relating the CSFs to the Business Processes by grouping the matrix into two sections:

(a) A 'Detail' Section, relating individual CSFs to the Business Processes.
(b) An 'Analysis' Section, which indicates the relative 'importance' to CSF performance of each Business Process, and forms the basis for the establishment of the Most Critical Processes.

The detailed steps which the team undertake to build the matrix are as follows.

3.7.3 Completing the 'Detail' Section of the Matrix

The first step is to insert the Business Processes and CSFs on to the matrix (see Figure 4). The management team focuses in turn on each CSF and considers the following question, 'Which Business Processes need to be performed particularly well for us to be confident of achieving this CSF?' Many Processes will influence a CSF's achievement, but the team is judging which are the truly critical ones.

After the first pass a 'sufficiency test' is applied. If the identified Processes are performed well, are they sufficient to manage the CSF in question? If the answer is 'no' then additional Processes need to be defined. This is where the team begins to be really creative, breaking new ground, agreeing what should be done in addition to what is already being done. Moreover, each new Business Process added for sufficiency must have an owner assigned from among the management team.

This analysis is repeated for all CSFs, each of which will have a different set of vital Processes. Again, the 'sufficiency' test must be applied rigorously.

Figure 5 shows a matrix in which all CSFs have been related to Business Processes. Note that Processes number 20 to 24 have been added in our example as a result of the 'sufficiency' test.

3.7.4 Completing the 'Analysis' Section of the Matrix

The matrix now contains much valuable 'raw data'. For this to be really useful an analysis of priorities must be undertaken, and this is done by using three indicators.

(a) The Count   The more important Business Processes are potentially those which impact most CSFs and a simple count is provided in column (A) in the Analysis Section of the matrix.

	1. Best–of–breed product quality	2. New products that satisfy market needs	3. Excellent suppliers	4. Skilled workers	5. Excellent customer satisfaction	6. Exploit new business opportunities	7. Achieve lowest delivered cost	(A) Count	(B) Process quality	(C) 'Big burners'
Critical success factors / **Business processes**								**Analysis** →		
1. Research the market place										
2. Measure customer satisfaction										
3. Advertise products										
4. Monitor competition										
5. Measure product quality										
6. Educate vendors										
7. Measure personnel satisfaction										
8. Educate/train employees										
9. Define new product requirements										
10. Process customer orders										
11. Develop new products										
12. Monitor customer complaints										
13. Negotiate manufacturing designs										
14. Pay vendors										
15. Define future skills										
16. Select and certify vendors										
17. Promote the company										
18. Track finished products										
19. Support installed products										

FIGURE 4   Business Process/CSFs matrix

(b) Assignment of a 'Quality' Rating   A 'Quality' rating for each Process is provided in column (B) in the Analysis Section. This rating is normally the subject of considerable debate among the team. The 'basic' ranking that PQM uses to assess the current Quality of the Business Processes is:

A = Needs no improvement
B = Works well, room for minor improvement
C = Functions, several areas for improvement
D = Process in place but not functioning
E = Embryonic

(c) Identifying the 'Big Burners'   In addition to 'Count' and 'Quality' a number of teams also identify the 'Big Burners'—those Business Processes which consume a significant proportion of the money, people or assets for which the team is responsible. The Processes to which this test applies are designated with an asterisk in column (C). A debate may well take place at this stage if a 'Big Burner' Process appears to have minimal impact on any of the CSFs.

The Matrix relating the Business Processes to the CSFs is now complete (see Figure 5). The raw material is in place, and potentially the relative importance of each of the Business Processes is itemised in the 'Analysis' Section. The team can now move on to establish their Most Critical Processes.

3.8 Establish the Most Critical Processes (MCPs)

Rule 8:   Those Business Processes designated as the 'Most Critical Processes' (MCPs) for improvement must be very limited in number. The team must not create a 'mission impossible' situation for itself by trying to manage too many MCPs.

The Most Critical Processes are those processes whose performance must be improved if the CSFs are to be managed successfully. Failure to improve the MCPs will mean that the CSFs with which they are associated will not be managed, and that consequentially the team will fail with its Mission. Identification of MCPs will follow the following steps.

3.8.1 Mapping Priorities

A 'Summary Grid' (see Figure 6) is used to map the 'CSF Count' against 'Quality' for each Business Process. Thus, Process 1 (P1) which impacts three CSFs and has Quality rating 'C' is inserted in box 3C (see Figure 6). Each of the Processes is transferred to its appropriate box on the Summary Grid.

The team can then use this summary to establish their Most Critical Processes. This is achieved by agreeing on 'zones' on the Summary Grid. Figure 6 illustrates this where the management team has decided that Zone 1 contains the Most Critical Processes. Of course, all the other processes are important, but

Business processes \ Critical success factors	1. Best-of-breed product quality	2. New products that satisfy market needs	3. Excellent suppliers	4. Skilled workers	5. Excellent customer satisfaction	6. Exploit new business opportunities	7. Achieve lowest delivered cost	(A) Count	(B) Process quality	(C) 'Big burners'
1. Research the market place		X			X	X		3	C	
2. Measure customer satisfaction	X	X			X	X		4	D	
3. Advertise products					X	X	X	3	B	
4. Monitor competition	X	X	X		X	X	X	6	D	
5. Measure product quality	X	X	X		X		X	5	C	
6. Educate vendors	X	X	X			X		4	E	
7. Measure personnel satisfaction				X				1	A	
8. Educate/train employees	X	X		X	X	X	X	6	C	*
9. Define new product requirements		X	X		X	X		4	C	
10. Process customer orders			X		X		X	3	B	
11. Develop new products	X	X	X		X	X	X	6	B	
12. Monitor customer complaints	X	X			X			3	D	*
13. Negotiate manufacturing designs	X	X	X			X	X	5	D	*
14. Pay vendors			X					1	A	
15. Define future skills		X		X		X		3	C	
16. Select and certify vendors	X	X	X			X	X	5	C	
17. Promote the company					X	X	X	3	C	
18. Track finished products					X		X	2	B	
19. Support installed products	X				X		X	3	B	*
20. Monitor customer's/prospect's business		X			X	X		3	E	
21. Announce new products					X	X	X	3	C	
22. Monitor legislation		X				X		2	E	
23. Develop/review marketing projects						X	X	2	C	
24. Monitor cash flows							X	1	D	

FIGURE 5   Business Process/CSFs matrix. © 1987 by the President and Fellows of Harvard College. All rights reserved)

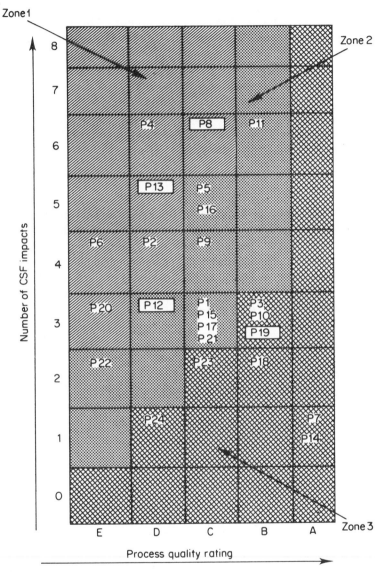

Note:
1. P = Business Process number from Figure 5.5
2. ☐P☐ = 'Big Burner'

FIGURE 6   CSF/Business Process summary grid

the higher risk/higher opportunity processes are those in Zone 1. The shaded zones in Figure 6 thus represent a view of the sequence for Business Process performance improvement (Zone 3 = least urgent). This is a judgement call by the management team. They have to decide where the zone boundaries on the grid should be.

'Zoning' of Business Processes to establish 'criticality' is the most commonly used technique by management teams. However, some teams prefer to assign a numeric weighting to the Process Quality Performance; for example A=1, E=5, etc. The processes can then be assigned a 'criticality' number equal to the number of impacts (count) times quality weighting and ranked in numerical order to assist in refining the Most Critical Processes.

3.8.2 The Influence of the 'Big Burners'

While all CSFs are equal in importance the Processes vary in their scope and the amount of the team's resource that is devoted to each of them. The general rule is that under no circumstances must the Quality rating of a 'Big Burner' Process be allowed to slip; and where it has a current Quality rating of 'D' or 'C', immediate attention in the form of improvement projects are required. The 'Big Burners' are identified by circling the Process numbers in the Summary Grid to which they apply (see Figure 6).

3.8.3 The Final Judgement

To bring a sharp focus to their activities most teams decide to restrict their attention to the Processes in Zone 1. They can now move forward to review the implications of the desired improvements to the MCPs on their general management activities and to review the implications for their use of IT-based applications and services.

3.9 Review Management Implications

Rule 9: The team should use 'business-as-usual' management systems to define and implement Process Quality Improvement Projects.

3.9.1 Commitment to Process Quality Improvement

It is vital that the team demonstrates its tangible commitment to Process Quality Improvement after the planning session by rapidly implementing a major improvement project appropriate to, at least, one of the MCPs.

So long as a team's CSFs remain valid, the Business Processes can only move horizontally (see Figure 6). If they are left alone, the tendency is to move to the left (Quality declining), whereas management desires movement to the right (Quality improving). This will normally only come about through hard work and concentrated management attention i.e. through effective Process Quality Management. Use of PQM requires that the management team deploys its resources to attain and sustain the desired improvements and it does this by use of Quality Improvement Projects.

3.9.2 Defining and Implementing the Quality Improvement Projects (QIPs)

Initially owners of MCP's and subsequently all processes should:

(a) Give a formal definition to the Process, and associated Sub-processes (assigning ownership for the Sub-processes)
(b) Conduct a strengths and weakness analysis to clarify the current Quality rating
(c) Define and obtain concurrence for the appropriate Quality Improvement Projects, relating these, if appropriate, to established QIPs
(d) Define the appropriate project management for each QIP

3.9.3 End Game

The progress being made by the team in implementing the Quality Improvement Projects should be reviewed as part of the business-as-usual management systems. The Sponsor has a significant role to play by ensuring that momentum on the projects is maintained. Major project reviews attended by the Facilitator normally take place three times a year.

One of these review meetings should be held as near as possible to the commencement of the enterprise's planning cycle. This meeting will be used to determine if the Mission has changed, and whether this change, coupled with significant changes in the environment (new competition, changes in regulatory legislation, economic cycle impacts, etc.), necessitate amendments to the CSFs, the MCPs and the existing set of Quality Improvement Projects.

The team must always concentrate on managing the QIPs to attain 'A' ratings for each of its Business Processes, and bring the QIPs in 'on time and within budget'.

3.10 Review IT Applications

Rule 10: Ensure full consideration is given to improving the current portfolio of IT-based applications and services (as well as to new developments). These can hold the key for major improvements to the MCPs.

3.10.1 Adding Value to the Business Process/CSF matrix

The team now capitalises on the work it has done to relate the Business Processes to the CSFs. (see Figure 5). The CSF/Process Matrix can be used to perform an audit of existing IT support for each of the Business Processes. This information can then be used to itemise those areas for possible future strategic investments in IT-based applications and services.

Figure 7 illustrates how a team adds value to the information contained in Figure 5. Two further columns under the heading 'IT' are added: the first for 'Business Quality' and the second for 'Technical Quality'. Each Business Process owner is asked to rate the current IT-based application/service support for his/her Process on a scale of:

A = Excellent
B = Good
C = Fair
D = Bad
E = Embryonic

and to assign this to the IT 'Business Quality' column.

The 'Technical Quality' column is completed by IT management who rate the technical quality of the systems that support each Business Process, again on a scale of 'A' to 'E'. Technical quality is taken to mean a combination of: the age of the application programmes, the maintenance spend each year, the ease of enhancement, the file technology used, the standard of documentation, the programming language used, the control software employed, etc.

This is usually a highly revealing analysis. The business community are frequently horrified to find their most important and highly regarded systems are only being kept afloat at enormous cost (and risk).

As an example one large Local Government team in England discovered at this point that their life support systems (payroll and local property tax collection) had been written in assembler language twelve years earlier. The documentation had long since vanished. The only remaining skill to monitor the programs lay with their 62 year old DP Manager. It was touching to see the solicitous way in which the Chief Executive suddenly began to look after the man's welfare!

3.10.2 Establishing IT Investment Priorities

(a) The Current Portfolio   The 'IT' information contained in Figure 7 can then be summarised to provide a 'Business/Technical Audit of IT Applications Support' (see Figure 8) which maps business quality against technical quality. This is a powerful diagram against which the team can determine IT funding.

Business processes	1. Best-of-breed product quality	2. New products that satisfy market needs	3. Excellent suppliers	4. Skilled workers	5. Excellent customer satisfaction	6. Exploit new business opportunities	7. Achieve lowest delivered cost	(A) Count	(B) Process quality	(C) 'Big burners'	Business quality	Technical quality
1. Research the market place		X			X	X		3	C		C	A
2. Measure customer satisfaction	X	X			X	X		4	D		B	A
3. Advertise products				X	X	X		3	B		E	–
4. Monitor competition	X	X	X		X	X	X	6	D		E	–
5. Measure product quality	X	X	X		X		X	5	C		B	D
6. Educate vendors	X	X	X				X	4	E		E	–
7. Measure personnel satisfaction					X			1	A		A	A
8. Educate/train employees	X	X		X	X	X	X	6	C	*	E	–
9. Define new product requirements		X	X		X	X		4	C		C	B
10. Process customer orders		X			X		X	3	B		A	D
11. Develop new products	X	X	X		X	X	X	6	B		C	C
12. Monitor customer complaints	X	X			X			3	D	*	E	–
13. Negotiate manufacturing designs	X	X	X			X	X	5	D	*	E	–
14. Pay vendors		X						1	A		A	A
15. Define future skills		X		X		X		3	C		B	B
16. Select and certify vendors	X	X	X			X	X	5	C		E	–
17. Promote the company				X	X	X		3	C		E	–
18. Track finished products					X		X	2	B		B	A
19. Support installed products	X				X		X	3	B	*	B	C
20. Monitor customer's/prospect's business		X			X	X		3	E		E	–
21. Announce new products				X	X	X		3	C		B	B
22. Monitor legislation		X				X		2	E		E	–
23. Develop/review marketing projects					X	X		2	C		D	D
24. Monitor cash flows							X	1	D		A	C

FIGURE 7   Critical success factors

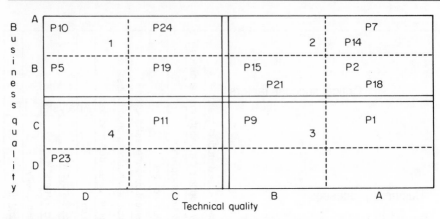

Processes currently without IT support

P 3 Advertise products
P 4 Monitor competition
P 6 Educate vendors
P 8 Educate/train employees
P12 Monitor customer complaints

P13 Negotiate manufacturing designs
P16 Select and Certify vendors
P17 Promote the company
P20 Monitor customer's/prospect's business
P22 Monitor legislation

FIGURE 8   Business/technical audit of IT

Systems in quadrant 2 are in good condition and are highly regarded for their contribution to the business. Funding nevertheless is most important with a focus on 'Maintenance'.

Systems in quadrant 4 need close scrutiny. The current IS support for these processes is poor and questions should be asked concerning the need and cost of improving the situation. If investment is justified funding will focus on 'Re-design' and 'Re-make', compared with Maintenance in quadrant 2, and correspondingly a different project management technique will be required.

Systems in quadrant 1 are a threat to the business. The longer a company has been using computers, the more likely it is to have a cluster of systems here; for example ancient accounts payable systems. Often such systems need the best skills available and often they do not get them until there is a crisis. At this stage somebody else's new development gets delayed, decibel management takes over and the image of the IT shop suffers. The funding focus for these systems has to be on 'Renovation' and the objective should be to move them to quadrant 2.

Systems located in quadrant 3 are less common than ten or fifteen years ago. They possibly are technically quite fascinating, but clearly are not highly valued for their contribution to the business. Here the funding focus has to be on improving 'business relevance', and a high degree of user input is required to ensure success.

The above analysis reveals how much new money is required to manage the current portfolio. It is not popular expenditure. It is not so glamorous nor so exciting as developing new systems, but it is necessary. This analysis shows the business managers why.

(b) Future Strategic Investments   But what about glamorous and exciting new systems? Simply maintaining the current stock in quadrant 2 of Figure 8 is unlikely to create any sustainable competitive advantage. Where should new investment be concentrated?

Two things should be considered: firstly, those processes which currently have no IT support (P3, P4, P6, P8, P12, P13, P16, P17, P20, P22); secondly, the current quality of IT support for the Most Critical Processes (see Zone 1, Figure 6), with special attention being paid to 'Big Burner' items.

(c) Debating the IT Priorities   In conjunction with the IT function the management team can now conduct a rational debate on its priorities for IT development encompassing both the current IT portfolio and future strategic investments. The debate centres on the use of scarce resources— user and IT personnel and capital and revenue expenditure—to produce a set of IT applications and services which give maximum support to those Business Processes which the team has identified as being critical to its business performance. The use of PQM tends to encourage a common will to succeed, thereby reducing the likelihood of priorities being established through 'megaphone' or 'decibel' debate.

But tough decisions still have to be made. The 'technical feasibility' of the desired developments has to be rigorously evaluated, as does the capability of employees at all levels in the business to gain the maximum benefits from them. Issues surrounding the certainty, and indeed the full scope, of the costs of development/renovation, running and maintenance for planned applications must be addressed. Factors concerning the quantification and scope of projected benefits, as well as the implementation of 'benefit management systems' to maximise the predicted benefits, must be debated. And of course risk analysis cases encompassing both costs and benefits must be prepared. (The issues surrounding costs, benefits and cost/benefit analysis from IT are addressed in Chapters 7, 10 and 11.)

3.10.3 Delivering the IT Priorities

Once the team have resolved their priorities for application development or renovation the required projects will be formulated, and appropriate project management techniques applied. Just as the entire 'team' was focused on the MCPs for the improvement of their general business activities, PQM ensures that this business focus is rolled forward into selecting IT priorities. This brings reality to the frequently stated requirement that 'the IT plan should reflect the business plan'. This extended use of the Methodology has enabled many management teams to achieve this requirement to their benefit and that of the entire enterprise. They have planned for maximum profit from their IT investment.

3.11 Summary of PQM Rules

1. Do not embark on a PQM planning session without the Facilitator completing an adequate briefing with the Sponsor.
2. All relevant managers must be present at the planning session. Do not run it if any key player in the team is missing.
3. The Mission must be defined and agreed by the team before proceeding to the next stage of the study—otherwise all that follows will be wasted effort.
4. Ensure that each member of the team makes his/her contribution to the Dominant Influences so that the real issues impacting the Mission are tabled.
5. A limited number of CSFs must be agreed on by the team as being the individually necessary, and jointly sufficient, list of essentials that must be achieved if the Mission is to be fulfilled.
6. Each Business Process must have an owner, and the owner must be a member of the management team that agreed the CSFs.
7. Take each CSF in turn and consider which Business Processes are required to manage it, adding new Business Processes if needed.
8. Those Business Processes designated as the 'Most Critical Processes' (MCPs) for improvement must be very limited in number. The team must not create a 'mission impossible' situation for itself by trying to manage too many MCPs.
9. The team should use 'business-as-usual' management systems to define and implement Process Quality Improvement Projects.
10. Ensure that full consideration is given to improving the current portfolio of IT-based applications and services (as well as to new developments). These can hold the key for major improvements to the MCPs.

Further guidelines for the successful use of PQM are contained in Appendix 5.

4 ALTERNATIVE USES OF THE PQM METHODOLOGY

Section 3 of this chapter discussed the 'classic' use of PQM which enables a management team to identify those IT-based applications and services which need to be enhanced or developed. PQM has been used to assist analysis of a broader range of issues as described in Notes 2, 3 and 4 and amongst these two have proved to be particularly successful. These are:

(a) Major organisation-wide projects
(b) The establishment of priorities by the IT team

which are described further below.

4.1 Major Organisation-wide Projects

4.1.1 The Problem

Many enterprises either have implemented, or are implementing, major 'culture change' projects designed to fundamentally change the way the organisation functions. Examples of these include delivering an improved customer service orientation and implementing electronic 'business communication' systems. Both examples can result in enhanced business performance through improved internal productivity and a growth in profitable market share.

Successful 'culture change' projects normally demand real ownership at the highest level in the enterprise and active participation by the entire Board. Failure of these projects frequently occurs where senior management delegate ownership to a lower level Project Manager. In order to minimise the risk of failure and maximise the chance of success for these 'culture change' projects a modified version of PQM has been used with Top Management teams to identify their project criticalities and the consequential Project-related Processes which they own.

This use of the Methodology enhances the capabilities of the Board in their role as the Project Team, and emphasises that each Director's performance is vital to the overall success of the Project.

4.1.2 The Planning Sessions

The planning sessions follow the same basic steps described in Figure 2. The key differences are as follows.

(a) The Team   In this case the 'Team' is the Board acting in its role as the principal Steering Group for the Project and the owner of the project is (normally) the CEO.

A Reviewing Director is often appointed to oversee the day-to-day issues and activities relating to the project on behalf of the Board. The Project Manager normally reports to the Reviewing Director.

(b) The Mission Statement   The project 'Mission' is described in an Executive Project Definition Statement (EPDS) of between fifteen and twenty pages. The production of the EPDS is vital if the Board is to play its required role in the

project and it represents the consensus view of the project. It is the 'Vision' of the project for the entire organisation. The EPDS is prepared ahead of the review, and is the subject of detailed discussion and, if appropriate, amendment during the meeting.

An EPDS will typically include:

* Introduction
* Management Summary
* Enterprise CSFs (if developed), and the way in which the project addresses one or more of these
* Key Elements and Boundaries of the Project
* Implementation Plans
* Project: Costs   (development, user, training, education, consultancy, etc.)
            Benefits (benefit management systems, benefit 'responsibility' of individual Board members, areas of benefit, specific benefits)
* Project: Risks, Assumptions, Critical Success Factors
* Project organisation and resources

The EPDS will be issued in a number of versions if the project has a sequence of discrete implementation steps which are scheduled to take place over a period of years e.g. in Europe, then USA, then Asia-Pacific.

(c) CSFs for the Project   The directors then verify, or amend, the CSFs contained in the EPDS. These are their collective CSFs for the project as a whole, reflecting their responsibilities as the principal Steering Group.

(d) The Most Critical Processes   Based on the CSFs the directors then build the matrix to relate CSFs to the Business Processes and establish the Most Critical Processes. Ownership of all required processes for the Project will then be assigned and the appropriate Quality Improvement Projects implemented. The relevant processes for the Project will be a mixture of Processes for the organisation as a whole, or sub-processes specific to the Project.

4.1.3 Follow-up Reviews

At appropriate intervals after the planning session the Project Reviewing Director, together with the PQM consultant, conducts a Review meeting with the Project Owner and each of the Directors to discuss their current views of the Project, based on the EPDS and the impact it is having on their Functional activities.

Current individual responsibilities within the project are confirmed and the CSFs amended if appropriate. Changing risks over time are thus identified and legitimise the establishment of major issues for further consideration.

The Processes to manage the CSFs appropriate to the Owner and individual Directors are also reviewed. This procedure provides the mechanism to implement and sustain the project across the enterprise.

4.1.4 Testing for 'Cultural Change'

From time to time it is appropriate to test whether or not the project is achieving the desired 'culture change'. This is done by interviews, led by the Reviewing Director and the PQM consultant, with selected levels in the management hierarchy and if appropriate with customers, suppliers and other outside parties. These interviews provided detailed information on the extent to which 'culture change' is taking place and point to corrective actions, especially at the middle management level, which may be required. They also provide an excellent judgement on the effectiveness of the Board in keeping the 'Vision' of the project alive.

4.2 The Establishment of Priorities by the IT Team

PQM has been extensively used to focus on the IT function in enterprises (see Note 4), and an illustration of this focus is provided by the two-day 'Information Systems Health Assessment Workshop', run for the IT management team (Appi, 1988). The objective of this Workshop is to enhance the effectiveness of the IT function by the team jointly identifying the Most Critical IT Business Processes, and then commiting to the relevant Quality Improvement Projects.

This work has led to the development of a standard IT Mission statement, related CSFs and Business Processes as shown below. Teams may elect to adopt these 'standard' items or to customise them, but either way they provide valuable input for the Workshop or for the Briefing and subsequent use of the PQM Methodology associated with a variety of teams in the IT function (see Note 4).

4.2.1 IT Mission Statement

'The fundamental objective of an IT department should be to exploit information technology to benefit the business and to produce 'value for money' products and services which meet justified user requirements exactly, are free from all defects, are available when required and are produced/maintained at minimum cost.'

4.2.2 CSFs for the IT Function

Typical CSFs for the this Mission are:

'We must ensure ... :

(a) IT priorities in line with strategic requirements of the business
(b) Maximum user involvement with clearly defined user roles
(c) An Information Systems organisation which is structured to promote individual accountability for performance
(d) The use of effective project management processes
(e) Efficient/effective delivery of user function
(f) Customer service orientation backed by Service Level Agreements
(g) Sufficient numbers of appropriately skilled people to meet all commitments to customers
(h) An effective communication system with our users

4.2.3 IT Business Processes

Those IT Business Processes tabled for use at the Health Assessment Workshops are listed in Appendix 3. These are used as guidelines, and may have Business Processes added or deleted to reflect the agreed remit of an IT Function in an enterprise.

The development of standard material for the IT Function has made a major contribution to the speed with which the IT management team can progress through the PQM Methodology steps at 'Health Assessment Workshops'.

5 SUMMARY

'Houston we've got a problem', said James Lovell, the Commander of Apollo Mission 13, when in April 1970 a major malfunction, connected with the liquid oxygen module of the spacecraft, occurred (fortunately Lovell and his crew all returned safely to Earth).

While their 'problem' may manifest itself in a less dramatic fashion many management teams (especially the Board) find that the identification of those IT applications and services, which will potentially bring the maximum contribution to the profitability of the enterprise, is fraught with difficulty. They readily acknowledge that IT can bring considerable 'competitive advantage', and that IT applications and services should be a major component to support the business plan. But how is the management team to break the deadlock and positively identify those crucial IT applications and services which will bring maximum competitive advantage and profitability to the enterprise?

In this chapter an approach to resolving this 'problem' has been described. Based on the experiences of the author, and many other consultants, it has been demonstrated that the use of the Process Quality Management Methodology has enabled management teams (especially the Board) to:

(a) Identify the key requirements for improving the overall business performance of the enterprise.
(b) Conduct an audit on the current investment in IT-based applications and services.
(c) Identify the principal opportunities and priorities for future investments in IT-based applications and services.
(d) Review the business relevance of current Quality Improvement Projects (if a Quality Programme exists).

PQM has been used to enhance the business performance of many types of management teams, with a multiplicity of functions, in a broad range of industries.

The formulation and implementation of projects to improve the quality of Business Processes provides an excellent framework for the team to follow up (over a number of months or years) those items which they identified as being critical to their business success. The project management framework for implementation of new IT applications or 'refurbishment' of the current portfolio again provides an excellent vehicle for follow-up. Experience suggests that both the Sponsor and Facilitator have a major role to play in keeping the team focused on follow-up projects.

Although the major part of this chapter has been devoted to the 'classic' use of PQM (which enables a team to establish its business priorities, and then its IT priorities), its use in the implementation of major organisation-wide projects and in assisting the IT team to establish its business priorities has also been reviewed.

Finally a fable to illustrate the harsh realities of today's business world!

> Every morning in Africa, a gazelle wakes up. It knows it must run faster than the fastest lion or will be killed. Every morning a lion wakes up. It knows it must outrun the slowest gazelle or it will starve to death. It doesn't matter whether you are a lion or a gazelle: when the sun comes up you'd better be running.

It is hoped that the reader and his/her management team will be sufficiently enthused by the contents of this chapter to use PQM to help them run as fast as they need to.

ACKNOWLEDGEMENTS

The author wishes to acknowledge the significant contribution made to his use of the PQM Methodology through joint research work and discussions with:

* Maurice Hardaker, IBM International Education Centre, Belgium

* Alex Mayall, Strategic Application Services Manager, ICI Corporate Management Services
* Alan Spall, Finance Director, ICI Colours and Fine Chemicals

NOTES

Note 1: Type of Industry

Where the team using the Methodology have a common focus and a real desire—indeed necessity—to succeed, then the type of industry has not been an inhibiting factor to the use of PQM. The industries where PQM has been used include:

* Insurance—Life and General
* Insurance Broking—International
* Building Societies (Savings and Loan associations)
* Financial Services Institutions
* UK Domestic Banking
* International Banking
* Chemicals/Pharmaceuticals
* Oil
* Gas
* Electronics/Computing/Office Equipment/Network Services
* Airlines/Airline Services
* Manufacturing—Food, Agricultural Equipment
* Brewing/Beer Distribution
* Retail—Furniture, Clothing, Food
* Private Health Care
* Central Government Ministries
* Local Government Authorities
* Universities
* Civil Engineering
* Distribution—Magazines
* International 'conglomerate'
* Heavy Industry—Steel
* Communications
* Cultural Festivals
* Environmental Agencies

Note 2: Types of Management Teams

While the 'optimum' use of the Methodology is obtained from a 'top-down' process, management teams at a variety of levels in the functional management hierarchy have found that its use has been of considerable benefit to them. Having carefully articulated their Mission, CSFs and MCPs, the team finds itself in a strong position when the bargaining process for resources starts!

Apart from using the Methodology with functional management groups, the Methodology has also been of to cross-functional management teams responsible for implementing major projects, managing Business Processes, 'Quality' initiatives, etc.

The types of Management Teams using PQM to assist their planning include:

- The Board of Directors
- Line and staff functional directors, and their reporting managers
- Functional teams below director level
- Territorial management groupings
- Boards for Joint Ventures
- Project teams
  —the Board as the principal Steering Group
  —the User Steering Group(s)
  —the Project Management team
- Business Process Management Teams
- Taskforce Teams
- Cross-functional staff groups
- Quality Councils
- Industry Marketing Teams (in 'product-led' enterprises)

Note 3: Functions/Activities Addressed

The types of activities which the Methodology has been used to address includes:

- Formulating business strategies
  —for the enterprise
  —for strategic business units
  —for major businesses/ divisions/territories
- Implementing major projects
  —to change market structures
  —to change 'corporate cultures'
- Improving performance of the following functional teams:
  —Research and Development
  —Manufacturing
  —Finance/Leasing
  —Communications
  —Personnel
  —Sales and Marketing

—Distribution
—Engineering (Customer Service Support)
—Property Management
—Corporate Services
—Planning
- Validating the 'management systems' of the enterprise
- Defining consulting strategy
- Enhancing the contribution of 'channel marketing' outlets

Note 4: IT SpeciFIc Activities

PM has been used in whole, or in part, by consultants in individual planning studies, seminars and workshops with IT management teams. These events either utilised the Methodology in its entirety—Mission to MCPs (see Figure 1)—or used parts of the Methodology (principally Mission and CSFs) as a major element in conjunction with other IT planning and evaluation offerings.

The 'topic' areas covered include:

- Linking the IT strategy to the Business Strategy
- IT strategy development and implementation
- IT Department organisation studies
- Objective setting for senior IT management
- Application Development group's strategy formulation
- Computer Operations—management issues
- Computer Services mission
- Office Projects—definition and benefits
- 'End User' computing strategy/justification
- Executive information requirements
- IT chargeout strategy
- Network strategy
- IT infrastructure strategy
- IT business case sanction

Appendix 1: PLANNING SESSION—BRIEFING NOTE

Planning sessions should be preceded by a note from the Sponsor to the participants. The following is an example:

Process Quality Management (PQM) Methodology

I believe it is important that as a management team we review the Business Strategy and our role in delivering it. This will be the prime purpose of our meeting. (Dates, times and location to be inserted.)

To assist our activities two consultants from IBM will act as Facilitators, and I will chair the meeting.

The meeting will be structured around the PQM Methodology which has been developed by IBM. A description of the PQM Methodology is contained in a Harvard Business Review article entitled 'How to make a Team Work', written by Maurice Hardaker and Bryan Ward. A copy is attached. Please make sure that you read it before the meeting.

The meeting will take at its starting point the following draft Mission Statement:

Insert '......................................'

Will you please consider the appropriateness of the Mission Statement to our activities, and the issues arising from it, to enable us to make a positive start to the planning meeting.

I also attach a draft list of the Business Processes applicable to our Mission. They are not meant to be exhaustive, some may not be relevant and I will undoubtedly have overlooked others. Again this list is a starter which I would like you to review before the meeting so that we will make rapid progress at the point in the PQM Methodology where we are creating and reviewing our Business Processes.

I look forward to a most interesting meeting, but more important to developing a solid follow-up programme to which we are all committed, and which we will actively pursue.

_____

Chief Executive Officer'

Where the methodology is to be used to establish IT requirements the following statements should be incorporated in the letter:

Would you please ensure that, prior to the meeting, you are aware of:

1. The major IT requirements to support your functional (or unit, territory, etc.) requirements of the enterprise business plan.
2. The current state of development of IT applications and services which support your functional (or unit, territory, etc.) activities.

Appendix 2: RUNNING A PQM PLANNING STUDY

The following steps provide a structure for running a PQM planning study which have been found to work well under a wide variety of conditions:

1. At the beginning of the meeting one of the Facilitators gives a presentation on the stucture of the Methodology, and the output which will be developed at each stage (see steps 3 to 10 in Figure 2). A copy of this briefing material is distributed to each participant, together with a timetable for the planning session.
2. The output for each stage of the Methodology is circulated to each member of the team as it is developed. To do this teams have used a number of alternatives including:
   (a) PCs using both text and data manipulation programmes with printed output.
   (b) flipcharts, foils and magnetic symbols. The material developed at each stage is then photocopied (after being transcribed if appropriate).
   The Facilitator gives a short presentation at the beginning of each step of the Methodology to remind the group of the tasks to be completed and the material which will be generated.
3. Use 'Brainstorming' Brainstorming Sessions have proved to be a very valuable way of collecting a wide variety of ideas in a short period of time. They should observe the following rules:
   (a) Maximum duration of 15 minutes.
   (b) Everybody should contribute.
   (c) Anybody can say anything, no matter how crazy or outrageous. Indeed, encourage wild thinking.
   (d) Nobody is permitted to challenge anything anybody says—until the end of the Brainstorm.
   (e) Be concise in noting ideas.

Appendix 3: THE IT BUSINESS PROCESSES

The material for the IT Business Processes shown below has been drawn from the Health Assessment Workshops (see Section 4.2) and from material contained in IBM G520-3998. 'Information systems management Architecture'.

1. Perform strategic planning and control.
2. Define technical architecture.
3. Conduct development and project planning.
4. Monitor services and service level agreement planning.
5. Conduct capacity planning.
6. Conduct skills planning.
7. Conduct budget planning.
8. Perform tactical plan management.
9. Manage change control.

10. Manage asset and data control.
11. Manage service and problem control.
12. Implement application development and maintenance methodology.
13. Develop application/software procurement.
14. Conduct hardware/facilities liaison.
15. Conduct tuning/systems balancing.
16. Monitor production.
17. Monitor systems and network support.
18. Monitor distribution.
19. Facilitate user support and help.
20. Monitor service measurement and reporting.
21. Implement services marketing.
22. Monitor finance and administrative services.
23. Conduct education and training.
24. Monitor staff performance.
25. Develop people management/recruitment procedures.
26. Implement quality assurance.
27. Conduct public relations.
28. Implement user liaison.
29. Manage supplier management.

Appendix 4: *BUSINESS PROCESSES FOR MANUFACTURING/PROCESS INDUSTRIES*

The material for the general Business Processes shown has been drawn from material developed by Tony Treadgold, Training Manager, ICI Chemicals and Polymers and the author. These have proved useful as a standard set to stimulate discussion, but would normally be amended.

1. Identify markets.
2. Conduct market research.
3. Develop portfolio products/services.
4. Formulate commercial strategies.
5. Monitor business/legal/political environment.
6. Prepare business plans.
7. Conduct competitor analysis.
8. Establish customer requirements.
9. Set price/cost strategy.
10. Negotiate product supply.
11. Negotiate raw materials supply.
12. Lobby legislators.
13. Agree commercial strategy.

14. Provide focused research targets.
15. Conduct research and development.
16. Develop channels to market.
17. Develop distributor network/communications.
18. Train distributors.
19. Monitor distributor performance.
20. Provide technical support to distributors.
21. Publicise/promote products.
22. Create/implement PR policy.
23. Develop capital investment plan.
24. Manage manufacturing.
25. Service customer orders (invoice/despatch/bill).
26. Conduct customer satisfaction audits.
27. Manage quality improvement process.
28. Conduct quality assurance control.
29. Monitor/control performance versus business plans.
30. Provide business information.
31. Manage cash flow.
32. Manage business planning cycle.
33. Plan organisation management systems.
34. Exploit organisation synergies.
35. Implement training strategy.
36. Consolidate personnel management systems.
37. Enhance communication processes.
38. Develop/implement IT strategy.
39. Manage/monitor change programmes.
40. Review strategy/operational plans.

Appendix 5: SUCCESSFUL USE OF PQM

Experience has shown that PQM studies are not always easy to run and some are more successful than others. This appendix itemises factors noted during many studies which have led to the relative 'failure' or 'success' of the PQM sessions.

'Failure Factors'

1. There was no common purpose in the group—a 'Mission' could not be agreed.
2. The management team was totally overloaded with 'guidance' from all directions; the PQM Methodology was simply regarded as yet another attempt to 'do' something.

3. The Facilitators did not insist on a rigorous briefing, adequate time to run the session, or only having those dedicated to the success of the Mission, MCPs, etc., at the planning session.
4. Organisation changes intervened between the briefing and the planning session taking place.
5. The Sponsor had created expectations which the Methodology could not meet.
6. The culture of the organisation did not encourage free and frank discussion.
7. A number of PQM concepts concerning 'criticality' etc. were considered too extreme.
8. The team had been instructed to participate in a planning session, with no follow-up envisaged.
9. The team created a number of short term action projects which withered away, instead of relying in their business-as-usual management systems to follow through.

'Success Factors'

1. An effective and thorough briefing was conducted.
2. The planning session stuck to the rules in terms of time, participants, etc.
3. The sponsor fulfilled his/her agreed role.
4. There was a strong desire to succeed.
5. The relevant output from the planning session was well communicated.
6. The business-as-usual management systems were effectively used to manage the follow up improvement projects for the Most Critical Processes.
7. A 'fast start' took place after the planning session; a major improvement project was identified and rapidly implemented.

REFERENCES

Appi, J. (1988) Systems Management Consultancy, IBM United Kingdom Ltd,Unpublished Material.
Boynton, A. C., and Zmud, R. W. (1984) 'An assessment of critical success factors'. *Sloan Management Review*, Summer Issue.
Daniel, D. R. (1961) 'Management information crisis', *Harvard Business Review*, September/October.
David, F .R. (1989) 'How companies define their mission', *Long Range Planning*, 22,1.
Demb, A., Chouet, D., Lossius, T., and Neubauer, F. (1989) 'Defining the role of the Board', *Long Range Planning*, 22,1.
de Geus, A.P. (1988) 'Planning as learning', *Harvard Business Review*, March/April.
Gulden, G. K. (1986) 'Neglected management systems can stall your strategy', *Indications*, 3,3, May.
Hardaker, M., and Ward, B. K (1987) 'How to make a team work', *Harvard Business Review*, November/December.

IBM GE20-0527 (1984) 'Business systems planning—information systems planning guide', July.

IBM G520-3998 'Information systems management architecture'.

Leidecker, J. K., and Bruno, A. V. (1984) 'Identifying and using critical success factors', *Long Range Planning*, 17,1.

Rockart, J. F. (1979) 'Chief executives define their own data needs', *Harvard Business Review*, March/April.

Shank, M. E., Boynton, A. C., and Zmud, R. W. (1985) 'Critical success factor analysis as a methodology for MIS planning', *MIS Quarterly*, June.

Chapter 6
MANAGING SUCCESSFUL APPLICATIONS

Mike Parker

1 INTRODUCTION—DOES A PROBLEM EXIST?

The Systems Development Manager today should be a happier man—confident that he can deliver what the user needs in a responsive way, giving good value for money, and consistently meeting his commitments. Yet is this true? Experience in many computing sites has shown that the average authorised backlog of system development workload is at least 18 months long. If this were not bad enough in itself, in most companies this represents only a third of the total backlog of requirements, which would keep the complete development group busy for 5 years! In this situation many of these users have given up asking their Systems Development Group to help them and are finding 'other ways' of solving their problems.

This should be the first warning bell to the Systems Development Manager. Many Users today have the budget and the technology and are quickly developing the know-how to 'do their own thing'. Whether they are right to do it or able to manage it is another matter—to them, it may seem like the only viable solution. If this is the case, what has the Information Systems (IS) Group been doing? Either it is fundamentally wrong from the Business control point of view for the User to do such computing or IS have not correctly considered all the alternatives available to satisfy a particular User requirement.

What, then, is the extent of the problem? Well, the problem has been compounded by the developments in hardware and software technology—which in themselves provide the solution as well. In the days when systems were predominantly written using symbolic language (3GL) software for running on the central mainframe, IS people were skilled through repetitive delivery and users conditioned to accept minimum leadtimes or interim manual alternatives. The Management process for delivering such systems was necessarily rigid, and the resource used in administering this process successfully was acceptable when compared to the total project cost.

But the world has changed! Alternatives have now arrived—choices in how to deliver the system, where it should run, and who should develop it. Exercising

Managing Information Systems for Profit.   Edited by T. J. Lincoln
© 1990 John Wiley & Sons Ltd

these choices bring with them complexity, and complexity has to be managed carefully.

In this chapter we will examine how we should choose the appropriate solution to the business requirement. Having made the choice, the next task will be to build a Development plan—a plan that is acceptable to both Users and Computer Operations. This plan will now contain a variety of solutions. We need, therefore, to explore how a single management process can be tailored to fit each solution. Lastly, how do we know we have been successful? What, indeed, is 'success'? We will examine ways of measuring the various aspects of Development work including achievement, quality and productivity.

The problems are real—but so are the opportunities!

2 HELP, MAKE, BUY, OR CHANGE—THE CRITICAL DECISION

2.1 Choosing the Right Solution

They say variety is the spice of life. Yet when faced with choice for the first time, people often make arbitrary decisions. Unfortunately, so it could be with many Systems Development Organisations. Figure 1 illustrates the choice now at our disposal.

In order to make a choice, we should have criteria to help us. Over the past few years, organisations have gained the experience to develop such criteria; we will discuss them in this section.

Before we do, however, the importance of the initial study should be

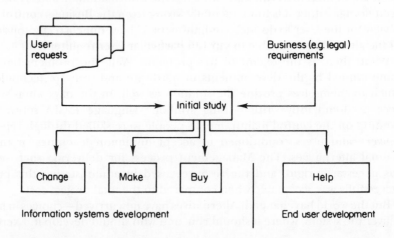

FIGURE 1   The critical decision

understood. Historically, Users may have developed a working relationship with certain individuals within the System Development project team who probably developed their installed systems base for them. However, if User requests continue to be directed to such people the solution most likely to be offered is to enhance the existing systems using the same programming language as that used for original development!

The element of choice is both part of the Systems Development Management problem and an area of great opportunity. There are so many ways of delivering a user requirement available to the developer today—ranging from traditional coding using 3GL languages through Application Generators and 4GL languages to buying a package which supplies the business function required. Typically, a Systems Development project team does not have the skill to make this judgement. Therefore, a separate group should be set up which has responsibility for both User Requirements analysis and IS Technical Strategy development. Another reason for this separation of responsibility is to allow the question 'Why should IS be providing the solution at all?' to be reviewed objectively. If the requirement can be satisfied by the End User himself, then we can address more of the requirements backlog, provide faster implementation with earlier benefits, and free-up Systems Development resource for more IS Development projects. To fully reap the benefits of this approach many IS Organisations must change their attitude from 'We write all the systems for Users' to 'We will advise the User on the best approach to his problem, and only write code as the last resort'! In order for both IS and User Management to feel comfortable that the right solution is chosen, understood and agreed criteria must be published.

But what is the 'right' solution? It should be the 'optimum' solution and not necessarily the 'cheapest'. The cheapest solution might not be strategic! That begs the question of whether the Organisation has an IS Strategy (see Note 1). The absence of a strategy can lead an IS organisation down a path of expedient solutions to individual requirements. This can result in a collection of unintegrated application and technical offerings, without the IS capability to support them or the collective ability of the systems to meet future business requirements. Very quickly these individual 'cheap' solutions become more costly than the optimum solution, and the cost of migration to the strategic environment once defined infinitely more.

The criteria which enable an organisation to evaluate the 'optimum' solution fall into the categories of help, buy, change, and make; these are examined below.

2.2 Help—If You Should!

Technology today, with greatly reduced costs of processing, the availability of personal computers, together with software development tools that can be used effectively by non-IT professionals, is enabling Users to satisfy their own computing requirements. This is not only satisfying for the Users but it is also one of the most effective ways of reducing the application backlog and brings early benefits to the Organisation. Yet, what is the right role for Personal Computing within an organisation? Should Users write their own Payroll System? Should IS continue to write report programs? The key to answering both these operations lies in the word 'Personal'.

Personal Computing is computing carried out by Users using interactive languages, such as APL or 4GLs, with appropriate support provided from a central Information Systems Group. All computing involves data. The data on which this computing is carried out is provided by one of three sources—the individual himself, public domain files (such as Market analysis data), or a copy data base provided by the central IS Group. The choice of software and hardware used (whether it is a central site Machine, a distributed machine, or a Personal computer on the individual's desk) should be made by Information Systems from within the Technical Strategy portfolio previously discussed.

Where, then, is Personal Computing appropriate?

2.2.1 Single User or Department Use

This limits the term 'personal' to an individual or a collection of individuals doing the same job within a department, where a common solution for everybody is possible. However, where the solution extends to multiple user organisations then the IS Department should develop or take over the management of this solution. Cross-Department Systems should be the responsibility of Information Systems!

2.2.2 No Direct Update of Company Shared Data

IS are normally the custodian of all the company master files and in discharging this role are responsible for the integrity of this data. Therefore, no User should directly update this data with their own developed code. However, it is possible for a user to develop a mechanised input file which mirrors exactly the format of previous input (e.g. key punching forms) and transmit this to IS as long as the file enters the system through the same edit programs as the previous input; i.e. no direct update of the company data files, only indirect.

2.2.3 Analysis and Exception Reporting on Company Data

Here a Data Administration role (which includes getting permission to access the data, confirming the data definition, ensuring the integrity of the data, and presenting the data in an appropriate file format) is carried out by IS.

2.2.4 Creation, Maintenance, Reporting, and Analysis of Personal Data

In this instance IS is providing the computing resource and consultancy support only.

2.2.5 Ad hoc or Frequently Changed Enquiries/Reports

Historically IS has hard coded reports and enquiries for Users which has necessitated the continual maintenance and enhancement resource being applied. This may no longer be necessary or justified. Many organisations have moved to a position of IS only providing the statutory company reports from IS developed systems, the rest being provided through personal computing from a reports data base provided by the IS system.

2.2.6 No Interface Problems

IS should not allow Users to develop in an area where either critical production scheduling dependencies or complex interfaces to IS developed systems exist. It is unlikely that the User has sufficient support resource or system architecture knowledge to unravel an interface failure in the middle of the night when the critical batch jobs are running!

   In order for the User to carry out effectively his personal computing role there must be an identified organisation within Information Systems to assist him in all these aspects—this organisation is the IS Information Centre.

2.3 Buy—The Next Best?

2.3.1 Why Consider a Package?

If it is not appropriate for Users to develop their own solution to a problem, then IS Development resource must be applied to this task. One of the first considerations should be to find out if anyone else has already developed a system which could be of use to our organisation. This may not be an easy attitude to adopt. Traditionally, our organisation may have developed every solution to its problems. But, does it have to any more? There is a rapidly widening market for application software packages both in specific business areas (e.g. payroll, accounts receivable) and specific industries (e.g. insurance).

   We need to ensure that the NIH syndrome (Not Invented Here) is not the reason why appropriate evaluations are not made of the opportunities now presented in the area. What, however, should we look for in an application package solution? First, let us define what we mean by a 'package'.

   The term 'package' in this context refers to application code developed outside the particular organisation that is considering installing it. This covers both applications developed in other parts of the same company being considered for local implementation, e.g. company common systems or shared systems, and those developed outside the company, probably with multiple customer implementation in mind. The considerations to be discussed refer to both sources and fall into two categories—firstly, evaluating the supplier and, secondly, evaluating the package. We will consider them in this order.

2.3.2 Evaluating the Supplier

Figure 2 below outlines the areas where questions should be asked of the potential suppliers. Although most of the points in Figure 2 are self-explanatory, some important points of elaboration may be helpful in assessing the suppliers capability to support you as a customer:

```
1. Deliverables?
   — Source code
   — Programming language
   — Test package provided
   — Standards used
   — Documentation
   — Data base structure
2  Usage?
   — Customer base
   — References
   — Experience from installed customers
3. Terms and conditions?
   — Contract details
   — Rights of use
   — Trial period before payment
4. Support?
   — Ongoing maintenance
   — Service level
   — Future enchancement releases
5. Organisation?
   — Size
   — Location
   — Parentage
   — Stability
```

FIGURE 2   Supplier evaluation

(a) The provision of source code to the installer is desirable to give it the ability to install *temporary* fixes to the production system in the event of a critical system failure (particularly in the middle of the night). The advantage to the Supplier is that the Installer can provide him with details of the area of code that has failed and, indeed, a suggested fix. A change to the source library is subsequently received from the supplier with the *permanent* fix contained. It also provides the implementer with a better evaluation of the quality of the product from seeing the standards used to develop the application. Obviously, the supplier might perceive this as giving away the 'crown jewels', but what is the risk in the installer using it only for the purposes above? The risk is obviously in what else the installer might use it for—and this is discussed under package evaluation.

(b) First users of a product can expect, and demand, extra support on site during the trial period. Conversely, if there have been many installations, their experience can be checked out, and less support accepted if the quality of the product is high.

(c) When considering installing the package in multiple sites, or even multiple CPUs, ascertain whether it is necessary to buy multiple licences or whether multiple copies can be provided free of charge.

(d) Assuming the vendor is providing ongoing support of the product, it is important to establish with him committed response times for different severity-of-system failures. Suggested severity codes are listed in Note 2.

(e) If the supplier is committed to enhancing the product for any of his customers, it is extremely likely that he will not want to maintain and support many multiple levels of the system for his installed customers. Therefore, it is important to obtain from the supplier (i) the committed enhancement and release plan for the system and (ii) the maintenance period for the previous release before support is withdrawn. The installer should remember that he may have little choice except to install the enhanced release (which may contain changes he did not request) or to maintain the old release himself when the support period expires. A way of ensuring that this unfortunate situation is never reached is to agree with the supplier a Management System for reviewing and agreeing changes to the base system.

How frequently should changes be released to the installed customers? From the IS Project Management point of view, one functional upgrade release per year is ideal; from a User point of view this may not be frequent enough to keep up with changing business requirements. On the other hand, more than two releases per year may be unmanageable!

(f) Some software suppliers are themselves subsidiary companies of large conglomerates. An installer needs to decide whether this relationship could lead to a conflict of business interest or, worse still, to the conglomerate gaining a market advantage because you are one of his package customers.

2.3.3 Evaluating the Package

In order to ascertain whether any package can be considered for implementation in a given business area (e.g. paying people), you need to analyse and record the individual business processes that your organisation wishes to implement. This would normally include the business functions, data flow and processing rules for this area. The capabilities of the package under consideration can then be mapped against this process and the degree of coverage, impact, and benefits in both cost and business terms determined. Normally, there is never a perfect fit—if there is, you are buying a tailor-made package (note that unless you have exclusive rights to the package, the second release might cause you to deflect from your 100% coverage position). The situation tends to be that represented by the picture at the top of Figure 3, with a Business area requirement as depicted by a 'round hole' and a package solution as depicted by a 'square peg'. Area A is the area of your business process not covered by the package at all, area B is a function in the package not relevant to your business, and area C is certain processing logic or rules that are not the way you would choose that business function to be calculated. The rest is good coverage!

So what is sufficient coverage? As a minimum it should deliver a business

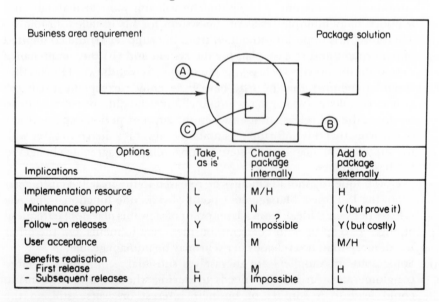

	Options	Take 'as is'	Change package internally	Add to package externally
Implications				
Implementation resource		L	M/H	H
Maintenance support		Y	N	Y (but prove it)
Follow-on releases		Y	? Impossible	Y (but costly)
User acceptance		L	M	M/H
Benefits realisation				
– First release		L	M	H
– Subsequent releases		H	Impossible	L

FIGURE 3   Package evaluation

benefit, preferably at 'local' installation level but certainly at company level. However, most installers are looking for at least 80% coverage against the business functions required of the application area, with a target of 90%+.

Before a decision to proceed is taken, the IS Department must agree with User Management what will be done to the package before implementation. Three options are usually open for consideration, as represented by the table in Figure 3:

(a) Take 'as is'.
(b) Change the package internally.
(c) Add to the package externally.

Some organisations may also consider combining (b) and (c). The decision on which option to choose is one of the most important decisions an organisation will take on embarking down the package route. As most major applications last over ten years the financial and business impact of a wrong decision will last for many years!

The table in Figure 3 summarises the relative weightings and trade-offs when comparing each option against various criteria. Let us look at each option in turn.

2.3.4 Evaluating the Options for Use

(a) Take 'As Is'   Here the installer will take the package as delivered by the supplier and install it 'as is', writing only those interfaces required to take transactions to and from connecting systems. From the IS point of view this is the cheapest and quickest solution, but the challenge lies in convincing the User to work within the limitations of the function and processing of the package capabilities. This challenge, however, should get easier as subsequent releases are received with more function provided, quickly implemented and good payback of business benefit versus cost to install, relative to all other options.

(b) Change Package Internally   IS could come under considerable pressure from the User in area C, previously mentioned, to change the processing logic to that desired by the User—in some instances, Users may make this a prerequisite before agreeing to take the system. Indeed, if IS has the source code and the capability, the temptation to change it might be strong. This must be avoided or else accept the consequence! Either convince the supplier to change the logic or put the capability in a table outside the system to vary the calculation, or challenge the User to prove that it is a Business 'showstopper' not just a 'nice to have'. If it genuinely is a showstopper do not accept the

package or consciously accept the consequences of changing the code.

What are these consequences? If faults are experienced with the package, the supplier, who cannot reproduce the fault condition because your code is different, will ask if the code has been changed—if it has, the maintenance agreement is invalidated and you are on your own! In addition, assuming one of the reasons the package was chosen was to take advantage of future enhancements made by the supplier, and bearing in mind his release support period regulations, it may be impossible to take future releases as both may have changed the same area of code! The same result occurs—the customer is on his own!

In summary, if this option is preferred, choose it knowingly with full Management support in the light of the potential consequences.

(c) Add to Package Externally   Many suppliers develop their packages with 'user exits' or 'hooks' designed into the system which allow installers to go out of the system at any 'exit', perform some locally written function, and then re-enter the system via a 'hook' to continue processing within the package. This gives, on the surface, great flexibility to the Installer. The User may well be pressing the IS Project Management to increase the package function to a more acceptable level. This potentially increases the benefits realised by the initial release as a consequence, and overall could increase the coverage from perhaps 80 to 90%. This may seem an attractive proposition if resources are available to contemplate such an option.

However, there are two adverse consequences of this decision. The first is that the onus is always on the installer, when reporting faults with the package, to prove that the fault lies within the supplier's base code and not the installer's add-on code. (Remember that the package supplier cannot reproduce your operational system in his test environment for fault analysis because of your 'Add-ons'.) Secondly, and much more serious, if the package will be continuously enhanced and re-released by the supplier to multiple customers, the functional boundaries of the package may change and what was once a 'square peg' now becomes an 'oval peg' and then a 'hexagonal peg', etc. This may cause the installer's IS group to rewrite the 'add-on' functions just to provide the same function back to the User again. At best, the installer must re-test all his 'exits' to ensure that the system processing still works. This is all additional resource installation cost with no benefit to the User. See Note 3 for an example of this cost.

(d) Another Alternative?   A package solution could have been discovered by user management which they regard as totally acceptable in its business function capability. Yet on evaluating the package from a technology point of view, the IS department rule it out as unacceptable for such reasons as data base

management, hardware or software dependency. Is there still an opportunity to proceed in some way?

Some organisations have entered into agreements with such package suppliers to buy the package outright, use the functionality contained in it as the 'Agreed Requirements Specifications', and, with or without the supplied design, rebuild the package locally to conform to the local technology standards.

What, therefore, are the conclusions that can be reached from studying the options? The preferred option is to ensure that, through involvement in the requirements gathering for the supplier's package where possible, the package has sufficient coverage of the business function required to achieve positive business benefit by installing the package 'as is'. Otherwise, accept the consequences!

2.4 Change—When Appropriate!

In many organisations, a large percentage of Development resource is tied up in making changes to installed applications. Is it all justified? Not normally! Could it be better managed? Usually! How?

2.4.1 Considerations for Any Change

Let us first look at whether it is wise to keep changing the application. The Systems Development Manager should ask the following questions:

(a) Is the application written in a technology compatible with today's and tomorrow's needs?
(b) Is the documentation up to date?
(c) Are there sufficient skills available to analyse the impacts of any requested change and then support the changed system?
(d) Is the requested change justified?
(e) Is the application capable of meeting the longer-term strategic requirements in this business area?

The answers to the first three questions do not need to wait until a new business requirement has been requested. We should have known this situation for some time now—only the criticality may have changed with the passage of time! If the answer is 'No' in these areas, analyse the continuing exposure to the organisation. One way to do this is to evaluate how to replace the application—does it have to be a total replacement, or could it be done in a modular fashion? A modular replacement strategy would have to be capable of having a new coded function running alongside the original code, with appropriate 'bridge back'. This can be extremely complex if new data base structures are introduced via the new modules.

Why is this evaluation necessary? If the User of this application could request a critical business enhancement needed for implementation say within the next few months, and you know that it will take you at least 2 years to replace the application, then you should have started over a year ago in order to meet the critical date!

This is why the last two questions are just as vital to this assessment. IS people are in the best position to explain to Users the technical and functional limitations of old systems. Such examples could be that this application could never be made on line/real time, or it could never handle an X times increase in transactions or customer records. IS has the responsibility to 'test' these areas with the application owner's strategic thinking so that funding can be obtained for a replacement system, and the solution made available in the time frame required to meet the business need.

2.4.2 *Considerations for Frequency of Change*

However, if continuing to incrementally enhance the system is the right decision, then how frequently should one change a particular application? What are the change drivers? They could arise from:

(a) Non-critical fixes (priority 3 and 4 as mentioned in Note 2) from the previous release installation
(b) Essential technical changes required to keep the application in line with the latest systems software level or new hardware installed
(c) Changes to interface with new release installations proposed by other systems, e.g. new transaction types or formats.
(d) Enhancements requested either by the Owner of the system to meet new business requirements or by the DP Operations Manager to make performance or operability changes (e.g. 'tune' the system to reduce run times, eliminate the need for tape mounting etc.)

If each of these changes were made and implemented individually then the application would be changing all the time. In some organisations, this is what happens! Yet this is both wasteful of development resource and risks production failure with the subsequent impact to the business and maintenance resource. Unfortunately for these organisations, it is proven that high levels of uncoordinated changes lead to shortcuts into production which in turn lead to production failures. So why cannot the IS department batch all the above changes into a single release and manage it as a Project, with appropriate Project Management disciplines? Is it opposition from User Management? Not normally! How often does User Management need (not want) his application changed to support his business?

2.4.3 Release Management

(a) The Rationale   Most User organisations have 'change windows' where historically changes either must happen (e.g. financial year start, tax year, new product launch, etc.) or must not happen (e.g. run-up to close of financial books, period ends, plant shutdown, etc.) The IS Project Manager should sit down with the User Manager (Application owner) and agree that all types of change will be incorporated into a new release of the system and when the mandatory change windows must be. The IS Project Manager's objective should be to limit the number of new releases of any application in any given year to a realistic minimum (two recommended)—with his argument based on value for money, manageability, user absorption rate, and risk to stability of the production environment. All these arguments will be elaborated later.

(b) Structure of a Release   The content of the releases does not have to be decided at this stage, but should wait until the requirements definition stage of the release. What should be decided now is the elapsed time for developing each release and from this IS can determine from their experience of 'fixed' length projects the maximum resource that can be applied to each release. All the outstanding negotiable requirements are then sized and prioritised during the requirements definition stage and committed up to the preallocated resource limit.

(c) Benefits of Release Management   One of the most powerful additional drivers towards implementation of the release concept with Users is the 'Value for Money' argument. To test an application properly, the developer must not only test that the changes have been correctly applied to the prime system but that all the secondary 'downstream' systems still process correctly. This normally is not an insignificant task in complex integrated environments. There are enough war stories around in most IS organisations on the impact of one line change not sufficiently tested. Unfortunately, some of the problems do not come to light until days or weeks afterwards—often in the period-end accounting runs! However, let us take the example of an organisation that will not risk taking short cuts into production for all good management and business reasons. Let us assume that the minimum system test cycle for the application is 1 week (5 days) and that we can make any number of changes from 1 day's worth of Development effort to 20 day's worth without increasing the test cycle from 1 week. If each change takes 1 day to develop then the cost of only one change is 6 man days and that of 20 changes is 1.25 man days per change i.e. $(5 + 20)/20$. What User would not prefer the latter 'value for money'.

2.5 Make—Where Essential!

If initial study of the Business requirement shows that a personal computing solution would not be appropriate, a suitable package cannot be found, and an existing installed system should not be changed to provide the necessary function, the last remaining option is to develop a new system. However, how should it be done?

One of the major dilemma's facing Developers is whether it is better to mount one large project, delivering all the required function in one 'deliverable', or whether it is better to stage the implementation through smaller and quicker projects.

Let us look at some considerations that should influence this decision.

2.5.1 Requirements Stability

To state the obvious, the role of the User is to define the requirements for a system that will meet the needs of the business from the moment it is installed, not at the moment it is defined. Yet, how many times have IS departments delivered exactly what the User asked for, but not what he needed at the time of installation! In my experience there are two main reasons for this:

(a) Most Organisations have two plan periods—a short term Operating or Tactical plan described and budgeted in great detail and a longer term Strategic plan outlining global direction and major goals. Any requirement stated today for implementation in the Operating plan period should be capable of exactly meeting the business objectives, whereas longer term business processes are far less well defined.
(b) Many businesses have to react to external market changes in a dynamic way in order to stay competitive.

How does the Development Manager, therefore, view these problems. Figure 4 illustrates the situation.

An element of change must be catered for in all projects—but in order for the original contracts of cost and schedule to be met, these changes must both be minimal and come at a time when changes can more easily be applied. Figure 4 depicts the User situation described previously with a continuous and increasing rate of requirements change as we move forward in time from those stated today.

If the Development Manager had committed in our example to a 'deliverable' in period 2, he is faced with a real problem. More and more changes are being requested late in the development cycle. Most of us have 'scars' from trying to reflect requirements changes in a project already into system test! Normally both cost and schedule targets are missed, and in worse

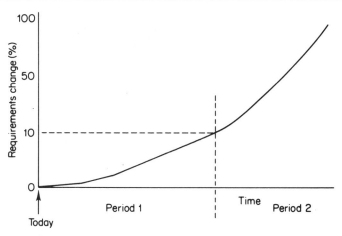

FIGURE 4   Business area stability

cases where changes continue to be applied the system may not be installed at all! Alternately, the Development Manager digs his heels in, rejects any change and delivers the originally committed function—which does not meet the needs of the business.

However, if the Development Manager has committed a delivery within period 1, when the requirements change does not exceed 10% of the original function requested, then change management can be applied to ascertain whether these can be applied without change to the committed resource levels.

2.5.2 Organisation

Although the previous section has concentrated on Requirements stability another area to consider is Organisation stability. If the company shape is regularly changing, then this in turn will reflect itself in potential requirements change to the Development Manager.

2.5.3 Technical Stability

A vast percentage of the change taking place in a computer centre is not caused by applications but by Operational changes. These changes include hardware upgrade, the introduction of both new levels of existing system software as well as additional system software, operability changes due to changes in transaction volumes and processing times, and network changes introducing new users and services to the TP network. Unfortunately, many of the changes are not transparent to the Application and, therefore, the Project Manager could be developing against a moving target of a DP environment. A most important element of the requirements stage is a definition and commitment of the performance and operability characteristics of the project at the time of cutover. Without a clear definition of the technical environment which will be in place at that time, the delivery of these requirements will be down to chance, with a high risk of non-concurrence from the computing Manager at Systems Acceptance Test time.

2.5.4 Manageability

Experience in IBM has shown that projects less than 5 man years of development effort can be delivered within 1 year elapsed time, and 20 man years effort within 2 years elapsed time. Yet these larger projects also bring with them potential Management problems. The size of the Development team will grow to more than twelve people. This will bring the need for significant project planning and control effort, supervisory effort and coordination effort. Also because of the significant elapsed time the personnel aspects of career planning, people replacement due to unexpected resignations, and clear role definition need to be managed. The fundamental size of the requirements generating the need for the larger project will probably imply that this is a significant change to the business process and may be involving multiple User Groups. This will necessitate additional project organisation effort, with the appropriate use of Review Boards or Steering Committees, and careful planning of user education and implementation activities. The larger the project the more complex the Management task, and the degree of Risk becomes greater.

Therefore, it is vital that the Development Manager consider what is the appropriate size of the project taking into account the above factors. In many organisations, the attitude will normally be to install the first 'deliverable' within 1 calendar year from the commencement of the project. If this cannot be the complete requirement, then a staged delivery process would be considered.

2.5.5 Staged Delivery

As discussed before, it is sometimes not possible to install all the required business function in a single deliverable within the appropriate elapsed time. Therefore, a staged delivery process must be used. Normally within any requirements statements there are some key areas that generate most of the business benefits offered up by the User, i.e. the 80/20 rule: 80% of the declared benefit could be provided by 20% of the Development effort required to deliver all the requirements. Some Development organisations have declared that this will become the first stage and, therefore, design to meet only the 80% defined benefits. Although it is possible for the Users to have a second stage it may be unlikely for two reasons: firstly, because most of the good payback items have already been taken, a follow-on may not be cost justified, and, secondly, no thought was given to the design requirements of follow on stages which may prove technically impossible or costly (therefore, not justified).

If there is a genuine business requirement for Staged delivery, then sufficient work must be done 'up front' in the Requirements and Design stages to ensure that the system can be progressively enhanced. Without a complete picture, you cannot put the various jigsaw pieces together with any confidence that you are right! What, therefore, is sufficient 'up front' work? A complete business process and data model of the business area must be completed in order to ensure that the correct data base design can be established for the whole requirements set. There are various System Design Methodologies that are capable of mechanising this development process and lead directly into the later stages of development. From the model, the Developer will be able to suggest the various staged deliverables for the User to provide the appropriate business case. However, stage 1 should not necessarily bear the total cost of the Requirements and General Design stage which has been completed for the whole project. You should consider spreading the cost across all committed stages. On the other hand, if the 80/20 rule can work for your stage 1 in this instance, then the initial stage could bear the complete cost.

2.5.6 Summary

Taking all the above factors together, it is recommended that the project manager endeavours to obtain user agreement to a 'Deliverable' in period 1 where both parties are confident that requirements can be held relatively stable (90%+). However, if the minimum elapsed time for any deliverable takes us into period 2 where requirements are predicted to change, then allowance in the project resourcing and scheduling must be made to accommodate such changes. The project plan must reflect the real world—not the theoretical world!

3 MAKE, BUY, CHANGE—BRINGING THEM ALL TOGETHER

From the previous discussion in Sections 1 and 2, a set of various IS projects (whether 'buy', 'change', or 'make') has been established which now need to be integrated into a single Development Plan for the Organisation. These individual projects, however, cannot be committed to the Users until we have completed the following stages:

(a) Building an integrated Plan
(b) Assessing the Plan
(c) Resourcing the Plan
(d) Managing the rate of change

Let us look at each of these in turn.

3.1 Building an Integrated Plan

Figure 5 illustrates the integrated systems implementation plan we are trying to build from the set of projects in our backlog. The sequence of build is as follows:

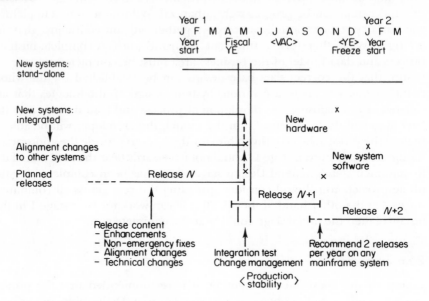

FIGURE 5   Building an integrated development plan

(a) Establish the 'change windows' as discussed previously in Section 2.4 which are either periods of known change, e.g. Fiscal year end, or periods to be avoided, e.g. Vacation close down and year end. These are listed across the top of our Development Plan.

(b) Plan the 'optimum' time for installation of New systems which do not require any or minimal integration with other systems. These should be planned to occur away from other types of change—to enable any problems to be quickly and effectively diagnosed and fixed with minimal impact to the business. In the illustration these installations occur in March and September.

(c) Align those new systems which require other systems to change at the same time. In addition, as discussed in release Management (Section 2.4.3), these aligned systems could have their own development plan integrating other types of changes in the same system release. Therefore, as shown in Figure 5, release N of the 'downstream' system has to be installed in May

in line with the new system required for the start of a new Fiscal year.
(d) The remaining enhancement releases, release N+1, etc., can then be planned in the frequency agreed by User Management and installed in periods hopefully between new system implementations, e.g. October in Figure 5.
(e) Incorporating Computing Environment Plans.

So far we have only described Application Development Projects and their integration. However, from the Computing Manager's perspective these are only part of the changes to be introduced into the computing environment—others are new hardware introduction and new system software releases. These must now be overlaid on the Development Plan. The implementations shown for November and January Year 2 respectively imply these have no implications to installed or proposed systems! If, as happens in many situations, the introduction of new technology does require application change then these changes are aligned and managed in the same way as any multiple project release.

3.2 Assessing the Plan

Aligning projects in this way provides the Development Manager with both an opportunity and a challenge. The opportunity is presented by the alignment of several project installations into a single change into production, albeit a significant one. The 'Change Manager' is far happier with this environment of fewer changes—if integration and acceptance testing can be successfully demonstrated. The challenge comes from managing the development of several projects together so that they are all ready to start the integration test. The risk is that if one aligned system is late, either that particular business function must be stopped (which in some cases is not feasible), or only the necessary alignment changes are implemented, or the whole integrated release of systems has to be delayed (which may be impossible because of business dependency). The whole onus is, therefore, on getting it right.

The practices discussed in Sections 3.1 and 3.2 illustrate a sensible management approach to the following principles:

(a) Minimise the incidents of change to correctly evaluate its impact.
(b) Manage each change correctly with appropriate testing prior to cutover.
(c) Work towards periods of production stability between changes (illustrated by June to September in Figure 5).

In building the above plan we now have the basis for turning it into a committed plan—after the next two elements are considered!

3.3 Resourcing the Plan

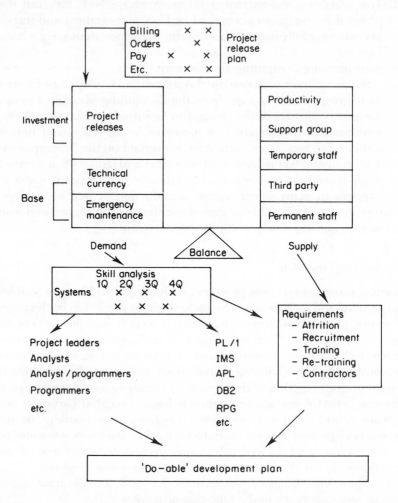

FIGURE 6   Development plan resourcing

3.3.1 The Demand Equation

(a) Are Maintenance Resources Necessary?   Before the Development plan can be turned into a resource plan, the resource to be planned for emergency maintenance should be decided. To reiterate the definition of maintenance, this is the resource necessary to correct all system malfunctions which have a critical business impact. How much should be planned? Good organisations

have statistics of failure rates by application, by release number, by type of failure, by severity, by period, by mean time to repair, as well as by the effort applied to make the corrections. From these statistics, project management can analyse the 'old' installed base and either accept that some amount of effort will continue to be applied or decide that the next project release will contain a small resource for fixing the old problems 'once and for all'. The latter attitude is strongly encouraged as maintenance effort ties up valuable skilled development resource and provides no added value to the business.

For a new system Development, plan *no* maintenance effort at all! This may sound a radical suggestion, even bordering on the naive, but it is a serious one. If proper business analysis has been performed, proper quality techniques adopted in the Development phase, together with the appropriate Management controls, then 'Defect Free' production is a practical proposition. Much of the maintenance subsequent to cutover is a result of the wrong attitude—an attitude which allows 'good enough' code to be implemented because we cannot be expected to find all the 'bugs' before it goes live. If the attitude, assisted by quality techniques, is to 'get it right first time' then there will be fewer bugs anyway. So, in my Development scenario, we only have Project Developers and a reducing amount of maintenance associated with 'old systems' which, in time, will be replaced. Hence, there is no need for a discussion on a separate maintenance department!

(b) Have We the Skills? The total demand on the Development organisation has now been established. The next task is to analyse it for skills required. This is a two way analysis. Firstly, determine how many Project Leaders, Senior Analysts, Senior Programmers, Programmer/Analysts, etc., are required? Secondly, what programming language, design methodology, data base skills, etc., are required? From this demand analysis the supply equation can then be balanced as follows.

3.3.2 The Supply Equation

The indirect element of the development resource must first be determined. This is illustrated in Figure 6 by Management, Support staff (e.g. Development Support resource planned for evaluation of new tools and techniques, etc.) and Productivity. An element of productivity may be given as a resource challenge by Senior Management or, preferably, offered up by the Development Manager as visible justification of the Development Support resource. The balance must now be made up of our systems development staff, 6 month or 1 year temporary students, and any sub-contract staff (if viable and manageable). Care must be taken to make a realistic plan for loss of people to the Development organisation, and the rate at which new people can be taken and absorbed into project teams. This balancing of supply and demand with skills available will highlight the type of people to recruit (both by level and technical skill) and their training required, together with the re-training and development of your own staff.

3.4 Managing the Rate of Change

The development of the Integrated Project Plan may have already taken weeks, if not months, to compile, including the right project definitions, the right level of resource, and the appropriate education, training, and recruitment plans. It is very tempting to say it is finished and submit the plan to the company planning process for agreement. However, before this can be done it is necessary to test:

(a) Whether the User can support the development plan with his resources
(b) Whether the 'end-using' Organisations can absorb the rate and degree of change which the plan will bring

3.4.1 User Resource Planning

How much User resource should be planned to support any project development? It is very dangerous to generalise as each project has different characteristics, but IBM experience has shown the following figures to be in the right 'ballpark'. The ratio of User effort to IS effort per stage is approximately:

	IS	:	User
Requirements	1	:	1
Design	2.5	:	1
Code, Unit and System test	4	:	1

Based on the IS development plan, therefore, this resource should be derived and planned by the User.

3.4.2 Absorbing the Change

The implementation of a project release usually implies change to some user operating procedures. These changes bring the need for training, and bring an element of risk to the day-to-day operation of the organisation. In fact, experience has shown us that many a well developed system has brought a business to a halt when the User is unable to effectively use the business function provided.

Figure 7 is one way to analyse the Risk to the organisation. Each of the proposed projects in the development plan should be analysed from the using department's perspective. All the individual User Departments operating the proposed applications should be listed and the degree of 'change' to their 'department' assessed by using Risk Assessment techniques (see Note 4). The assessment produces a High, Medium, or Low rating appropriate to the impact of change to each individual using department.

Impact to users:							
		End user depts					
Projects		Orders	Billing	Accs	Payroll	etc.	
Order proc	rel 1	H	H	L			
Billing	rel 2		H				
Billing	rel 3		M	M			
Payroll	rel 1			M	H		
Ledgers	rel 25			M	M		
etc.							
			*	*			

H/M/L assess degree of change and/or risk
  - Technology
  - Process
  - Training
  - Culture/organisation
User absorption guidelines:

Rate of change
  H   1 per year
and/or M   2 per year
and/or L   1 per quarter
  *   Unacceptable degree of change

FIGURE 7   Project release planning—user absorption rate

Following any change, there is a learning period where the User more fully understands and becomes comfortable with the changed way of working. If another change is implemented before this period is complete, then confusion and total loss of business control can easily emerge. Therefore, guidelines should be established linking degree and rate of change in any organisation— a suggested rate based on experience is shown in Figure 7. From the example of this evaluation shown, the Billing department cannot absorb the rate of change (two high degree changes) and nor can the Accounts department (three medium degree changes). Either the Business function proposed should be changed to reduce the 'degree' of risk or a project moved into the following year to reduce the 'rate' of change.

3.4.3 Summary

Only when the proposed development plan is complemented by the User support plan and an acceptable absorption rate can the total plan be *committed* as achievable and forwarded for company agreement and funding.

4 DELIVERING THE PLAN—THE PROJECT MANAGEMENT STRUCTURE

4.1 Learning from Experience

Many books have been written on the correct way to manage a project—almost as many as the different types of project management methods 'on offer' to the System Development Manager today! In this section, we are not going to analyse the various pros and cons on offer, but concentrate on the essential ingredients of any process selected. These ingredients have been borne and bred out of hard experience, both failures and successes. The infamous phrase 'learning from your mistakes' is never better illustrated than in managing projects. Here is a list of lessons learnt—I am sure you can add some of your own.

Why do projects fail?

(a) Undisciplined Management Process
(b) Uninvolved Users
(c) Ineffective communication
(d) Uncontrolled change
(e) Poorly defined end products
(f) Inappropriate focus on technology
(g) Too large
(h) Incompetence

This, therefore, begs the question, how do we define success? I propose that when a project is completed, success is defined by the criteria:

(a) On time
(b) Within Budget
(c) To agreed Specification
(d) With satisfied Users
(e) Defect free
(f) Value for money

In this section we will discuss the following aspects:

(a) The definition of different types of project
(b) flexibility in breaking the project into stages
(c) The Organisation, and roles and responsibilities, appropriate to the Project being developed

4.2 Flexibility—In Project Definition

Our Project Management process must be capable of delivering projects that meet these criteria consistently. Also the method must be capable of managing all types of project—large, small, installing 'vendor' code, enhancement projects, etc. Some Development managers confuse the subject of Project Management with Design and Programming methods. The essential ingredients of Project Management discussed in Section 5 are independent of the delivery mechanism and, therefore, can cater for whatever application generators, design methodologies, etc., are chosen as the technical development tools.

What, however, is the definition of a project in this context? It is a discrete piece of development—having a beginning and an end. Although the examples we will be using are typical of Systems Development (as previously discussed in Section 2), the definition and Management method are just as applicable to the Computer Operations Manager and Systems Programming Manager when installing new systems software or hardware, or moving a computer room!

Let us look, therefore, at the flexible approach that allows all types of project to be managed. Let us return to our three types of Development Project (Make, Buy, and Change) discussed in Section 2.

The 'Make' projects need first to be estimated for total size—with correct emphasis on early delivery as discussed in the new development section. However, most organisations end up with a mix of project sizes. The organisation I was familiar with ended up with three, as shown in Figure 8. From experience, the definition associated with the various sizes was as follows:

Large   >24 man months of IS development resource
Medium 6–24 man months of IS development resource
Small   <6 man months of IS development resource

Figure 8 illustrates the different number and definition of the development stages through which a system will pass. However, there are two fundamental principles contained in our Project Management stages:

(a) A Management Review, which will sign off the completed work and authorise the next stage, will take place normally within 6 elapsed months from the start of the stage.
(b) The total Project Management effort (e.g. Planning, tracking, reporting, etc.) should not constitute more than one-eighth of the total project resource.

In order for this latter principle to be applied, not only have the number of Management reviews been tailored to suit the project size but the amount of documentation associated with Project Management should similarly be tailored. Some examples of this will be discussed later.

Unfortunately, some organisation's answer to the high level of effort applied to Managing 'smaller' projects is to allow them to eliminate elements of management control or, worse still, be developed outside of any Project

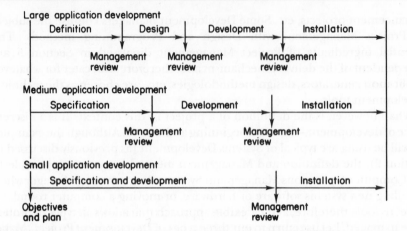

FIGURE 8   Management stages for application development

Management process. This is not acceptable or necessary. The key word is 'tailor' not 'eliminate'.

The Stages applicable to 'Change' and 'Buy' projects are shown in Figure 9. Here the stages contain different elements dependent on the type of project. In the enhancement 'Change' project, the first stage compares the installed system with the new business function requirements, 'designs' the enhanced system, and agrees which business requirements are going to be contained in the next 'release' within the resource levels planned (see Section 2.4).

The next stage carries out the changes and the latter stage in *all* projects is the User and Computer Operations Acceptance Test.

In the Acquisition 'Buy' project, the first stage is the comparison of the vendor package with the new business requirement to determine whether there

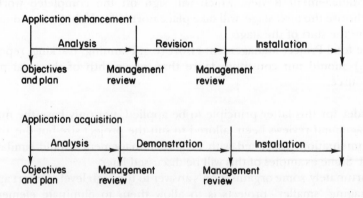

FIGURE 9   Management stages for application adaptation

is an 'acceptable' match and which of the options previously described in Section 2.3.3 will be chosen. The 'demonstration' stage will show the User what he is getting, including completing any 'optional' work together with any interface changes to integrate the vendor package into the system architecture. Then the 'common' installation stage follows as mentioned before.

What, therefore, in the context of all systems shown in Figure 8 and 9 is a project? Each Management Stage is a discrete Project requiring Project Management. From this point onward, any mention of project will be in this context.

4.3 Organisation—The Platform for Success

One of the key elements of Project Management is the Project Organisation (see Figure 10). This includes not only the communication between all parties but a clear definition and agreement on their roles and responsibilities. Experience has taught us that an ineffective project organisation will almost certainly bring failure, but a sound one will give the platform for success.

Business success depends on good customer/supplier relationships, and building computer systems is no different. The customer is the 'sponsor' who wants the system, the supplier is the 'Project Manager' who delivers the system, and the agent who represents the customer in the negotiations is called the 'Project Administrator'. These three roles are discussed next.

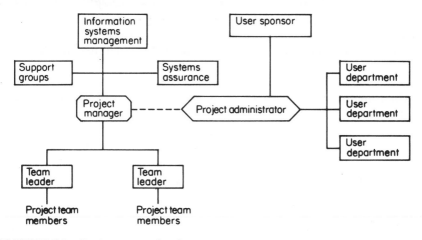

FIGURE 10   Project organisation

4.3.1 The Sponsor

Normally the Sponsor is a Senior Manager (in many instances, the Director) of a Business Area, e.g. Personnel, Finance, Distribution, etc. This essential role will be carried out in addition to his line capabilities. His duties are to:

(a) Represent all potential users of his system
(b) Ensure that user requirements are clearly defined
(c) Develop and obtain approval of the business case
(d) Appoint the Project Administrator
(e) Establish which parts of the organisation will bear the cost of the project and how the cost will be apportioned across users
(f) Approve and ensure availability of user support resource
(g) Identify Security, Auditability Requirements, and Business Controls, e.g. access control, record counts, etc.
(h) Initiate a post-installation review after cutover to production status

4.3.2 The Project Administrator

Because of the vital nature of the above tasks, the Sponsor appoints the Project Administrator to work for him in discharging his responsibilities. The Administrator is always a User experienced in the business area under development and normally of a similar stature to the IS Project Manager. As could the Project Manager, he may be responsible for more than one project for his business area at any one time—but this must not give him a priority conflict, and *must* be for the same Sponsor. This will bring the advantage of facilitating decisions across projects in the same business area. However, it is essential that the number of projects, and the associated workload, under one Administrator is limited to that which can all be delivered successfully.

The role of the Project Administrator is to:

(a) Coordinate all user activities and manage the approved user resources for the project
(b) Act as prime contact to the IS Project Manager
(c) Act on behalf of the Sponsor on day-to-day matters relating to the project
(d) Carry the authority to make decisions on behalf of users

4.3.3 The IS Project Manager

The IS Project Manager, who reports through to the Development Manager, has the Analysts and Programmers under his control. He may be developing multiprojects for a Sponsor. This Manager has the responsibility to:

(a) Review the user request for work and accept the definition of requirements
(b) Develop the overall project objectives as a basis for project initiation
(c) Develop the overall plan and schedule, identify the work products, sign

offs, responsibilities, reports, etc., as determined by installation standards

(d) Manage the project, allocating work, tracking, controlling, escalating as necessary and coordinating user activities through the Project Administrator

(e) Carry responsibility for satisfactory completion of the project into production status (including ensuring that other systems affected by this project can successfully process output produced from this system)

4.3.4 Multiple Projects

The environment created by integrating and aligning Project Releases, as discussed in Section 3.1, creates an environment which introduces a new ingredient of multiproject management. This, in my experience, needs an additional Project Management structure. Recently, the Development organisation I was managing implemented some major new business function into an Order processing system which necessitated changes to contracts, billing, and accounting and costing systems. In all, eighteen different systems had to be changed, many with their own project enhancement releases, and installed in the same accounting month. One way for this to happen might have been to encourage the individual Project Managers to work together and rely on their system dependence to ensure it would all work on the final day. This was not the approach used because of the unacceptable risk associated with a single project failure affecting the integrated Project Release. The approach, which had been in use prior to this example, was to give the 'Upstream' Project Manager, in this case in charge of the Order processing project, an additional responsibility for *assuring* that all associated 'downstream' Project Managers (e.g. Billing, Accounting, etc.) can process successfully the changes needed to align the new system releases. In no way did this make him responsible for their individual project development—this was the responsibility of the respective Line Management—but he was responsible for the following activities:

Planning
— Ensuring that related systems are aware of his development plans and plan sufficient alignment effort
— Developing a consistent release plan
— Identifying adequate resources for testing
Requirements
— Identifying interconnection testing requirements
— Outlooking production cutover approach and timetable
— Agreeing optimum business solution across all systems
Management
— Identifying key checkpoints for related projects
— Monitoring overall progress against checkpoints

— Reporting overall status

Cutover

— Ensuring all related systems have successfully completed testing
— Producing detailed cutover plan for related projects
— Agreeing the production schedule

Even with the increased complexity introduced by the above approach, the benefits in release quality and resource management are worth pursuing.

4.3.5 Critical Projects

(a) Definition   The vital link between the IS Project Manager and the User Project Administrator is maintained by complementary sets of responsibilities and experience of working together in the same business area. In most cases this is effective and all that is required. However, in some cases the link does need strengthening when a critical project is being developed. What is a critical project? Normally it has at least one of the following characteristics:

— Fundamental change of process as seen by the Users (e.g. High risk). One of the key indicators is normally the number of days of training required for the end users.
— An 'extended' elapsed time for the project, taking the Developer into the 'unstable requirements' period. This is typically projects greater than 5 man years of IS effort and a duration greater than 1 year.
— Cross-functional User Impact. This implies that some of the Users of the system wanting their requirements satisfied are outside the direct authority of the Project Administrator, and maybe the Owner. The User role now embraces negotiating and 'political' skills not normally expected in a Project Administrator, and which can be very time consuming—diverting him from his essential day-to-day duties.
— Business and/or Political sensitivity. Another dimension of this is the visibility the project will have either to Executive Management or Customers. The implications of Project failure are not acceptable within the organisation!

(b) Strengthening the Organisation Structure   Where some of these characteristics are present, the project organisation is strengthened by the appointment of a Project Implementation Manager reporting directly to the Owner. This appointee is normally a relatively senior User Manager, well respected for his knowledge of the business, his management skills, and his previous record of achievement. He is singly accountable for a successful project implementation by giving operational direction to both the IS Project Manager and the User

Project Administrator. This relationship is depicted in Figure 11. He could well be appointed full time for the duration of the project—if the project requires it! Because of the nature of the project, he reports regularly to a Steering Committee consisting of the following people: Sponsor, Functional Manager(s) of other involved User Functions, the Systems Development Manager, and/or the IS Director. Other Senior Managers such as the Financial Controller and Personnel Manager should be considered where applicable. The role of the Steering Committee is to provide guidance to the Project Implementation Manager, review project status, and resolve escalated issues and concerns.

Whatever project organisation is adopted a monthly project status report should be available for Senior Management review. The contents of this report will be discussed later.

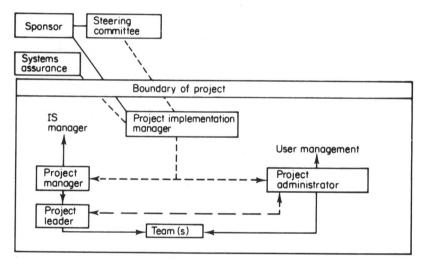

FIGURE 11   Critical development of project organisation

5 MANAGING THE PROJECT—THE CRITICAL PROCESS

Having chosen a stage approach relevant to the size and nature of the project proposed, and established the correct roles and responsibilities both within IS and User Management to manage the project, the next stage is to ensure that the system can be successfully developed.

The Essential Elements

In this section we will discuss the essential elements of any Project Management Process—essential because the absence of any of these elements could result in a project failure, not apparent until it is too late. The elements to be discussed are as follows:

(a) Project Objectives
(b) Risk Assessment
(c) Project Status Reporting
(d) Project Reviews
(e) Change Control
(f) Project Completion Reporting

A complete diagram of the process and the relationship of the elements is shown in Figure 12.

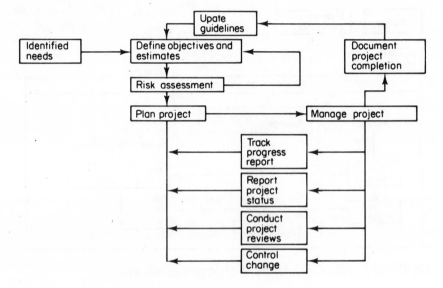

FIGURE 12   The project management process

5.1   Project Objectives

At the commencement of all projects the IS Project Manager and the User Project Administrator complete a document or form which becomes the project *contract*. It must contain the following definitions and descriptions:

(a) What the task is (e.g. requirements definition) and how it is to be tackled (e.g. use of a prototype)
(b) The deliverables from this project, e.g. a requirements document
(c) Who needs to participate in completion of this deliverable, e.g. project

team, operations, technical support, data management, other project managers, etc.
(d) Who is responsible for what activities needed to complete the deliverable
(e) How much effort is to be put in by all those participating and over what time frame
(f) The overall project schedule and cost

This document is then circulated to all the Managers of the areas mentioned for their sign-off, together with the Risk Assessment form explained next in Section 5.1.2.

For a large project this document may amount to many pages necessary to obtain the degree of understanding and commitment from all the parties. However, for small projects a 1- or 2-page document may be all that is necessary. Remember that this reduction is in line with the 'scaling down' principle previously discussed.

5.2 Risk Assessment

Before the project can start it is important to assess whether it is wise to start at all! That is to say, is the risk of failure too high? In order to answer these questions the following areas of the complete system to be developed should be analysed:

Project scope   —size, elapsed time, number of users, etc.
Project definition   —conciseness and stability of requirements, etc.
Resources involved   —skill levels of IS and User, resource availability, familiarity with similar projects, etc.
Hardware and Software considerations
                      —newly released by manufacturer, new to installing organisation, product history, etc.

The recommended method of assessing each of the above areas of risk is by use of a questionnaire completed jointly by the Project Manager and Project Administrator which puts a numeric value on each element of risk. Each area can then be 'scored' and the relative level of risk determined from a matrix. Project Management can then consider taking appropriate action to reduce the risk to an acceptable level. Such actions could be to assign more skilled resource to the project, or use a prototype to confirm the requirements, or use proven software and hardware, or even increase the resource and elapsed time of the project. It should be noted that taking these actions is not adding contingency. Contingency is a buffer for totally unforeseen circumstances; risk actions are for events that probably will happen. Manage risk rather than add contingency! At the start of each project (at the Project Stage as defined in

Section 4.2), it is recommended that the questionnaire is completed again for all systems other than those previously determined to be low risk. The risk score should be reducing stage by stage as further progress is made and increased knowledge gained. If the score is not reducing the project will probably not meet its Project Objectives Document contract. If the score is increasing the Project may never complete!

However, the Development Manager should not undertake only low risk projects. He should have a mix of risk projects—however, he should consciously commit to high risk projects supported by the appropriate Senior IS and User Management.

Only when the Project Objectives Document is signed and the Risk Assessment accepted can the Project commence.

5.3   Project Status Reporting

With the correct recording of time and tasks, together with a project plan compiled in the same level of detail, it is possible for the same base data to be used by the team members in their weekly meetings and by Senior Management in monthly status reviews. The Development Manager should receive a single-sheet report monthly on each project under development—the form shown in Figure 13 told me enough either to be satisfied or ask for further information from the Project Management.

5.4   Project Reviews

The organisation charts shown earlier in Figures 10 and 11 included a System Assurance Group reporting outside of the project teams. This is essential as their main role is to provide for IS Management an *independent* assessment of project status. The most effective assurance role I have seen practised came when reviews were carried out unannounced on the official project file. The Project Manager was responsible for keeping the file containing Project plans, task assignment sheets, monthly status reports, change control documents, sign-off sheets, and tracking data—everything anyone needed to know about the project. The principle of these reviews was 'show not tell'. If the Project Manager had reported that the Specification Project was complete, then the reviewer should check the file for the deliverables and all the signatures—if they are not there, it is not complete. The reviewer then writes a report to the Project Manager with recommendations for action. The Project Manager subsequently formally accepts the recommendations and acts accordingly. If either the recommendations are not accepted or the actions are not effectively carried out then, and only then, is the report escalated to both the Systems Assurance and Project Manager's Managers. In this way, the Systems Assurance

Group are perceived by Developers as a necessary check and balance function providing added value to the Project Manager and not as a personal threat.

5.5 Change Control

One of the key management responsibilities is to have an effective change control system in place during the development of a project. Unfortunately, many Managers feel that the imposition of a change control process turns the Development group into a negative, bureaucratic organisation. This should not be the case. Change Control is not practised to eliminate change, but to manage it. It should be used, for instance, to prevent a user informally approaching the programmer requesting a 'minor' requirements change during the system test, and, thereby, corrupting the whole data base because the implications had not been thought through. An uncontrolled change can throw an otherwise well managed and planned project into total chaos.

The change control process must be used to assess the impact of the request on the resources, schedules and deliverables committed in the Project Objectives Document. The process should have the following steps:

(a) Document the change request
(b) Agree to carry out an investigation
(c) Investigate impact on project
(d) Decide whether to implement
(e) Revise the project plan where necessary
(f) Communicate to the affected parties

The completed form should be jointly signed by the Project Manager and Project Administrator and filed in the project file. The new project against which 'success' will be measured is now as follows:

New project = original project objectives document $\pm$ change controls

5.6 Project Completion Reporting

A completion report should be the last deliverable of every project. In all projects (i.e. each development stage) except an installation project, this report should be completed at the point in time when all signatures to the completed work have been obtained and all issues resolved. For an installation project, this is completed when the cutover to production has been achieved. The report is essential to measure project success and document the experience gained during the development cycle. It should contain the following:

(a) Actual elapsed time
(b) Actual resource consumed (both IS and User)

IBM	INFORMATION SYSTEMS PROJECT MANAGEMENT REPORT	Page 1 of 2	Account Code:

Project Name:		Date:
IS Project Manager:		Report Month:
Change Numbers:		Plan No. :
Current Project Review Classification:		Date of Classification:

Yes	No	Status Summary
		1. Are the man hours to date within 10% of the approved plan?
		2. Is the number of tasks completed to date within 10% of the approved plan?
		3. Will the project products meet specification?
		4. Will project products be on time relative to the estimated schedule ?
		5. Are the users' responsibilities on plan?
		6. Are user and management relations acceptable?

Manpower Status:

Attached Resource Plan Summary	Plan Date :	Date of Actuals:

Task Status:

Attached Manpower Phasing Summary	Plan Date :	Date of Actuals:
Attached Cumulative Task Summary/Plot	Plan Date:	Date of Actuals:

Status in NET MAN HOURS

Planned hours as at last month ___ / ___ / ___   . . . .

Approved changes since last month ___ / ___ / ___   . . . .

New plan as at this month ___ / ___ / ___   . . . .

Actual hours spent to date ___ / ___ / ___   . . . .

Estimate to complete   . . . .

Total outlook at completion   . . . .

Approvals :			
IS Project Manager:	Date:	Systems Group Manager:	Date:

FIGURE 13   Information systems project management report

IBM INFORMATION SYSTEMS PROJECT MANAGEMENT REPORT Page 2 of 2	Account Code:

User Responsibilities Status:

Milestones/Keydates:

Event	Plan Date	Outlook	Actual

Problems and Planned or Recommended Action:

Inspections

Planned:	Actual:
Month: To Date:	Month: To Date:

Change Control Status

PCR(s) Submitted:	PCR(s) Investigated:	PCR(s) Approved:
Month: To Date:	Month: To Date:	Month: To Date:

(c) Quality statistics (see 'Measurements' in Section 6)
(d) Good aspects of the project
(e) Bad aspects of the project
  — Function Point Value (see Note 5) (only recorded when installation is complete)
  — Tools and techniques used

Senior Management (Development Manager, Owner, etc.) then sign off the document and hence the project. The document is then used for many purposes such as:

(a) Formal closure of the project
(b) Updating the estimator with 'actual' figures
(c) Costing the project for cross charge purposes
(d) Updating the development process with documented experiences
(e) Feeding the actual figures into the Development Measurements (to be discussed in the next section)
(f) Learning from experience

If all Project Managers ensure that the six elements previously discussed taught and practised within their project, then with intelligent use and judgement applied to the information they receive more projects will be successful.

6 MEASURING SUCCESS

6.1 Fact or Fiction

How good are you? It is an objective of any development organisation to be successful. Yet in many companies it is a matter of subjective opinion whether this objective is achieved or not. The Development Manager can probably 'reel off' the major successes in the last 12 months, whereas the Users will vividly remember other projects. As both sets of Management have the same objective to install systems successfully, then both should be motivated to put in place measurements which can assess the real situation and thereby, initiate improvement actions where necessary.

The definition of success of any Project should be as follows:

(a) On time/within budget/to agreed specifications
(b) Satisfied Users
(c) Defect free
(d) Good value for money

All these elements are capable of being objectively measured, as will be demonstrated in the following sections.

6.2 Measuring Achievement

The Project Objectives Document (POD) contained the contract for resource, schedule, and deliverables which may have been subsequently amended by authorised Change Control forms (CC). The Project Completion Report (PCR) contains the actual statistics from which success measurements can be derived. As shown below, both time and budget success can be calculated when the actual < POD ± External Change Controls. Only those change controls requested by the User should be taken into this equation, e.g. 'External' to IS.

	RESOURCE (HOURS)				SCHEDULE (DAYS)			
PROJECT NUMBER	POD	CC	PCR	SUCCESS	PD	CC	PCR	SUCCESS
10	100	—	98	Y	20	—	20	Y
20	300	—	300	Y	50	5	55	Y
30	120	20	130	Y	30	5	32	Y
40	180	40	230	N	35	10	45	Y
50	150	60	210	Y	25	15	45	N
60	180	—	185	N	30	—	30	Y
70	400	120	500	Y	60	20	90	N
80	250	20	240	Y	50	—	60	N
90	110	180	280	Y	20	30	45	Y
100	300	—	150	Y	50	—	35	Y

HOURS SUCCESS RATE = 80%, SCHEDULE SUCCESS RATE = 70%
TOTAL ON TIME/WITHIN BUDGET SUCCESS RATE = 50%

Note that a failure on either time or budget is a project failure.

6.3 Satisfied Users?

Unfortunately, it is possible to complete a project successfully as measured by the above criteria but still have a dissatisfied user. The reasons could be that he did not like how the project was managed, that he was not correctly involved, that there were too many surprises, that the education was inadequate, etc.

The only way you are going to find out how satisfied he is is to ask him! This in itself is a major step forward in the eyes of many User Managers when initially asked. You see, they never thought the Project Manager cared about this aspect of the project. The most objective way to assess User satisfaction is to derive a standard questionnaire which can be given to the User Manager(s) within the Sponsor's organisation. An example of such a questionnaire is shown in Figure 14. The questionnaire is issued by the Project Manager to User Management the day the project is completed, for return to the Project Manager within six weeks. The reason for this period is to capture the development experience while fresh

Project name : _____					
Release No. : _____ First production run date : _____					
Please rate IS performance in this project against the following criteria. You may find it useful to refer to the guide to completion attached. How satisfied are you with the IS performance in the following areas? Score =>	Very good 5	Good 4	Fair 3	Poor 2	Very poor 1
1. Gathering and agreeing requirements					
2. Estimating and scheduling of project					
3. Applying appropriate level of control					
4. Communication of design of solution					
5. Allowing user to comtribute to development					
6. Assessing and managing change controls					
7. Responsiveness to user queries/concerns					
8. Addressing audit/security aspects					
9. Quality of solution/function provided					
10. Ease of use of solution/function/provided					
11. User documentation/education provided					
12. IS/user relations during the project					
Totals					
User satisfaction index = $\dfrac{\text{Sum of totals}}{\text{No. of questions answered}}$ = ___ = (please calculate to two decimal places)					
Which one of the above areas do you feel IS should most concentrate upon to improve the overall service they provide ? : _____					
Completed by : _____ Title : _____					
Function (e.g. Admin, Personnel, Finance, etc.) : _____					
Signed : _____ Date : _____					

FIGURE 14   User satisfaction index questionnaire

in the User's mind. In addition, six weeks is normally sufficient to cover most of the processing options, i.e. on-line, daily, weekly, and monthly processing cycles. In order to assist the User to be more objective in his individual marking, a guide should be issued with the questionnaire explaining the meaning of each of the 5 to 1 options within that particular question.

When the questionnaire is completed and duly authorised by the User Management, it is analysed by Development Management. Firstly, a definition of the minimum satisfaction index to be achieved for 'success' should be decided by the Development Manager. For the questionnaire shown, an overall index of 4 should be the minimum. Then this success rate (%) should be combined with the on time/within budget rate to determine an overall project installation success rate. Of equal interest to the Development Manager should be an analysis of all the completed satisfaction forms, and an average score by question determined. For instance, an analysis of question 6 from every project questionnaire would give feedback on the effectiveness of the Change Control process. Again, any individual question with an average score of less than 4 should be followed up to determine if the Development process needs changing or strengthening, or Project Managers need more coaching or counselling.

Although some Project Managers may feel very nervous about formally asking User Management if they are satisfied, experience has shown that the User Management's delight at actually being asked does not justify this apprehension. However, the data once collected needs acting upon and communicating to all the relevant parties.

6.4 Measuring Quality—Defect Free

One of the prime objectives of any Project Manager should be to deliver a product which contains no defects. Defects are defined as those items not 'conforming to specification'. Yet many Project Managers have been guilty in the past of an attitude which allowed 'good enough' systems to be implemented, using the first few weeks of production to get the remaining bugs out of the system. This has been demonstrated in some organisations by not allowing the project to be handled over to maintenance until 3 months after cutover; others call the first period after cutover the 'probationary production'. All this implies is that this period is an extended testing period! Yet, what is the problem?

6.4.1 The Problem

Errors cost money to correct, and cause the loss of availability when the system is down. Just how much errors cost is illustrated by the analysis shown in Figure 15. The top half of the graph shows that an error costs orders of magnitude more to fix in later stages compared with the early stages of development. The point made by the lower half of the graph is that most errors originate in the early stages of development. Therefore, a 'good enough' attitude is costing the company a lot of money.

There are two types of measurement needed to address this area. The first is Defects in Development, the second is Defects in Production.

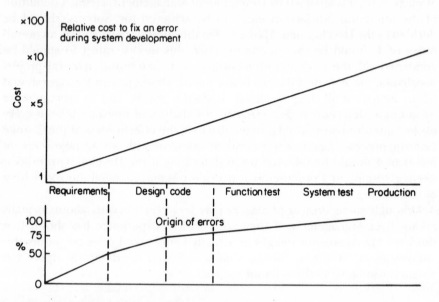

FIGURE 15   The quality problem

6.4.2 Defects in Development

Throughout each phase of the development process there should be *independent* quality reviews or tests of each item of completed work. These are to ensure that conformance to final quality objectives can be assessed *well before* the developed system goes into production.

Independent reviews can be carried out on requirements and design documents, program code, test plans, etc., using formal processes such as Simulation and Inspection. Endproducts are tested using the Unit and System Test processes. Defects found during these processes are formally recorded (and corrected) and the defect data collected and analysed in a number of different ways using simple statistical techniques. It is recommended that the data from production defects attributed to development is also analysed using these simple techniques so that a complete 'cradle-to-grave' picture can be understood.

There are three main types of analyses:

(a) Percent defects by Defect Type
(b) Defect Density
(c) Phase Efficiency

which are shown in the tables in Figure 16.

(a) Percent Defects by Defect Type   Total the defects for a given phase or deliverable. Analyse the significant percentages and look for opportunities to take corrective action. Look for trends across different projects and over past years.

(b) Defect Density   This analysis concentrates on the 'impact' of errors relative to the size of the deliverables being inspected or tested. Establish a value for defects per line/page etc of inspected or tested material. In the example shown, deliverable Transaction 1 had eight defects in 200 lines of external design document. This gives a Defect Density of: 8 divided by 200 multiplied by 1000, giving a (round number) Defect Density = 40, and this is 10 above the average for the phase.

Analysis should now concentrate on the extreme deviations above and below the average. High density may mean poor work or a very good test and, conversely, a low density may mean good work or a poor test. It is up to the analysis to take advantage of the opportunity presented by the statistics to see if a real out-of-line situation is occurring. Corrective action may then be required on deliverables Transaction 1 and Conversion. This same analysis can be done for Internal Design, Coding Testing, or Production. Comparisons should then be made and trends analysed across this development, and with previous releases, and other developments, until an exhaustive picture of quality performance is fully understood.

(c) Phase Efficiency   The matrix shown in Figure 16 is a record of all defects found during the development and production phases of a product.

Defects are initially recorded against the phase in which they were discovered. If, then, on further detailed analysis, some of these errors are attributable to previous phases, e.g. they should have been found in that phase, then the score of that prior phase is adjusted accordingly with an entry in the appropriate row. In the example, the Internal Design phase identified 95 defects, but of those, two were attributable to External Design and one to Requirements phases. Likewise, during System Test, 65 defects were recorded—all must be attributed to the Build phases and eight of them came from Internal Design. Therefore in terms of which phases are efficient or inefficient at removing defects, a simple percentage calculation of—Defects

Defect Types

Error category	Total numbers	Error (%)
Previous phase	20	5.5
Logic	55	15.2
Performance	12	3.3
Standards	16	4.5
Maintenance	29	8.0
Issue	22	6.0
Software A	18	5.0
Software B	31	8.6
Documentation	100	27.6
Software C	52	14.4
External routine	7	1.9
Totals	362	100.00

Defect Density
External design

Deliverable	Number of errors	Lines	Defect density	Fraction
Transaction 1	8	200	40	+10
Transaction 3	4	134	30	Average
Batch progress 1	3	102	29	− 1
Transaction 4	7	245	28	− 2
Conversion	12	490	25	− 5

Phase Efficiency

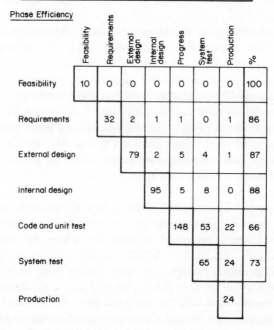

	Feasibility	Requirements	External design	Internal design	Progress	System test	Production	%
Feasibility	10	0	0	0	0	0	0	100
Requirements		32	2	1	1	0	1	86
External design			79	2	5	4	1	87
Internal design				95	5	8	0	88
Code and unit test					148	53	22	66
System test						65	24	73
Production							24	

FIGURE 16   The main types of analyses

found in Phase divided by Total Defects for that Phase will show where the low percentage inefficient phases are. The example shows that the Code and Unit Test phase needs improvement.

The calculation is: 148 divided by 223 multiplied by 100, giving a Phase Efficiency of 66%.

This can be on-going or can be stopped after an initial 3 month period in production.

The objective for all phases is an efficiency of 100%. That is to say, all the errors found were caused by the task just completed.

The other key measurement is to assess whether the number of defects per Function Point developed is decreasing either year on year or project to project (Function Points are discussed in Note 5). This measurement supports the other important quality concept of 'Get it right first time'.

The collection and analysis of defect data should be carried by each development project, and corrective action taken as appropriate. The most important part of the exercise is to understand what the various statistics are showing. Is there or is there not a quality problem with this development that should be given some attention and follow-up action?

In addition, the Development Centre (Development Support Group) or Quality Assurance group should also be reviewing project quality statistics to see if any positive or negative quality trends are appearing at a group-wide or process level. Appropriate escalation/action should then be considered in order to foster the 'good' and eliminate the 'bad'.

6.4.3 Defects in Production

A good IS organisation has a comprehensive Problem Management System usually administered by the Computer Operations Manager for all production systems. Any incident occurring during production running should be logged and allocated to a cause code. Cause codes normally to be found include the following: Application, Hardware, System Software, Network, User Error, Environment, etc. Each incident has a severity code as previously discussed in Section 1.2.1 to enable the owner of the problem to understand the urgency of the response.

The Systems Development Manager should request from the Problem Management system the following information:

Application Name, Type of Error (e.g. application code, JCL, documentation, etc.), severity code, and, after the error is corrected, resolution time and effort.

Until the Development Group consistently achieve defect free production, the following measurements are suggested:

(a) Calculate the total score of all *outstanding* production defects each month by multiplying each defect by the inverse of its severity code (i.e. each severity code 1 defect scores 4, severity code 2 defect scores 3, etc.). Plot the monthly figures with the target for the development group being a reducing trend score.

(b) Ascertain the number of *new* problems found in that month and score as above. The objective is to have a lower score for this release compared with the previously installed release. Each Project Manager can be given this personal objective as the statistics are available at the application level as well as the total organisation level.

(c) Capture the total score of defects found in the first 3 months of production running and divide this total by the total of function points changed and/or added by the completed project. (Function Points are explained in Note 5.) This will take into account the fact that projects vary in size. An alternative, but much less desirable measurement, could be lines of code. Again this measurement when plotted by month is useful at both the individual project, project manager, or total organisation level.

6.5 Measuring Value for Money

It may be obvious to most managers that all the previously mentioned success measurements can be met by overestimating the cost of the project, adding unjustified contingency, and testing 'the application far beyond that which is required. However, although we might install the application within the inflated plan resources, the project in no way gives the users value for money.

However, until recently, there has been no objective way of demonstrating value for money. Many users have an 'affordable' cost in mind (maybe based on a benefits assessment already completed) which when the Project Manager quotes a lower figure they accept, if more it is rejected. Neither side then had the means of demonstrating that the quotation was reasonable for the function requested.

In addition, Users are under continuous pressure to increase their productivity by taking the benefit of the new applications delivered. Yet how many Development organisations can show the benefits achieved by their investment in new tools and techniques? There is now a measure of both value for money and productivity and it is 'Function Points'.

Many papers have been written on the use and counting of Function Points and some of these are referenced in Note 5. However, I would like to discuss how the Development Manager can intelligently interpret the results of function point analysis.

Where, therefore, can the Development Manager apply this measurement to benefit the organisation? A Function Point count is carried out on all systems entering production—right from enhancement projects, through the acquisition of packages, through to new development. This data should already be recorded on the Project Completion Report together with the total IS resource used. Dividing one by the other, the Function Points per man month of effort can be derived. From this the following analysis can be made.

6.5.1 Productivity Versus Size of Project

Plotting the data obtained from completed projects normally produces a graph as shown in Figure 17.

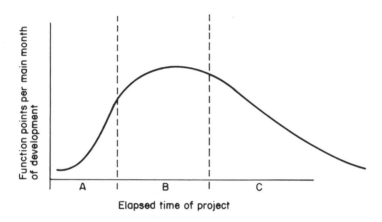

FIGURE 17   Elapsed time of project

Period A depicts the period where either making single changes or committing too many enhancement releases per year for a particular user is not good value for money. The incidence of testing far outweighs the added business function value. On the other hand, Period C represents projects whose elapsed time continued into the period when the original requirements become unstable due to changing business demands. This meant that the Project Manager was faced with making changes, perhaps affecting the basic design of the system, very late in the development process. Assuming that these changes were duly authorised due to their business criticality, the effect on the project is to apply significant additional resource with very little net change to the overall Function Point Value.

Therefore, Period B is where the optimum productivity and hence value for money is given to the User. With this data in hand the Development Manager should be able to convince a businesslike User Manager that phasing Project releases with the elapsed time within Period B is the sensible thing to do!

6.5.2 Productivity Versus Type of Project

Function Points, although originated for counting new development projects, have over the years been extended to allow the effective counting of both installing other people's software (e.g. common code, vendor packages) and enhancement projects on installed systems. The Function Point count should be part of the initial study evaluation, as a productivity test can be applied as soon as the initial estimate of installation cost is known. To this cost, of course, must be added the cost of the package. You should recall the discussion earlier in this chapter on the options open to package installers. The use of function points will confirm the wisdom of your choice to take the package 'as is' versus adding changes externally and/or internally.

When a subsequent release of a package is installed, if enhancements had previously been added externally, the only additional function point value is that contained within the enhanced package. However, the local installation group must apply significant resource to re-test the local add-ons and change them where appropriate. This normally is zero added value to the organisation—just cost. The function points per man month of installation effort will confirm this!

6.5.3 Productivity Versus Tool

We have all read some manufacturers claims that by using their particular mechanised tool the development process will be improved by x per cent. Yet how many customers have any means of evaluating this claim? Many of these tools are bought as an 'act of faith' by the Development Manager and probably some benefits in schedule and quality obtained. But did it justify the original outlay? Function Points (being a measure of output to the business) and resource cost are independent of the tool used and can, therefore, first evaluate potential benefits from the tool's use and then confirm their achievement. However, do not forget to include a share of the 'tool' cost in all the developments using it.

6.5.4 Development Organisation Productivity

The System Development Manager is faced annually with the task of submitting a budget for at least the following year. This will normally consist of Analysts and Programmers and the amount of money he would like to invest in new tools and techniques. Historically, in my experience, there follows a debate with Senior Line Management and, usually, Finance on whether last year's resource could achieve more next year, thus avoiding an increase in budget, or whether the requested increase can be cut back without decommiting any workload. This is a subjective 'no win' debate. The most senior subjective opinion always wins! If, however, the Development Manager could show the following, the debate would be very different:

(a) The average function points 'developed' per man month of development effort
(b) The man months of maintenance effort per one thousand installed function points

The first measure when compared period to period (e.g. this year versus last year) will show the percentage productivity improvement for his whole organisation for all types of projects. The second measure when compared period to period (if reducing) will show the maintenance productivity and improved quality of installed systems.

As both of these are objective measures they can be used both to show that this year's investments were good business decisions and secondly next year's investments will bring an X percent increase, thus substantiating the budget request.

6.6 Summary

Measurements have come a long way in the last few years when applied to Systems Development Organisations. However, for any measurement to be effective it must be meaningful. They can be very motivating for all concerned when the concerted management and professional efforts made to improve the situation are reflected in better measured results. However, if all this well directed effort does not move the measurements, then goodwill will be lost followed quickly by the cessation of effort. If the Application Group's reward system can be geared to measured results, then this can also correctly 'focus the mind'!

7 CRITICAL SUCCESS FACTORS FOR THE SYSTEMS DEVELOPMENT MANAGER

In this chapter, I have endeavoured to put forward ideas for consideration which have all been practised in Development Organisations. As my role has now taken me to many customers, some with a Development Organisation of 20 people, others with more than 500, I can say with certainty that none of these ideas are only applicable to my organisation. In fact, many customers are adopting them, with or without local tailoring.

With this in mind, I urge you to assess your company's status against the following Critical Success Factors for the Systems Development Organisation:

(a) IS leadership in selecting the optimum solution
(b) Published criteria assisting the selection process

(c) An appropriate stage approach for all systems development
(d) A minimum set of Project Management standards
(e) Measurements which cover achievement, quality, and productivity

The means to be successful are now available—it is the Development Manager who must provide the leadership to achieve it.

NOTES

Note 1

A Strategy embraces all aspects of Application architecture and design, Software selection, Central and remote processing including choice of User workstation, and Networking of Voice, text, data, and image.

Note 2

1. System unusable, critical business impact, no alternative/workaround available
2. System unusable, critical business impact, bypass/alternative available but costly
3. System degraded, not critical to the business, but restricted function and/or operational impact
4. System degraded and/or component unusable, circumvention possible, not critical to the business, but inconvenient

Response times from the supplier could vary from Type 1—the supplier will stop all other work and provide you a fix ASAP—to Type 4—the supplier will include a fix in a future formal release of the package.

Note 3

Recently, a re-release of a large common system comprising more than 1 million lines of PL/1 code was installed by one installer at a cost of 4 man months of development effort. Another installation, which had used the exits extensively in release 1, took 44 man months of development effort and three times as long to provide the same functionality to the User. When you realise that this system is over 10 years old and released twice a year, the latter installation site has paid dearly for the initial decision to provide local 'Add-Ons' time and time again!

Note 4

In assessing the risk caused by 'Change' the following should be evaluated:

1. Technology. Consider the degree of change in the departments use of technology, e.g. moving from a manual process to a rules driven on line system might be considered 'high' risk.
2. Process. Consider how the processes used by the department will be changed when the Release is installed, e.g. it could be that the method of placing an order has been substantially changed or a new product has been introduced requiring a different process from other products.
3. Training. An indication to the degree of risk could be gauged by the length of 'classroom' training needed by the users before they can operate the new system.
4. Culture/Organisation. Companies may consider new systems, or new releases of installed systems, as a means of introducing a reorganisation. Alternatively, companies devolving responsibility and authority to Business Units may fundamentally shift the operation of business processes to new departments. This could introduce a period of 'instability' and therefore risk.

Note 5

Function points are a measure of a project in terms of the amount of business function it delivers to the User. It is a measure that the User can understand and relate to as he participates in the Function Point counting of any project. It is a consistent measure of size and is independent of technology. The use of lines of code to demonstrate value for money was thrown into disrepute first with the introduction of common code or vendor packages, and then with the introduction of application generators and 4GLs. Function Points can cater for all these environments.

Much has been written about function points. The following publications would assist the reader in further understanding.

REFERENCES

Albrecht, Al (1985) 'Function Points and Measuring Installed Application Support', IBM Guide 63, November.
Jones, Capers (1986) *Programming Productivity*, McGraw-Hill, January.
Vacca, John, (1985) 'Function Points: the new measure of software', *Computerworld*, 18 November.

Note

In assessing the risk caused by a change, the following should be taken of

1. Technology. Consider the degree of change, in the departmental use of technology, e.g. moving from a manual process to a fully driven on line system might be considered high risk.

2. Process. Consider how the process used by the department will be changed when the Rules are modified, e.g. it could be that the method of placing an order has been abandoned, changed and new product has been introduced requiring a different way or new office modules.

3. Timing. An indication to the degree of risk could be gauged by the length of time a user is going to be able to use to minimise the impact on the user ...

4. Culture/Organisation. Companies may consider new systems, or new release of installed systems, as a means of introducing a reorganisation. Alternatively companies desiring to reorganise and adhering to business ... may find it necessary to shift the operation of business process to pre dominant. This ... had to reflect a period of instability and therefore ...

Note b

... purpose, a measure of apparent ... top of ... the main or business ... that ... to the that ... are the that the or ... that ... related to as the particulars of the Function. Unfavourable or any profit ... is a constant measure of size and is independent of structure ... The use of ... both periods to reconcile value for money, see through and therefore that ... with the ...

... has been written about this ... justice. The to library much about ... would assist the reader to further understanding.

References

Morecki A. (1992) Enhanced software and M ... Intelligent Application Support, 1994, pp. 62 N November.

Jones Capers (1994) Assessment Productivity, McGraw Hill, January.

Loveridge (1980), System Points and new mechanism of software, Cambridge, J ... describes ...

Chapter 7
GEARING IT IN THE OFFICE TO BUSINESS NEEDS

Julian Smith

1 INTRODUCTION

Many people are confused about what happens when you give terminals to office workers. Above all, directors and executives doubt if they are cost-effective (Note 1). They ask for evidence from other firms' experiences, with costs and benefits, but they have yet to see a convincing case. Some go so far as to say they will wait until office systems mature before investing. Five years ago this was a tenable view but much has happened since then. It is now becoming clear that giving terminals to office workers can contribute significantly to the success of a business.

This chapter describes how to achieve benefits from office applications. It looks at the office and some of the ways that technology can support it. A description follows of one way of studying the needs of the business and selecting the best applications, i.e. those with the most attractive benefits. The chapter concludes with a look at what determines whether those benefits are actually obtained.

2 THE OFFICE

In businesses and consultancies, as well as in the literature, people define and discuss what an office is, who the office workers are and which applications constitute the office system. This section suggests that such debate is interesting rather than fruitful. It contrasts the difficulties of justifying office applications with those of justifying data processing applications. This analysis points to three suggestions for the basis of the business case for office applications.

2.1 Who Is an Office Worker?

Some see the office as an information factory (Note 2) while others see it as a bureaucracy dragging down the rest of the organisation.

There are likewise diverse views on who should gain from use of technology. Poppel (1980) points to knowledge worker productivity as the key to office

Managing Information Systems for Profit. Edited by T. J. Lincoln
© 1990 John Wiley & Sons Ltd

productivity. By knowledge workers he means managers and professionals (Note 3). Hirschheim (1985) seems to take a different view, but this is explained by his focus on office automation as distinct from office applications in general. He divides office workers into principals and non-principals, where the principals equate to Poppel's knowledge workers (Note 4). Because non-principals have more structured jobs they are more suitable cases for office automation. The choice between Poppel's and Hirschheim's views resolves into a choice of which section of the workforce to concentrate on.

An example will put this point differently. One way to put the question is to ask whether salesmen, who spend 80% of the time travelling or with customers, are office workers. The other way is to ask whether we should concern ourselves with salesmen. The second question is more helpful because it leads to a judgement that can be tested against business criteria. If we answer no, saying salesmen will not figure in the business case, we discount their communication needs and much else besides. We can then decide whether that is sensible in the light of the aspects of the business under consideration.

The scope of a business case can be the whole business at one extreme and a single section at the other. The widest view gets closest to the goals of the business and its relation to the external world. The narrow view goes into particular problems in depth. Later in this chapter (Sections 5, 6 and 7) there is a description of one successful method of studying the needs of large numbers of people.

2.2 Differences between Office and Data Processing Applications

Early computer systems tackled repetitive tasks where procedures were defined, or were relatively easy to discern. Tasks and processes were formalised and then translated into a computer system. Payroll is the classic example. Once on the computer, the payroll takes less human effort and is done faster with less mistakes. It is not difficult to put a money value on these improvements. Furthermore, the simple fact of putting in the system and using it ensures that the improvements are obtained. The way the payroll department uses this new system is determined by how it was designed and the payroll clerks, for example, have to change their way of working to suit the system. Instead of filling in a form, they key into a terminal. Their only choice is whether to use it or to seek alternative employment. While data processing has moved on from such simple applications it is still the case that many present-day uses of computers have these same characteristics.

Office applications, however, are not so straightforward. Frequently the system goes in but improvements that were hoped for do not materialise. Staff who were supposed to use terminals let them gather dust.

The problem is that the characteristics of data processing applications do not apply to office applications. For many office staff it is difficult to define the office tasks and processes they carry out, let alone formalise them and translate them into computer systems. Reductions in human effort, time taken and numbers of mistakes are not automatically obtained. Changes in ways of working may or may not happen as expected. It is difficult to order people to use a terminal when they have alternatives to hand—to make them send an electronic message when they can pick up a phone or send a memo.

To summarise, office applications differ from data processing principally in being less structured. That goes for the tasks, for the processes and for the information. Information that resists being coded, activities that cannot be captured in flowcharts and people who have to be persuaded rather than told to use a terminal characterise 'the office'.

2.3 Justifying Office Applications

We can assume that the whole idea of applying technology to what goes on in the office is to bring about improvements of some sort. Productivity is often the reason given for investing in data processing (Note 5), but other reasons include jobs otherwise impossible because of time, cost or complexity; and reducing elapsed time. There are usually, of course, intangible benefits that are also made possible by the investment.

Similar arguments do not work as well when justifying investment in the office. Many cases have been built on productivity savings but the difficulty lies in proving them. Office productivity is notoriously hard to measure.

Proving that time (or labour) has been saved is not possible unless there is an observable difference in the way people work. Let us take a very simple case in which the system has been put in and each individual has decided how to take advantage of it. With no direction from above, those who come in late and leave early will very likely come in later and leave earlier. Others will choose differently. The sum total of all these changes will be the evidence of productivity improvements. A case study along these lines is included towards the end of this chapter.

This example shows that benefits will only be obtained if people use the additional time to some purpose. The business case must show that the office applications make business sense. It must show what is to happen to the time saved by productivity improvements.

It is useful to distinguish between the financial aspects of the justification and the impact on the business. Let us move on from the simple case and suppose that time savings are being directed towards some worthwhile goal. An easy one to consider is a reduction in the workforce of 5% (say). Avoidance of an increase of 5% that would otherwise be necessary is another version of this goal. The financial view of the investment sets the costs of the office system against the smaller salary bill. If the saving is greater, we have a positive justification and if the costs are greater, a negative justification. Either way, there may be advantages in having a smaller workforce—less difficulties in recruitment perhaps.

This distinction between the cost case for investment in office technology and the impact on the business provides a way of dealing with intangible benefits, always a source of difficulty. In the first case (positive justification), the advantages of the smaller workforce were a bonus. In the second, the intangible advantages were obtained for a net cost (gross costs minus financial savings from the smaller workforce).

If the only argument that is acceptable to the directors is a strict cost justification, attempts must be made to put a financial value on the intangible benefits. This is the point where cost justifications can start to look unreal for it is not easy to value such things as improvements in customer service or staff morale.

If arguments about business impact as well as about financial savings are acceptable, a clearer presentation of the business case becomes possible. The financial case can show the net cost of the system. The business impact on customer service or whatever can be described. Senior management then face the decision of whether it is worth spending the net figure in order to improve customer service in the ways detailed.

The business case should also address another point made earlier—voluntary use of the system (Note 6). If people can choose whether or not to use the system, the reasons why they will so choose should be detailed. This will be because they see some advantage to themselves as individuals.

There are thus three components to a business case for office applications: cost justification, business impact and user motivation. They are not tightly linked to each other. No one component ensures that the other two are there.

To see why this is so, imagine a project with definite advantages to the users but where no-one has thought about the business benefits. Everyone will be keen to use the system because it saves time and avoids boring tasks. If staff take the benefit in the form of leaving early, there is no business benefit. The impact of the project on the business is, in other words, indeterminate even though users are keen to use the system.

The converse, a project with good benefits but with no attractions to users hardly needs consideration. It will be problematical how much of the potential benefit will be realised. There are many ways to avoid using a system. The usual response of managers who do not like a system, for example, is to place someone else between it and themselves. A secretary will do admirably for this purpose (Note 7).

A case with a good cost justification but with no business impact will resemble the situation where staff come in later and leave earlier. This sort of case has well-researched productivity improvements but no plan to use the time saved.

In justifying office applications, therefore, we must make sure that the business and the people both get their share of attention. It is to the people that we turn next.

3 THE OFFICE WORKERS

This section looks at those who work in offices and the relevance to them of any proposed office applications. This aspect of the business case requires insights into the range of people's activities, interests and motivations. The purpose of this section is therefore to illustrate and not to define.

The characters who appear in the following paragraphs are a personal selection drawn from experience. The representative views of the various types of staff are drawn from many user surveys of the type described in Section 5.

3.1 Clerical Staff

Many of the earliest uses of computing were to assist clerical operations, which is why we no longer see rows of clerks and a supervisor on a podium facing towards them. Today in many organisations, the clerical worker is someone who sits at a screen and works through it. The clerk's job has improved because the work is easier, less mistakes are made and much routine has disappeared. These changes have come about because they have been designed into the computer applications used by the clerks.

A longer term effect is that as more and more tasks are automated, the scope for judgement in a clerical job increases. Where previously many clerks were needed and only a select few did anything out of the ordinary, we now have a tenth of the number getting through the same amount of work. The routine work is now just a matter of keying into the computer. There are as many one-offs as before but most clerks now handle them. Less straightforward cases, in other words, loom larger in the job. The type of person required for the job therefore evolves to match: more initiative is needed and more understanding of policies.

Clerical staff often complain about delays. These include slow computer response times, people not being available on the phone, out-of-date directories and misleading or incomplete information.

3.2 Secretaries and Personal Assistants

These people are expected to think for themselves and to get things done. They must be able to find their way around and be good at dealing with others. Their to-do lists are always very long and interruptions are a way of life.

They like good communication channels that help you be in the know and reduce interruptions. Efficient communications also speed things up and reduce panics. Anything that helps find people is good news, whether that be radio-phones or an electronic diary system.

Secretaries are associated with typing, or these days with word processing, the excellent business case for which has been proved time after time over the last 10 years. There must be few businesses where just about anyone with a clear need for word processing does not get it.

The other thing worth noting about secretaries and personal assistants is that there are, as a proportion of total headcount, not many of them. Accordingly, unless they are part of a wide-spread communications network, there is little productivity advantage in giving them more than word processing.

3.3 Professionals

Professionals have a degree of expertise and are paid to exercise judgement. They work sometimes to a formula, sometimes as they see fit. They do not care for work that is not, as they see it, related to their jobs. Such activities as reporting upwards, documenting cases, form filling and updating whereabouts boards are frequently neglected. Clerks, as we have seen, are becoming more like professionals.

Some jobs demand a large amount of data, in the sense of structured information. Some require access to a lot of unstructured information—textual, diagrams and images, catalogues and directories, works of reference, news reports, etc.

Professionals' use of communications is strongly influenced by the management style of the organisation. We can see how this is so in terms of the styles described by Feeney (Note 8). He distinguishes four different ones: personal informal, personal formal, written formal and written informal.

In any organisation, of no matter what style, professionals spend a lot of time communicating—writing, reading, making telephone calls, and attending meetings, formal and informal. The style cannot be deduced from a study of these activities by themselves. However, the management style will profoundly affect what the professionals will value. For the formal written culture, for example, it is reasonable to suppose that anything that makes the preparation and revision of reports and position papers better will be welcomed. Once prepared, papers have to be circulated for review, so improvements in communications will be attractive. Were it an organisation whose style was personal informal, to take a different example, the same features would be less significant and simple messaging would be attractive. Only when the role these different means of communication play is understood can the attractions of technology to the individuals be imagined. The proposed tools must fit in with the way professionals work.

Professionals are often charged with bringing about change. Broad examples include developing and announcing new products; setting up new facilities;

rationalising services; and, of course, installing computer systems. This kind of activity is increasingly being formalised under the name of project management, often with computer systems in support. The value of this to the business is clear but our concern in this section is the value to the individual, which can vary. If it appears as more bureaucracy it will be unwelcome. With good management, it will appear like a smoothly running project.

The field force are professionals in the sense used here. They spend a lot of time away from the office and so are particularly dependent on communications.

3.4 Supervisors and Junior Management

Management needs and motivations overlap those of professionals. There are, however, three principal differences between professionals and junior management, relating to their activities and to their position at the start of the management tree:

1. Junior management attend more meetings than professionals and they spend less time investigating or researching decisions.
2. They form the end of the management channel for news, directives and policies.
3. They are the start of the chain of accountability, often having responsibilities for people, money and other assets.

Communications are consequently more important to junior management than to professionals. Improvements in informal communications and in the flow of official information will be attractive.

3.5 Higher Level Management

Moving up the management levels is once again a matter of degree rather than of kind: still more time in meetings, virtually no research into issues (passed via assistants to professionals), lots of travel and above all the continuous press of events. There is too much paper to get through and too many people to see. Too many decisions refuse to stay down in the management tree where they belong.

Any technological solution will have to offer advantages over those to be had by working through a secretary. Those at the top of any organisation deserve and get good assistance. They do not suffer difficulties with getting things out of the typing pool or tracking down someone on the phone. This leads to tough targets for technology to meet. It also explains why many projects where directors are supposed to use terminals themselves are not as successful as hoped. The idea of those at the top giving a lead by personally using technology is fine in principle, but the applications offered to them have to be truly excellent to sustain use of a system once the initial novelty has worn off.

4 EFFECTS ON THE BUSINESS

Having reviewed the diversity of people who might come within the scope of our business case for office applications, we should examine the benefits to the business as a whole. This section considers some individual applications in order to show the range of effects they can produce. Once again, the intention is not to define but to illustrate. The richness of the range of effects is both a strength and a difficulty. The difficulty is that starting with any particular application you cannot immediately say what benefits it will bring. The strength is in the versatility of the applications, which allow the area of benefit to be chosen and the applications to be focused accordingly.

4.1 Office Communications

Many, when they think of electronic mail or E-mail, have in mind the combination of facilities described here. Using these systems people write notes and create documents which are then sent to and fro. These notes and documents should be kept in their electronic form to facilitate follow-up and to reduce the need for printed copies. There is a better record of what is going on than with phone calls, because few people record their phone calls comprehensively. There are less delays than with internal mail and no items go missing.

A good record combined with a short circuit to the internal mail cycle is a blend of features that attracts users. Electronic communication steals traffic from both phone and internal mail.

The quantifiable financial savings are usually modest and are seldom the reason for building the system. The real value comes from new work patterns of which the most important are:

1. The electronic system leads to less phone calls which mean less interruptions. As an advantage to the individual this has already been discussed. Its value to the business is intangible and comes from more effective use of time. There can be no doubt that interruptions waste time insofar as it takes time, after the interruption, to get back to where you were before.
2. The electronic communication channel is more business-like than phone calls. A phone call has a spurious appearance of immediacy but many phone calls are merely an interactive way to work out a request, and not the best way either. Furthermore, the other party has to react off the cuff.
   Using the electronic equivalent the thought goes in before the note is

sent. The request is a less amateurish piece of work. The recipient has the chance to provide a considered reply.
3. The electronic system allows people to be much more responsive. This scales up to a more responsive 'office', both in speed and in effectiveness. The hours or days that were spent getting an answer are reduced to minutes or hours. As to effectiveness, no-one can say they did not get the phone message or that the memo must have been lost in the mail. Requests are re-sent if they are not attended to quickly enough and expectations rise as 'quickly enough' comes to mean 'quicker than before'.

The foregoing benefits are generalities. They can be turned into real business benefits in countless ways.

4.2 Whereabouts

The electronic diary is a component of many office systems despite the well-worn jokes about lugging around a computer in order to use it. The benefit of diaries in the office, whether electronic or kept by a secretary, is seen by others, not those who maintain them. Individuals have therefore to be motivated to keep them up to date. This may come from realising that everyone benefits or from management pressure. An example of the latter is a sales force 'encouraged' to maintain diaries for the benefit of customers. The most common benefit is improved service to others, internal or external.

Another benefit is finding key people when they are wanted. The electronic system is less intrusive than bleeps or radio phones, while naturally not as immediate. An actual case was the senior management team of a social services department. When stories are about to hit the newspapers they need to respond very quickly. That means finding people quickly to provide facts and agree policy statements. The manager of a service may have to meet with an area manager in order to finalise an action plan. In this case the management decided there was clear benefit from a whereabouts system.

4.3 Professional Support

The jargon word here is decision support. As is true of so many applications of computers, the words tend to mean different things to different people.

Professionals' information requirements are not as straightforward as are those of clerical workers. When they require large amounts of data, it is probably different analyses on different occasions and not standard reports at regular intervals. Analysis and research lead to conclusions which have to be presented clearly but with the backup available.

Professionals as agents for change deal in schemes, for example plans supported by piles of figures; projects supported by timetables and estimates; forecasts supported by statistics.

The shift from manual methods to use of computer tools for these tasks has brought large productivity improvements. A spreadsheet, for example, is recalculated with a different assumption for the dollar exchange rate in seconds. Despite this productivity improvement, the effect on businesses has been qualitative. Assessments are more thorough, more alternatives are evaluated, and so on. These applications can even lead to increased workload as management realise what can be done and call for in depth work instead of educated guesses.

4.4 Common Files

Common files provide access to shared information, such as correspondence; notes and minutes; forms, blank or filled in; drafts and reports. What these have in common is that they are produced by the workers who share them.

There are many advantages of sharing working papers. The information is available to anyone working on the topic wherever they may be with no delays. It is always complete—no-one can borrow an item from the file. A good report is kept to answer later questions.

4.5 On-line Procedures

Printed procedure information can suffer from a number of difficulties, such as not being used, not being up to date or being misinterpreted. Updating is troublesome and costly. People photocopy extracts for themselves that may or may not get updated.

The simplest on-line procedure manual takes existing information and makes it available on the screen. This removes some, but not all, of the difficulties. For example, individuals will still decide for themselves when to refer to the on-line procedures and when not to bother.

The fullest advantage comes from reshaping jobs and matching computer assistance to them so as to ensure that all relevant information is always applied. A system of this type will have no clear distinction between procedure information, help information, a prompt for input to the computer, an item of data entry, application of a rule, a link to a set of supplementary questions, a suggested decision, possible wording of a letter, inclusion of a mandatory phrase, and so on.

If such a system is easy to use, staff with less skill and experience can be as effective as more senior staff with no such assistance. Other effects on a business include better service to customers; more uniform treatment of cases; greater adherence to company policy and external regulations; capture of a full record of decisions with the reasons for them; simpler and faster introduction of changes in rules, etc., and diverting out-of-line cases to the experts.

4.6 Links with External Parties

This is a fast-growing use of terminals. Electronic data interchange, or EDI, is widely used to assist supermarket chains to submit orders to their suppliers. Manufacturers using 'just-in-time' techniques, relying on the arrival of components before the small quantities held at the point of assembly run out, find it useful to link their suppliers into their own systems. These examples are perhaps not what is usually meant by 'office applications' but they show how value can be got from linking to the outside world.

By connecting outsiders to the kind of office communications described in Section 4.1 above, a different range of benefits can be obtained. Information can be provided via these links. Customers or suppliers can get information quicker. The sorts of errors and misunderstandings that creep in when a query is passed from person to person and a reply is passed back along the chain do not arise. The productivity of both parties is improved.

4.7 Summary of Effects

We have looked at six different office applications, chosen to be quite distinct from each other. The possible benefits overlap, illustrating that they cannot be tied exclusively to any particular application.

	Productivity		Effect on working methods	Effective-ness	Attractive-ness to individual	Benefit
	those affected	across board				
Office communications		Medium	Large	Large	High	Responsive
Whereabouts	High	Low	Slight	Medium	Low	Finding people
Professional support	High		Large		High	Well prepared
Common files	High		Medium	Medium	High	Less confusion
On-line procedures	High		Large	Large	Depends on how introduced	Zero defects
Links with external parties	High		Medium	Large	Medium	Partnership

FIGURE 1   Office applications summary

In summarising the effects of each application on a business Figure 1 risks oversimplification. Its purpose is to suggest different aspects of each application that are worth investigating. Benefits, for instance, have to be identified and translated into a change in the business. Two other columns note that an effect on working methods is not the same as a change in effectiveness. Productivity is shown in two columns because improvements for individuals do not necessarily multiply up across the whole organisation. Where the productivity rating is shown in the 'across the board' column, critical mass is important.

5 A METHOD FOR BUILDING THE BUSINESS CASE

The previous two sections have looked at the raw material of an office business case—the workers and the applications. Their purpose was to convey the diversity of the subject matter.

We shall now look at the POINT study technique as an illustration of how to build a business case. The components are, as Section 2.3 stated, cost justification, business impact and user motivation. We shall see how it is possible to pick a way through all the permutations and combinations and select a good office application.

POINT stands for Planning Office Information Needs and Technology (Note 9). A major part of it is a top-down business study which stems from Business Systems Planning—a general technique not directed specifically to studying the office (Note 10). The method also involves the study team surveying the staff. The study delivers recommendations on the uses of information technology that offer most promise to the business. Figure 2 shows how a study is done and gives some idea of the results at each stage.

The technique does not depend on enumerating office processes, forms used, items of information and so on. Studies along those lines tend to focus on structured, repetitive information handling and produce detailed solutions. The POINT study focuses on a wider issue—the use that can be made of information technology to address some of the fundamental needs of the business.

Studies call for two kinds of experience: how to do them and what the business is about. When external people are brought in to do a study they bring the doing experience with them. They proceed to learn about the business, often using questionnaires or interviews. When Information Systems staff do a study, they know something of the business but may lack the outsiders' experience in conducting studies. The POINT approach is to pick a team of users who understand the business and then supply the study expertise from outside.

Many methods of studying office needs have been documented. Hirschheim (1985) reviews several of them (Note 11), but none have the mixture of business analysis and staff consultation that POINT has.

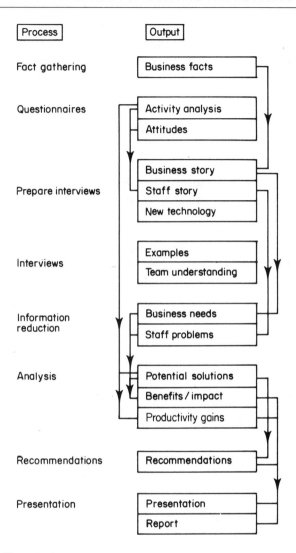

FIGURE 2   The study process

There is no claim that this is the only way to study business needs. The full method is unnecessary when there are simpler ways of bringing together the elements of a business case.

We will first describe what goes into a POINT study before looking at the activities during it, finishing with the results. An example of a study runs on the facing pages. This illustrates the description of the method. The example is based on an actual study, though it has been made anonymous to keep it confidential.

6 THE INGREDIENTS OF THE METHOD

6.1 The Scope of the Study

Any organisation can be studied using this method. The limit on size is set by how well the team can understand the chosen scope, i.e. the staff to be studied. Two things affect this: the range of experience gathered together in the team and the amount of detail they can afford to go into. As a rule of thumb, anywhere from 100 to 3000 people can be studied. For less than 100 people less formal methods are probably more effective. (See also Section 2.1.)

6.2 The Executive Sponsor

The team will be picking out the most important questions facing senior management. To have any chance of success in this they must have the backing of a senior manager or director, who must have confidence in them and understand what the study will achieve.

The results from studies correlate very well with the seniority and seriousness of the sponsor. Someone with limited responsibility who has been told to do a study is not going to be a good sponsor. Such a manager will not preside over anything more than some thoughts on how a bit of word processing would help his overstretched secretarial staff.

The sponsor has to be visible. This is because the team will need to use the sponsor's authority to persuade others to help the study.

The sponsor must be determined to follow up the study. There is no point in spending time and effort on a study of the key aspects of a business and then putting the report on a shelf. If there is no backing, it is as well not to do it. The study will indicate the next tasks to be done and they will have to be given to suitable people. The sponsor will lend weight to freeing such people. Besides people, there is money. The study has not yet been done that did not recommend spending on information technology of some sort. If there is no chance that money can be spent, no matter how good the case for it, the study will be futile.

LOCAL AUTHORITY CASE STUDY

Some care has been taken to make this case study anonymous. It is nevertheless drawn from an actual POINT study. Studies should start from the way things are and that always means some good news and some not so good.

1 The Scope of the Study

This local authority department ran about 500 establishments, whose activities were outside the study. The main focus was the head office staff servicing the establishments. The small management team in each establishment was included. Caretakers were counted as management because they had responsibilities for the buildings.

Nearly 2500 staff were within the scope of the study; 2000 were out in the establishments but spent only a proportion of their time on administration. This preponderance of staff outside head office was quite consistent with the focus on head office.

2 The Executive Sponsor

The director of the department sponsored the study, although he was at first inclined to delegate it to his deputy. What changed his mind was the realisation that his own people would be studying his department. He had recently been criticised by an external study that he felt had taken too little account of his circumstances. The study could provide him with better grounds for change.

6.3 The Staff

The staff are as much the subject of the study as is the business. They will receive any equipment that results from it and, depending on the application, they will individually decide to what extent they wish to use it. Their wishes should if possible be considered when deciding to what uses information technology can be put. They clearly need to be aware of what is happening.

A POINT study appears to the staff as a consultation exercise. It involves two way communications, both formal and informal. The first news filters out as the study is set up, with members of staff being nominated and freed up from their regular responsibilities. Formal channels are not far behind since all staff within the scope of the study receive a letter from the sponsor. As the study progresses, the grapevine continues to work: some people receive questionnaires to complete; some go to an interview; some have friends on the study team. When the study ends there will be more talk. Management can influence this by formally explaining the results.

All these channels of communication are exploited by a POINT study. The study team draw on their contacts. Interviewees talk about the views of their colleagues as well as about their own. In a very real way all of the staff become part of the study, and this is one of the strengths of the method.

6.4 The Study Team and Its Leader

There may be between six and twelve members. They will be selected for their ability to think through all sorts of business questions. The team will range over the whole organisation and make judgements on many topics, so they must between them understand all major departments.

The best team is made up of a mix of people. Senior managers provide understanding of the goals and objectives of the business. Junior members of staff appreciate how things are near the base of the pyramid, which is where most people are. Secretaries have a completely different viewpoint and a very good knowledge of how the business works.

One or two of the team should be from the Information Systems department. They will contribute to the debate on ways of using information technology to support the business. They will also carry back the knowledge they gain from the study and provide continuity for subsequent project work.

The team leader is responsible for completing the study on time and for maintaining the sponsor's confidence. One idea is to pick a junior manager who is being groomed for higher things. The combination of work on the basics of the business, the relevance to them of information technology and leading a project is an excellent experience for someone on their way up.

3 The Staff

Staff were analysed in eight groups: senior managers, managers and senior administrators, professionals, section heads and administrators, clerical, secretarial and typing, operational and ancillaries.

4 The Study Team and its Leader

Twelve people made up the team. The leader was a first level manager and not actually the most senior person on the team. No-one worked in an establishment but several had experience of what went on nearer the sharp end. Three of the team had IS experience, one of whom was responsible within the department for the use of information technology. The other two came from the authority's IS department.

6.5 Assistance to the Study

The role of the Information Systems members of the team has already been outlined. Besides their input, the team will gain some education in what information technology can do from the consultant. A useful source of ideas is to go and see suitable demonstrations. To have a dozen staff gain insights into the uses of technology as well as an appreciation of the major objectives of the business is a further advantage to the organisation.

A team assistant is valuable throughout the study. The distribution of questionnaires, getting them returned, the transfer of their contents into a PC, analysing the numbers and arranging interviews amounts to quite a bit of effort. An assistant to do all this will lighten the load on the rest of the team.

6.6 The Study Room

Some studies use a large room such as a conference room. Others have used two or three rooms and reduced the interference of different pieces of the work with each other. The essential things are for the study to have a base and to have somewhere suitable for interviewing staff.

The board room makes an excellent study room. Its prestige will show people that the study is important and has strong backing. Staff attending interviews will form a good impression. Whatever room is chosen, it should have a long stretch of wall for posting up charts and exhibits.

There are other practical considerations, of which the principal ones are the availability of power for equipment, phones for contacting interviewees and security arrangements if it is felt the study material is sensitive.

7 THE STEPS OF A STUDY

With the six ingredients described in the previous section we are ready to do a top-down business study, a bottom up staff study and some business analysis. They are done in eight steps.

Figure 3 lists them, showing how long each may take. The study should be done to an agreed timetable and not allowed to drift. Entirely satisfactory studies have been done in the minimum period of twelve working days from preparing the interviews to presenting to the sponsor. It should be noted that this does not include time for preparing much in the way of a written report. The full team, however, is not needed for that.

5 Assistance to the Study

Most of the team had no experience of using a workstation or PC. Two half days were spent visiting the authority's computing department and attending a briefing given by IBM. Care was taken in both sessions to describe how computing could affect a business and not to confuse the team with details of particular items of software.

Two junior operators keyed the details from the questionnaires into PCs. The manipulation of the information was done by two of the team.

6 The Study Room

One of the large meetings rooms used by councillors for committee meetings was handed over to the study. It had two small rooms opening off it and the PC was installed in one of them.

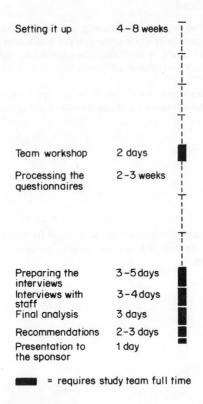

FIGURE 3   The steps of a study

7.1 Step 1—Setting It Up

The start-up phase involves briefing and selling the sponsor; deciding on the scope of the study; selecting the team; identifying the room and other resources; and sending a letter to all staff.

The first five items have already been covered in the previous section.

The importance of publicity to staff has been mentioned earlier. There are all sorts of consequences of good publicity backed by the sponsor's name, not least is the signal given to staff and management that the subject is being taken seriously.

The major motivation for people to resist the introduction of new technology is fear for their jobs. The sponsor will know whether such fears will arise. If so, the announcement letter or other publicity should take pains to deal sensibly with them.

7 Step 1—Setting Up

Much of the detailed work in setting up the study was done by the deputy director, who was largely responsible for picking the team. The director sent a letter to all members of staff.

7.2 Step 2—Team Workshop

This step is to plan the questionnaires and the gathering of business material. The team meets for the first time, about three weeks before the full-time period. The object of this two-day exercise is for the members to start forming themselves into a team and to understand what the study is all about. The sponsor will address the group, saying why the study is important.

The sample questionnaire has to be customised to the team's satisfaction. It has two sections. The first asks people to estimate how many hours per week they spend on each of about sixteen office activities.

The second section seeks people's attitudes towards their jobs—their frustrations and their time wasters. The team uses this information later in assessing how well staff will accept different office solutions. By starting with how people see the job today, the study team can choose between solutions. The test is not 'is this the best answer for the individual?' but rather 'does our chosen solution meet individuals' needs well enough for them to wish to use it?'.

Then the team decide who should receive questionnaires (Note 12). The number of questionnaires sent out lies between 200 and 300. Much more than 300 gives little additional information for the extra work, as handling that number of responses begins to become a major chore.

Fact gathering refers to work ('homework') the team have to do before the full-time part of the study begins. The preparatory work is to research aspects of the business for presentation to the rest of the team. It is the starting point for the top down view of the business.

7.3 Step 3—Processing the Questionnaires

The questionnaires are printed and sent out. The POINT method assumes a high response rate and is geared to ensuring this. The sponsor's signature on the covering letter should encourage those who receive a questionnaire to respond. The other encouragement comes from the team assistant personally chasing up replies. A response rate of 90% is quite usual.

Processing the questionnaires is usually what threatens the overall progress of the study. The gap between the team workshop and the start of full-time study must be at least the two weeks shown in Figure 3. Three weeks is still not generous.

8 Step 2—Team Workshop

The workshop was squeezed down to one day and a half instead of the two days stated in the plan. All the work was done although one or two items had to be tidied up afterwards by the department's IS manager and her two assistants. The director attended the first half of the afternoon that started the workshop.

Tailoring the questionnaire did not present any particular problems. It was decided to leave operational staff to put the time spent on their 'real' jobs in the catch-all activity at the end of the list. Caretakers, for example, did not find an activity specially aimed at their caretaking tasks. They reported this time under the heading 'Other activities: all significant activities not mentioned above; please explain'.

Sampling of the large number of staff out in establishments was done by selecting 36 establishments that represented the range of sizes, type of neighbourhood and function. Within each of these, the four or so staff who were the principal channel into the department's management processes received questionnaires. Besides the caretakers already mentioned, the responsible manager and principal secretary were the sort of people who were picked. In this way, about 150 respondents were picked to represent the total of about 2000. The remaining 500 staff were covered by another 150 questionnaires.

The following fact gathering subjects were shared out between the members of the team:

— The department's purpose, aims and objectives
— Its critical success factors
— The environment it operated in
— Its strengths and weaknesses
— The existing structure and systems
— Findings of the external study

9 Step 3—Processing the Questionnaires

A little less than 75% of the questionnaires were returned, below average for this kind of study. The assistants spent time on the phone chasing up replies but there were only eight working days between the end of the workshop and the start of the full-time work. During this time the questionnaires had to be printed and distributed. They were sent to the selected establishments by external mail and within head office by internal mail. Not many replies came in after the cut-off for finalising the analyses, but more time for chasing would have generated more replies.

7.4 Step 4—Preparing the Interviews

The team reconvenes and spends the first three to five days preparing for the staff interviews. They discuss the results of the fact gathering exercise in the form of two or three charts on each topic. Each team member will explain the whole story during the interviews and so needs to be familiar with all the material. The charts, amended as necessary, go up on the walls as the business story. Tables and graphs are made from the questionnaires and posted up as well.

The assistant prepares a list of interviews from those who completed a questionnaire. A cross-section of people are invited, including some of those whose responses look interesting and also some of those who appear to have no views at all.

The size of the study team sets the number of interviews. Each team member should do six or so interviews, enough to become familiar with the material and not to become bored. A ten man team will thus do some 60 interviews. There is no case for interviewing everyone who completes a questionnaire.

7.5 Step 5—Interviews with Staff

The interviews last for about an hour each and spread over three or four days. The interviewer walks round the charts with the interviewee, explaining the story and listening to the reactions. The object of the exercise is twofold. First, the team gets examples of what goes on in the business, which help to flesh out the dry facts from the earlier research. Second, during the succession of interviews they become very familiar with all the material. This is important as the subsequent analysis depends on the whole team having a grasp of it.

Valuable insights are gained by talking to a variety of staff members and by answering their questions. Most teams say the interviews are the most enjoyable part of a study.

10 Step 4—Preparing the Interviews

Five working days were spent on this.

The first section of the interview was the top-down story. Apart from meeting statutory requirements, the aims of the department were, as one might expect, to provide the best possible service.

Critical success factors included confidence on the part of local politicians; the allocation of resources; planning ahead, albeit with flexibility to cope with change; and committed and adaptable staff.

Environmental factors included several on the finance front; the impact of privatisation; and trends in central control (Whitehall) and local control. Consideration of the public, for whom the services are provided, produced social trends and an assessment of pressure groups and other agencies.

The second section of the interview was based on the questionnaires. There were profiles of how different grades of staff spent their time. Professionals, for example, estimated that they spent on average twelve hours each week in meetings. Managers and senior administrators spent seven hours per week in meetings but eight hours per week on the telephone.

Staff expressed many opinions in their responses to the attitude questions. Only about one in seven had no comment to make. The two biggest categories of comment were Communicating and Organisation. Communicating included remarks about the postal system and difficulties with phones being engaged or left unanswered. Difficulties in getting decisions came under Organisation as well as other views on delegation and irrelevant paperwork.

11 Step 5—Interviews with Staff

About 60 people came for interview. The nine non-IS members of the team averaged nearly seven interviews each. Staff were keenly interested and were obviously proud to have been chosen for interview. Best suits were much in evidence. There was no difficulty in persuading those the team selected to take the trouble to attend. The deputy director had to be found quickly when those travelling in from establishments asked if they could claim mileage expenses!

Some tried their hand at word processing on a PC. Others welcomed the chance to see how spreadsheets had been used in analysing the questionnaires.

The interviews were spread over four working days.

7.6 Step 6—Final Analysis

By the end of Step 5 all the material has been collected. The top-down and the bottom-up views of the business have been formed. The final analysis picks the best avenues for the organisation to go down. The approach is to see how each of a range of possibilities measures up to the needs of the business. As well as this, the team assesses how attractive each possibility will be to members of staff, and how much potential it offers for productivity improvements.

This part of the study, lasting three days, defies succinct description and is best illustrated by the case study opposite. The experience of the consultant is crucial in guiding the team through all the issues without floundering.

The staff attitudes and business needs are listed and the solutions selected. The heart of the analysis is to investigate how each solution relates to each staff problem and to each office activity. Each set of comparisons is done on a matrix.

The most important matrix relates solutions to business needs. It represents how valuable each solution is across the range of needs. It therefore contains all the elements of the business case. Wherever a solution strongly supports a business need, the team have found a piece of justification. The discussion may identify a particular feature that would make a solution much more useful. Such discoveries are invaluable later on when it comes to making more detailed plans.

After they have completed the needs and problems matrices, the team can tackle the activity matrix. This estimates how much time could be saved, as a percentage, in each activity by adopting each solution. The totals of time spent on each activity are multiplied by the percentage and an overall percentage for each solution is calculated. The team will assess the solutions in a consistent manner, albeit subjectively. The overall percentages can be used as a way of ranking the solutions and later as productivity targets.

By this time the most promising solutions are emerging. They will show a good impact on the business needs, be relevant to people's problems and offer useful productivity gains. It is quite usual for the same solutions to look good from each of these three vantage points. My experience does not support Rudy Hirschheim's assertion that 'major technology changes in the office will inevitably cause conflict' (Note 13).

12 Step 6—Final Analysis

There is not the space to go into the results of the study in any detail. By looking at examples of what was discussed we can form an impression of how the analysis went.

The staff attitudes were summarised into a list of seventeen staff problems.

The list of business needs came from the top-down story presented at the interviews (Step 4) supplemented by the insights gained through the interviews. Needs were summarised under seven headings, shown on the left of Figure 4. Each heading was supported by a lot of detail.

The solutions selected for evaluation fell into three groups: non-computer systems (three solutions), computer-based systems (four solutions) and management actions (four solutions). The computer and management solutions are shown across the top of Figure 4. Training included appraisals, objective setting and staff development. Organisation included forward planning and resource allocation. Communications included public relations.

The matrix relating systems and management solutions to business needs is shown as Figure 4. The question for each combination of need and solution was 'what exactly does this solution do for this particularneed?' This question was posed 56 times in order to complete this matrix. Each answer is either 'nothing', 'something' or 'a lot'.

Some interesting findings emerge. It is apparent that technology is not going to do very much to address the needs under the Staff and Training heading. Stand-alone Equipment scores less well than the other systems, indicating that the business case for PCs is best made at lower levels than the department taken as a whole. The strongest solution is Shared Filing and Records, with Office

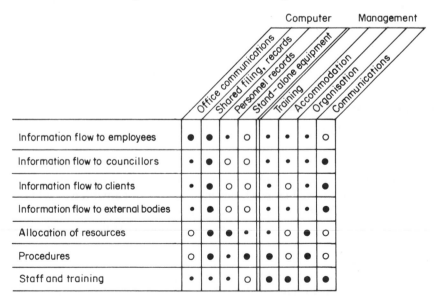

FIGURE 4   Analysing how solutions address business needs

7.7 Step 7—Recommendations

The preferred solutions, electronic or otherwise, are not the end of the story. The team will need two or three more days to develop recommendations. Some of the solutions will be longer-term ones and for these it is particularly important to have early milestones that will show progress to staff and sponsor alike. This reflects the well-known honeymoon period for anything new. POINT studies create a climate of expectation and enthusiasm. It is clear to all that change is afoot. If the months go by and nothing is visible, everyone gets disillusioned.

As well as preparing the presentation for the executive sponsor, the team will by this stage have written much of their report.

We have reached the end of the study. A senior executive commissioned it and put a trusted manager in charge. The team has worked diligently and covered a lot of ground in its three weeks together. The sponsor is looking forward to hearing about the organisation he or she heads up. Two hours,

Communications probably being a lower priority. Personnel Records was the major item in the authority's application backlog and clearly offered worthwhile benefits to this department.

A very similar analysis was done using the staff problems. The biggest impacts were from Organisation and Training, in that order. Shared Filing and Records showed enough useful impact to be easily saleable to staff.

The productivity assessment showed the most potential to come from Shared Filing and Records. It was assumed that the system was fully installed. Each activity was considered and a productivity target for it estimated. It was judged, for example, that a 50% reduction could be made in time spent retrieving information. The different categories of staff surveyed spent on average between 25 minutes and 2 hours 20 minutes per week on this activity. Knowing the staff numbers (within the scope of the study) in each category, it was possible to calculate the overall effect of this estimate. All told, the Shared Filing and Records solution was estimated to offer an improvement of nearly 12% against the total hours worked by the staff surveyed.

13 Step 7—Recommendations

Eight working days were spent on analysis and recommendations. Recommendations were made for each computer-based solution and for two of the management actions.

Clearly, the most promising solution was Shared Filing. The full benefit required all manner of information to be within the system and that was not going to be achieved quickly. The team picked information on manpower and budgets as the place to start. One reason for this was that a mini-computer system for the department was being looked at and this information could be held on it. The business case reasons included removing duplicate information held in different sections of the department.

A prime reason for recommending PCs was that they could be introduced in parallel with the other solutions. This would speed up the rate at which the department could exploit information technology.

In the area of management actions, Communications appear to be the strongest solution. This area, however, was put over in a low key. Since Communications lines up closely with the target audiences (councillors, etc.) not much emphasis was open-ended, has been put aside for an excellent opportunity to review the operation as a whole, its strengths and its weaknesses.

7.8 Step 8—Presentation to the Sponsor

The presentation starts with a walk round the interview room. Everyone then sits down to listen to the findings and recommendations. The team leader outlines the action plan and asks for the sponsor's agreement to some immediate items. It is important not to lose momentum and it is quite reasonable to make some decisions at the presentation, e.g. to pass the results to the Office Project Manager for action.

One thing remains: feedback to the staff, without which studies can lose credibility. One way is a presentation by the study team of the study's findings. This will include agreed actions and dates so as to convince people that management is committed to following through. An alternative is to re-open the study room for those interested to walk round. Either way, a foundation for introducing the solutions is laid.

7.9 The Advantages of the POINT Study Technique

POINT studies produce agreed findings and avoid the 'not invented here' syndrome. Members of the study team will have to live with its aftermath. Some of them may well be involved in making it happen. These thoughts strongly influence them towards making practical recommendations.

Everyone will be committed to taking the next steps. Executives without understanding and confidence will not commit themselves to electronic tools. Clear away mystery and confusion, recommend some simple actions and commitment follows. The study, in other words, lets senior management select clear, agreed goals.

A further outcome affects the success of the project that follows the study. Office projects are no different from systems ones in that experts and users tend to find themselves on either side of a solid wall. This is bad enough with data systems but can be fatal with office projects. The answer is, of course, to have people on either side of the wall who appreciate what is happening on the other side. Such people are scarce but members of the team add to their number.

Finally, the whole staff becomes more aware of the business and technology through the study. It is a useful base on which to build awareness of the business felt necessary. The Organisation and Training recommendations were expressed much more strongly.

14 Step 8—Presentation to the Sponsor

The presentation was made twenty working days after the start of the full-time part of the study. The team spent seventeen days together and re-convened for the presentation to the director and his management team. Presentations were subsequently given to councillors and staff, separately. The last presentation was six weeks after the first. The typed report was published two weeks later.

The recommendations on technology were accepted without alteration and the department's IS manager was charged with turning them into more detailed action plans. The suggestions on Training were turned over to the responsible manager. Organisation triggered more debate, but the phrasing of the recommendations recognised that this was the domain of senior management. Study teams have a line to walk between suppressing useful observations and encroaching on areas outside their scope.

reasons for the office project. Known staff views make it easier to decide how to explain what the new system will do. Although the planned business impact will not motivate individuals to use it, no-one can produce benefits if they do not know what they are.

In summary, the business case built from the recommendations of the study will be agreed and practical. The next steps will be committed and there will be a wider understanding of information technology on which to build the project. Above all, there will be a clear, planned impact on the business—the source of the benefits for the business.

8 MANAGING BENEFITS

The earlier sections of this chapter have reviewed the key components of a business case for office systems and described a practical method of building it. Assuming that the analysis provides a good case, we must now turn to perhaps the most neglected area—ensuring that the benefits identified are actually achieved.

8.1 Case Study—Linked Word Processing Terminals

In this case study links have been installed between word processing terminals in different parts of the country. The idea is for secretaries and personal assistants to be able to move important draft papers and approved reports to and fro. The managers and professional staff they support are responsible for commissioning the reports, agreeing terms of reference, drafting and reviewing drafts and so forth. The directors want high quality material at the time and place of their choosing. A speech must be picked up at the agreed office on the way to the engagement.

The equipment is installed and usage is good. Users are happy. They can turn documents round faster than by using the typing pools and there are fewer panics. The people they support are also happy. They have happier, more relaxed support staff and they get better service from them. The old struggle to get stuff out of the typing pool in anything under two days is fading from memory.

No problem, you would think. That would be correct if the business case had been agreed on the basis of investing the money in order to make people happy and to cut down on panics. In real life that is seldom the kind of benefit that justifies spending. The business case in this case study spoke of productivity improvements that would save x per cent of secretarial and typing effort, valued at £y per Annum. It predicted less use of fax machines and telexes, saving both capital and running costs. For good measure it also quoted savings in postage. It was a simple matter of observation that no secretaries or typists had left and no fax or telex machines discontinued. In short, the claimed benefits were difficult to see on the ground.

The lesson is that it is not enough to hope for benefits. Installing office applications may very well not, of itself, produce any tangible benefits at all.

8.2 The Need for Management Action

Figure 5 shows the case study diagrammatically. The intention was to turn the old staff with no system into a new staff with a supporting system. A string of benefits were to be extracted: less people, discontinued equipment, faster document preparation and other less tangible benefits. A project was set up to install the system. What was missing?

The answer is that some of the benefits are of direct interest to individual staff while others are not. Secretaries, for example, like to gain the approval of their bosses and the others they support. As intelligent and motivated employees they also take a pride in their work. Both factors impel them to improve turnaround on work if they can, and sure enough that was what happened.

Nobody likes panics. Exploiting the system to reduce them is not surprising. This is the kind of benefit that brings advantage to the individual—the kind of benefit that needs little encouragement to emerge.

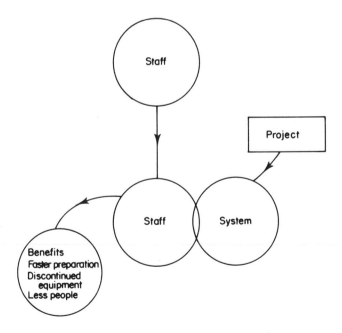

FIGURE 5   Getting benefits from a system (maybe)

By contrast, no individual has an interest in firing others or in sending equipment to the breaker's yard. Responsibilities for such things have to be given to someone. To put it more generally, management action is needed if benefits are to be assured. Without it, it will be a matter of chance whether the intended benefits, or indeed any benefits at all, are obtained. This very simple point is frequently overlooked.

Figure 6 shows how the whole thing should have been set up. A manager can be made accountable for the benefits and a suitable executive can take an interest, keeping everyone's eye on the ball. However, as this is not a book on management techniques we will not pursue the question of managing change any further.

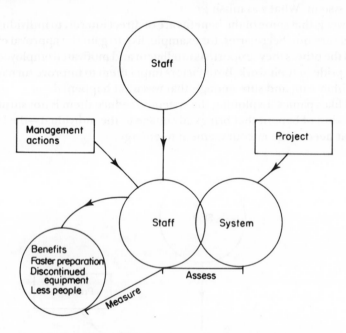

FIGURE 6   Management actions ensure benefits are obtained

8.3 Measurement and Assessment

The word 'measurement' is used here to mean gathering the evidence for beneficial change. The benefits need to be recognised, which ideally means measured, in order for all to be happy that they were obtained.

Putting 'measure' on Figure 6 suggests that the benefits are obtained by the management action, which is fine. Where does that leave the system? Maybe it played little or no part. It is a valid question. By loosening the link between solution, or system, and benefits we have let in this possibility. The way to check is to assess the ability of staff and system together to provide as much as the staff alone did beforehand. This is much easier than attempting to measure directly the benefits arising from the use of the system.

An illustration would be if the system gave productivity improvements and the time freed was used to improve customer service in purely manual ways. In this case it would be fair to say the system supported the staff but its direct contribution to the improvements in customer service could not be measured.

There are thus two topics to discuss—measurement and assessment. We will deal with measurement first.

As Philip Crosby (1979) says in *Quality Is Free,* anything can be measured if you have to (Note 14). What often happens is that the work required to measure things seems excessive. People then fall back on anecdotal evidence and feelings about how things are going. For this reason, the subject of measurement should be aired before any electronic facilities are given to people. Managers can be relatively dispassionate before the event as to what will and what will not amount to reasonable evidence of an improvement. No-one is then claiming success or trying to strike down someone else's achievements.

Whether or not benefits are tangible is not too relevant in deciding on the measurement plan. Take a simple example in which the objective was to reduce workload and improve speed of service—good territory for quantitative measures, at first glance. In this case, the office recorded overtime and turnaround times for some key transactions—two quantitative measures and both found a place in the list of measures.

Not everyone was paid overtime, however, so that particular measure left something to be desired. Likewise key transactions, almost by definition, were common but far from the whole story. Many kinds of service did not involve them. This gave two choices. One was to set up many new measures, with associated records and reports. The other was to admit less formal signs of improvement onto the list. An example of the latter was to have an 'indicator' for time spent chasing Head Office. It was a collective judgement by branch staff and 'less time' equals goodness. There were other such indicators.

Staff in the office, as well as management higher up the organisation, were able to agree a set of measures and indicators before the system went in. The managers of the offices, knowing what the measurement plan was, had plenty of incentive to focus attention in the right areas.

Another objective of the same solution was to improve the effectiveness of service—an intangible objective if ever there was one. As you would expect, the plan relied on indicators rather than quantitative measures. However, even in such a judgemental area there were two or three factual and quantitative measures. Examples were:

1. A greater number of types of response to customers generated within the branch, i.e. without the need to refer to Head Office
2. Longer hours of service each day from computer systems

The judgement was that these, in conjunction with six other measures and indicators, would be useful pieces of evidence in deciding whether the effectiveness of service had improved.

Given that the benefits are being obtained and that discussion about their size is based on hard, agreed evidence, given, in other words, that all is well on the benefits front, we now have to answer the sceptics who say it was the management attention that produced the benefits, by which they mean that the technology was irrelevant. The assessment programme should answer this kind of question. It will probably be based on classic techniques like questionnaires and interviews but there are two additional possibilities worth mentioning.

1. The system's features may have a predictable connection with the intended benefits. If so, that can be investigated after the fact. Sticking to our aim of improving customer service, we may have put salesmen's diaries on-line and let secretaries and message-takers look at them. We want customers to find out where their salesman is and when they may expect to contact him or her. Assuming the disciplines on the sales force are there, the linkage between the system and benefit is clear. Part of the assessment in this case is to find out if the system, electronic and human, works and has the hoped-for effect.
2. How much the system is used can be a valuable part of the assessment. We may have a system which is not forced on users. Let us suppose, in the previous example, that branch managers were expected to tell customers more accurately where their salesman was, but were not forced to use electronic diaries. It would be open to a branch manager to set up a whereabouts board and to lean on the salesmen to tell message-takers where they were. If this course had been taken the usage statistics would show the system had not helped. In this simple example it would be evident that the branch was not using the system. Other cases, however, may not be so clear cut.

Finally, there are usually benefits and improvements that were not foreseen in the original business case. As the users of the system become familiar with it they will think of ways to exploit it. The assessment programme should watch out for these uses so that they can be extended elsewhere in the business.

8.4 Key Questions for Management to Answer

To ensure benefits are achieved, management should ask themselves the following questions:

1. Have the benefits been picked out and agreed?
2. Has the sort of evidence of improvements that will be acceptable been agreed?
3. Will the mere fact of installing and using the technology produce the benefits? If not, where will the motive force come from?
4. Will the organisation be overloaded with too much change at one time (i.e. benefits management coming on top of other changes)?
5. Will the pressure for change be kept up or will management attention move on to the next business opportunity, operational crisis, company re-organisation or whatever?
6. Finally, will management review progress and compliment all concerned?

9 SUMMARY

The business, and the needs of the business, are paramount in deciding which office applications to install. It is less important to define who are office workers than it is to decide which aspects of the business should be studied. The range of jobs and the range of office applications are so wide and rich that neither form a good starting point. The goals of the business provide a surer basis for assessing the potential of technology and indeed non-technological solutions.

A good business case considers the business impact of the recommended system and the motivation of staff to use it as well as the financial justification. The POINT study method was used to illustrate the building of such a case.

The business case and the installed system do not, of themselves, cause any benefits to happen. If the system is attractive, staff will use it and the business impact becomes possible. The realisation of the intended benefits then has to be managed—the final aspect of gearing information technology in the office to business needs.

NOTES

Note 1

The Kearney report (1984) asked what the main barriers were to success. The most frequent answer was 'difficult to cost justify', given by 45% of those surveyed. Next came 'economic factors', given by 41%.

Note 2

One clear exponent of this view is T. Aklilu (1981). He describes the office as a place where information is 'manufactured'. Data is first created, then converted into information and finally used, for example in making decisions. This is an attempt to cast office automation in the data processing mould and it is difficult to see a practical way of defining all the items of data, their processing and use so as to develop some kind of usable system.

Note 3

The well-known Booz Allen and Hamilton study (Poppel, 1980) looked at how 300 managers and professionals spent their time. They recorded their time and activities. It was found that 25% of time was being taken up by 'less productive activities'. Poppel stated that previous efforts to improve productivity had been 'focused almost exclusively on clerical and support staff'.

Note 4

In a survey of the implications of office automation Hirschheim (1985) covers the optimist, the pessimist and the pluralist positions. Optimists see employment increasing (or at least not decreasing) as a result of the application of technology. Pessimists see a steady decline. Pluralists think it could go either way and so concentrate on what will drive it in a positive direction.

Note 5

The Kearney report (see Note 1) also asked what contribution was already being made by IT. While this question is not limited to conventional data processing, it is influenced by its achievements. The first two answers were 'maximising office productivity' and 'reducing/controlling staff costs'. The examples quoted under both headings rely greatly on data processing applications.

Note 6

Use of an office system is not always voluntary. If structured letters, with standard paragraphs or whatever, are put on the computer they replace the forms with ticks in boxes that were used previously. This is a perfectly good office application but the staff producing the letters will not have the option to go on using the old forms.

Note 7

Wilbert O. Galitz (1984) gives eleven responses to poor design. 'Those unable to cope with poor design', he says, 'may exhibit a variety of responses ranging from the psychological to the physical.' An example of a psychological response is indirect use of the system. An intermediary is placed between the would-be user and the computer. 'This requires high status and discretion; it is a typical response of managers.'

Note 8

The written formal management style is outlined in an exhibit used in interviews with managers. 'Important interactions are initiated through papers, memoranda, proposals, submissions, minutes, etc. Meetings are held, but they tend to be explanatory or supportive or "rubber stamping" in intent, the substantive work having been in the exchanging of documents and written commentaries on them. Meetings, therefore, follow the papers. Many of the papers are produced to a calendar and they have established distributions and sign-off procedures' (Feeney, Edwards and Earl, 1987).

Note 9

POINT was developed in the early 1980s in South Africa by Martyn Harper, then of IBM. The method has been used by many consultants in many different countries to study organisations in every type of industry.

Note 10

The origin of IBM's Business Systems Planning was in 1966 when a group was set up to look at what was being done with data processing throughout the business unit responsible for all of IBM's US data processing business. Engineering, manufacturing, marketing and service divisions were covered. A set of strategies was established. An integrated set of information systems was then defined and responsibilities for development assigned. The Business Systems Planning programme was established in 1970.

One of the base principles of the planning process is a top-down approach to getting people committed and involved, and to studying the business. In outline, the top-down analysis starts by defining the business objectives and going on to define the business processes. From these, the business data can be identified and used as the base for an information architecture (see IBM, 1984).

Note 11

Nine different methodologies are reviewed. Some attempt to analyse what is going on in offices, e.g. ISAC from Sweden, OFFIS from Arizona and Information manufacturing, referred to above in Note 2. Other methodologies emphasise the social aspects of office work. Enid Mumford's Ethics and Pava's sociotechnical design methodology are examples. None of the methodologies seeks the kind of business impact that POINT does, although Tapscott's user-driven design methodology includes discussions with senior management.

There are few structured ways to get potential users to participate in the implementation of office applications. Most of the elements in Hirschheim's discussion (1985) can be picked out in the POINT method.

Finally, none of the methodologies appears to lay any foundations for the management of benefits as discussed in Section 8 of this chapter.

Note 12

Responses to the questionnaire must represent all the staff within the scope of the study. Analysis will be wanted by type of staff, by geographic location, and so on. For this to be soundly based, there should be enough responses in each analysis group. This does not mean that the sampling rate has to be uniform across all the staff. There are, for example, relatively few senior managers. To get enough responses from them the sample has to be a high proportion of them, often 100%. Further down the organisation a much lower sampling rate will produce plenty of responses.

Note 13

The argument is that there are several parties involved in the introduction of technology. Hirschheim (1985) lists top management, middle management, clerks and their union, and technologists. He conducted a role play experiment using outsiders to represent these parties. Each group was briefed to look at the consequences of introducing technology from their own viewpoint only. All the groups then presented and, predictably, there were conflicts.

My own experience with the POINT method is that conflicts do not occur. This is partly because the study team is briefed to look for ways of bringing about change smoothly. It is also remarkable how often solutions that are good for the business also bring improvements for the individual. Furthermore, many POINT studies have included a union representative to ensure a good (two-way) communication channel in that direction.

Note 14

The full quote is 'There are those who will assume that some tasks are just plain unmeasurable. To them, you must raise the question of just how they know which people are the best at what jobs, whom to fire, and whom to reward. Anything can be measured if you have to do it' (Crosby, 1979).

REFERENCES

Aklilu, T. (1981) 'Office automation—office productivity—the missing link', Office Automation Digest, AFIPS.

Crosby, Philip B. (1979) *Quality Is Free*, McGraw-Hill Book Co.

Feeney, David F., Edwards, Brian R., and Earl, Michael J. (1987) 'Complex organisations and the information systems function', Oxford Institute of Information Management.

Galitz, Wilbert O. (1984) 'Humanizing office automation', QED Information Sciences.

Hirschheim, R. A. (1985) *Office Automation: a Social and Organisational Perspective*, John Wiley.

IBM (1984) 'Business systems planning—information systems planning guide'.

Kearney: Management Consultants (1984) 'The barriers and the opportunities of information technology—a management perspective', Institute of Administrative Management and the DTI.

Poppel, Harvey L. (1980) 'Managerial/professional productivity', in *Outlook*, Booz Allen and Hamilton.

Chapter 8
DELIVERING IS SERVICES EFFECTIVELY

Bob Jones

1 INTRODUCTION

This chapter is concerned with the issues involved in ensuring that IS services are delivered to the end-users as effectively and efficiently as possible. In order to address these, I will assert that the Mission of IS comprises two fundamental elements:

- To provide the services necessary to facilitate achievement of the business goals of the enterprise
- To deliver to the end-users responsive, high quality and secure services at an affordable cost

The first of these is the responsibility of a Development department and the second that of a Service Centre. The assumption is made that the range of services required by the business has been identified and created by the Development department for an architecture optimised for this enterprise's IS environment.

The chapter focuses on the role of the Service Centre in delivering IS services effectively to the end-users and this requires that the key management processes are put in place and function properly. To achieve this it is necessary to define the Goals of the Service Centre, develop a Strategy to achieve them, create an Organisation to execute the Strategy, establish an implementation plan and allocate the necessary resources and lastly measure actual achievement against objectives. The details of an implementation plan will vary from installation to installation. However, in my experience, there are three areas: the network, automation and the management of multiple Service Centres which are of key significance and merit more detailed discussion in a general paper.

Accordingly, the topics addressed in the sections which follow are:

- Service delivery goals and strategy
- IS organisation
- The network

Managing Information Systems for Profit.   Edited by T. J. Lincoln
© 1990 John Wiley & Sons Ltd

- Automation
- Managing multiple Service Centres
- Measurement systems

2 SERVICE DELIVERY GOALS AND STRATEGY

If the mission of the Service Centre is as stated in Section 1, it follows that the key goals must be directed towards:

- Responsive User Support
- High Quality Service
- Cost Effectiveness

Let us investigate each of these in more detail.

2.1 Responsive User Support

A fundamental objective for an effective IS organisation must be that the services provided should have the functions required by the user and be available on schedule; it is of equal importance that they should be easy to use and have consistent interfaces to all users. To achieve this, special emphasis must be given to user support and experience shows that the following three elements need particular attention.

2.1.1 Documentation

One of the tasks of the Service Centre is to ensure good documentation of all services, so that the user knows where to find the necessary information. This will normally take the form of a Users' Guide covering the range of services, with more detailed information available in documents relating to the individual services. In addition, wherever possible, the services themselves should have on-line Help facilities. The Users' Guide should be supplemented by regular Newsletters of a chatty nature, indicating either new facilities which will in due course be fully documented in the Guide or hints on how to obtain maximum benefit from the services.

2.1.2 Service Support

A Service Support group should exist in the Centre with full knowledge of all services, together with the ability to educate users on the functions available and advise them on their use. Since information stored in the systems is becoming an increasingly vital asset, steps must be taken to ensure that this information is protected against access by unauthorised users and against loss resulting from human error, system malfunction, environmental failure or disaster.

2.1.3 The Help Desk

The single most important element of user support is almost certainly the Help Desk. This is the shop-window for IS and for most users creates its image. A user must feel in contacting the Help Desk that the staff will be sympathetic to his/her problem, be sufficiently knowledgeable to discuss the concern, be able to initiate action to resolve the problem and ensure good communication on the status of resolution. The Manager of the Help Desk should identify with the users and be seen to do so. If the Help Desk is not effective, much of the good work done in all other areas of IS will be nullified.

In the IS Organisation discussed later in the chapter, all of the above functions are contained in the User Services group.

2.2 High Quality Service

In order to attract and retain customers in a competitive environment and to ensure a good image with internal users, it is essential to provide high quality service. In both cases this is a vital contributor to the productivity of the users. Quality, of course, starts with the Applications, since it is impossible to deliver high quality service if the Applications have not been designed with this goal. Accordingly it is vital for the Service Centre Manager to have approval rights for each phase of the process by which the Development department creates new services. There are five key steps in ensuring a high level of service quality and these are outlined below.

2.2.1 Define Service Parameters

The first step is to define the parameters against which the quality of service can be measured. These should, of course, be relevant for the services provided and for the users, and would typically include most of the following:

- Service Hours
- Accessibility
- Availability
- Mean Time between Interruptions
- Batch Turnaround Time
- Average Response Time
- Consistent/Predictable Response Time
- Network Added Delay
- User Satisfaction Index

As regards the actual service levels achieved, the complaints received at the Help Desk are normally a fairly accurate indicator of the progress an installation has made on quality of service. The list of parameters suggested above is in a logical sequence of accomplishment. The further down the list the complaints are received, the better the overall health of the installation. For example, if the Service Hours are unsatisfactory, the rest of the parameters do not matter. If availability is poor, then few complaints are received about response times, etc. When availability is well over 99%, Mean Time between Interruptions is a better measure, since users normally find 99.1% with one interruption in a week less disruptive than 99.6% with two interruptions. In fact, it is more accurate to add, to the time lost for any interruption, 50% of the average session time to reflect the actual disruption of the users' work; this gives a more meaningful figure for percentage availability.

2.2.2 Establish Service Level Agreements

The second step is to establish Service Level Agreements with the users, documenting, for each parameter, the objective which is necessary to meet their business needs, and against which the quality will be measured (the process is described more fully in IBM, GE20-0749). This is a two-way document, since the agreement should be based on the business volumes defined by the user and included in the document. The last point is important, since response times, in particular, can be affected adversely by a workload greatly in excess of that predicted. Ideally a Service Level Agreement comprises two parts, the first detailing the service level objectives for each service and the second defining the workload as indicated by the user.

The service level objectives should be defined and measured over the most demanding and critical service period. This is normally the Prime Shift appropriate to the *user's* location, particularly for response times. In many installations, the number of hours per day included in Prime Shift is increasing steadily as services become more and more interactive and critical to the business. The Service Level Agreement represents a *commitment* by the Service Centre and it is advisable to measure weekly achievement over a 4-week, 10-week or 13-week period or alternatively as an *N*-week rolling average. The reasons for this are twofold. Firstly, the measurements week by week tend to be rather erratic and can obscure the general service trend; secondly, if commitment were required on a weekly basis, the objectives would be set much lower to give a reasonable guarantee of success. This is undesirable since the Service Centre should have demanding targets.

2.2.3 Measure Service Levels Provided

It is essential for the Service Centre to have a comprehensive system to measure service levels provided. This will show actual achievement against objectives and indicate what commitments can be made to the users in the future. The types of measurements required are discussed in detail in Section 7.1. Both the Service Level Agreements and the measurement system are vital for the Service Centre Manager, not only in helping him to manage the services but also in providing an objective record of achievement, rather than subjective views of the service provided.

Achievement of high quality service is a classical case of perspiration rather than inspiration, particularly in the area of reliability. The requirement most users would state initially would be 100% availability with no interruptions, and this is clearly the ultimate goal. However, it would be very expensive to guarantee this level of service, since substantial duplexing would be needed. It is, however, possible to commit to ongoing improvements in reliability and to approach 100% without interrupts asymptotically at little extra cost in financial terms. In one of the functions I managed, we committed to decrease time lost through unreliability by 20% per annum. Hence if in one year we had achieved 99% availability with 1.0 Interrupts per week, the next year's objectives would be set at 99.2% and 0.8 Interrupts. The general approach should be to anticipate and prevent problems rather than to repair them. To this end, all new services should be subjected to rigorous acceptance tests by the Service Centre before being put into production.

Improvements in performance are achievable with systems tuning and even more with Applications tuning. However, if this tuning has already been done and the user still requests a dramatic improvement, this will normally result in extra cost to the user, since it involves either reduced loading of existing resources or purchase of additional resources.

2.2.4 Apply System Management Controls

Within IBM, Service quality has been significantly improved by application of what are called the System Management Controls (IBM, GE20-0749 and IBM, GE20-0751). They comprise the following management disciplines:

- Change Management
- Problem Management
- Recovery Management
- Performance Management
- Capacity Management
- Interactive Processing Management
- Batch Processing Management
- Management Reporting

The controls are fundamental for effective service management and both management and staff have received comprehensive training in the relevant areas. The purpose of the disciplines is fairly obvious, but let me describe briefly the first and probably the most important of them.

Change Management requires that *all* changes are approved before they are made, with exceptions only in emergencies. These changes may be in the applications, the software, the network, the hardware, the facilities or any other aspect which could affect the service. The person wishing to make the change must describe the nature of the change, the purpose, the testing that has been performed, the potential risk, the back-out plan, the date of the change and why it has to be made then. Those changes which are approved at the Service Centre Change Control meeting are then scheduled for a specific date and time.

At a subsequent Change Control meeting, the success or otherwise of each change approved is subject to review and the actual impact assessed. Any person with a poor track record in making changes would, of course, be subject to more rigorous checks in future. The objective is not to prevent changes, since these are clearly required to introduce new services or to improve existing services, but to ensure that, as far as possible, changes do not adversely affect the quality of service provided to the users.

One of the most important tasks of the Service Centre is to ensure that vital services are fully protected and that, in the event of a disaster, service will continue to the users. This is covered in Chapter 9 of this book entitled 'Securing Vital IT Services'.

2.2.5 Define Responsibilities

The Service Centre Manager is responsible to every user of the centre's services regardless of where the user is located and the actions taken should indicate that full responsibility for resolution of all problems is accepted. Indeed the Service Centre Manager sets the tone for the whole organisation and, in my experience, high quality service can be achieved only with his/her personal and active commitment to excellence. It is necessary that the management team is carried along and they must in their turn educate their staff to achieve the highest standards. Service levels attained should be displayed prominently throughout the Centre and the information should be freely available to the users. As the levels improve, the staff identify with success and become increasingly self-motivated.

2.3 Cost Effectiveness

This is always an important objective for the Service Centre whether it operates as a Profit Centre, in which case it must be given a target for the cost of services provided as a proportion of the revenue accruing, or as a Cost Centre, where there is always pressure to reduce costs.

In order to be cost effective, it is necessary to optimise resource utilisation in two areas primarily:

- Human Resources
- Systems Resources

Human resources comprise all staff including contract labour; Systems resources include Hardware, Hardware Maintenance, Software and Telecommunications. Recent surveys have indicated that in a typical Service Centre, human resources represent 15 to 25% of the cost, while the systems resources represent most of the remainder. In a multi-centre environment, further savings can normally be achieved by consolidating centres.

2.3.1 Human Resource Efficiency

(a) Organisation   One of the most significant contributors to efficient use of staff is the existence of a sound Organisation with all responsibilities clearly defined and strong accountability. This ensures that each member of the staff understands his/her role, thus avoiding areas of redundant effort or areas where necessary effort is not applied. This is discussed further in Section 3.

(b) Rationalisation of Services   Another source of potential saving is in rationalising the services provided. It is much cheaper to provide one service to a thousand users than to provide a thousand services to one user each. Hence a clean-up of services to provide as much replication as possible will lead to significant savings in support staff.

(c) Automation   Increasingly automation is being applied to increase productivity. This has dramatically reduced the number of Console Operators and Network Operators and allowed unattended operation to become a reality. Software is available to manage data more effectively, to reduce the volume of information which is printed and generally decrease the number of Input/Output operators. Expert systems are being investigated in connection with the Help Desk, Systems Support and other areas. The subject of automation will be addressed in more detail in Section 5.

2.3.2 Systems Resource Efficiency

There are four key steps in ensuring efficient use of systems resources and these are discussed below.

(a) Design IS Architecture   In order to ensure optimal use of the systems resources, it is necessary to develop an IS Architecture which defines a standard environment for which all Applications will be designed and within which the Service Centre will operate.

(b) Plan Capacity Required   Capacity planning is a significant contributor to efficiency and it should cover CPUs, Data Storage and the Network. In order to do this, measurement systems must be available to record resource utilisation for all components and relate them to service level attainments. In order to do Capacity Planning effectively, it is necessary to understand thoroughly the services being provided and the service levels required. From this information, capacities of various systems can be developed and plotted against the predicted workload. It is very seldom that users' forecasts are accurate for more than 6 to 12 months ahead; on the other hand the Service Centre's planning horizon has to be much longer. The Service Centre therefore has normally to derive its long-range forecasts from a combination of extrapolating growth of current services from past usage and information on new services planned.

One of the areas to be investigated in looking at the workload is the proportion of capacity which is consumed internally by IS in general and the Service Centre in particular. Since this is not chargeable to the users, it can have a serious impact on unit cost if it is not carefully controlled.

(c) Manage Data Storage   In many installations, the cost of Data Storage is increasing steadily as a proportion of total expenditure. Indeed, as regards computer room space, data storage is by far the most dominant factor. In my experience, however, little attention is given to capacity planning for data storage in comparison with work on CPU and Network capacity.

Particularly where there is a high incidence of interactive services, it is very common to find that only a small proportion of the data sets held on-line on DASD is actually referenced on any given day. Hence in many installations, a premium price is being paid to store inactive data. This problem and an approach to solving it are discussed in Note 1.

(d) Use Modern Technology   The cost effectiveness of Hardware continues to improve and economies can be made by using the latest Hardware, although this may require careful timing of investments. The same considerations are becoming increasingly appropriate for software.

2.3.3 Consolidation of Centres

In a multi-centre environment, savings will almost invariably be made by consolidation of centres. This will be particularly true if there is a high incidence of common applications. The savings are made primarily by a significant reduction in the number of staff needed, and also by reducing the spare and backup capacity by consolidating it into a smaller number of centres. These savings normally exceed the additional network costs considerably.

3 IS ORGANISATION

The creation of an Organisation designed to implement the IS strategy is a vital element in effective management of IS and is a significant contributor to optimal use of human and systems resources. A large variety of organisations exist and perform successfully; the key objective is to ensure that all required functions of IS are included and primary responsibilities assigned. To illustrate the roles and responsibilities involved, let us consider the organisation shown in Figure 1.

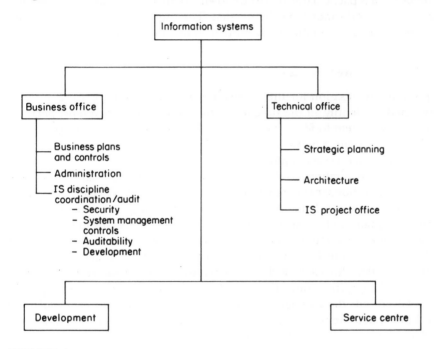

FIGURE 1

This organisation has two line management positions (Development and Service Centre) and two staff management positions (Business Office and Technical Office).

The role of the Business Office is to handle all financial aspects of IS and to provide an internal audit function for a number of IS disciplines. The Technical Office has three main responsibilities: firstly to develop a Strategic Plan of Services which are designed to provide maximum support for the business goals of the enterprise; secondly to design in conjunction with the Development and Service Centre Managers an IS architecture optimised for this enterprise's service environment; and thirdly to coordinate management reviews of key IS projects. A possible option is to have a single staff manager to whom both the Business Office and Technical Office report.

The responsibility of Development is to provide and maintain the Services identified in the Strategic Plan. The decision may be to develop new applications, buy the applications from another company or modify either an existing application or a purchased application. The services must be designed for the agreed IS architecture and should address such areas as ease of use, security, continuity and manageability. Where applications and/or software are purchased, it is particularly important to ensure that these criteria are met and significant modifications may be needed. The functions of Development are covered in Chapter 6 of this Book entitled 'Managing Successful Applications'.

3.1 Service Centre Organisation

A possible organisation for the Service Centre is shown in Figure 2, where I have tried to identify all the functions which a Service Centre must perform and allocated them to four groups. At the bottom of the chart are shown for each group the most important focus areas. The functions can be allocated differently; it is, however, important that they are included.

This IS organisation assumes a reasonable level of maturity in the telecommunications/networking area. Hence network development is in Development, network planning in Service Planning, network systems in Systems Support and network operations and line technicians in Operations. In a less mature organisation, it might be appropriate to have a separate Telecommunications Department including most of these functions.

It is vital that, for each of the principal functions, prime responsibility is assigned to a specific group. The word 'prime' implies that other groups may be involved, but the manager of the specified group is held *accountable*. By this I mean that the responsibility is written into the manager's job objectives and he/she is assessed on the success in meeting the agreed standard. Figure 3 illustrates this point by suggesting the allocation of prime responsibility for some of the most important Service Centre functions.

3.2 IS Director's Role

In practice the organisation selected by the IS Director will always reflect:

• The political or cultural approach of the enterprise
• Current problems perceived by top management in the enterprise
• The maturity of the IS function
• Calibre of IS management and staff available

The IS Director has a special responsibility to ensure good communications:

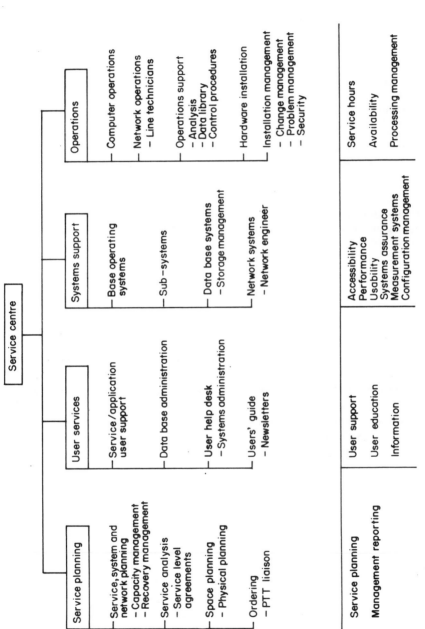

FIGURE 2

Function	Prime responsibility
— Processing management	Operations
— Batch	
— Interactive	
— Change management	Operations
— Problem management	Operations
— Recovery management	Service planning/systems support
— Performance management	Systems support/development
— Data storage management	Systems support
— Capacity management	Service planning
— Usability	Systems support/development
— Systems assurance	Systems support
— Security management	
— Physical	Operations
— Data	Systems support
— Information/communication	User services
— User education	User service
— Management reporting	Service planning/business of ce
— Service level management	Service planning

FIGURE 3

firstly with the users to ensure that their goals are understood and that IS is seen to be helping them to achieve them; secondly with higher management to inform them how IS is contributing to the business and to tell them of the successes of IS. This last point is important, since most meetings with higher management are held to discuss the shortcomings of IS; normally its successes are taken for granted and greeted with silence. It follows that in many meetings the IS Director is in a defensive position so it is incumbent on him/her to organise meetings which show IS in a good light. Chapter 11 of this book entitled 'Demonstrating the IS Contribution' discusses how this might be achieved.

4 THE NETWORK

The Network is the enabling technology for access to all services and also for remote operation of those services. As such it is one of the most vital elements for delivery of IS Sevices. This is particularly true when providing services from multiple Service Centres. Further functions which are facilitated by the network are portability of applications, Disaster Recovery and load balancing. In this section, I will discuss briefly network objectives, network design and network management.

4.1 Network Objectives

There are six objectives which in my experience are key to the success of a network.

4.1.1 Access to Services

The most common objective is that any user should be able to access any service provided by the enterprise without knowing or wishing to know the geographical location of that service. It is the task of the network to establish the connection. A corollary of this is that the user should not be able to access services for which he/she is not authorised and the security of networks is of increasing importance. Information stored on processors represents a vital asset to the users and it is essential that the network is designed to prevent users from outside the enterprise from gaining access to any services.

4.1.2 Connectivity

Connectivity should be as extensive as possible to allow a variety of workstations to access the services. When providing services to customers outside the enterprise, they may wish to connect either their own private network or workstations they already own in order to avoid expenditure.

4.1.3 Network Service Quality

Since the service level commitments relate to the service received at the user's workstation, service quality is fundamental to the success of a network. The most important service parameters are Service Hours, reliability and response time and each is affected by the network. For example, if the Network Added Delay is excessive, the response time can never be satisfactory, regardless of the service host processor's performance. Each link in the connection has a potential degrading effect on reliability and response time.

4.1.4 User Friendly Interface

Since the network is the first element accessed by the user, it must provide a consistent interface to all services which is easy to understand and is user friendly. In the international environment, it must provide this interface in the language of the user.

4.1.5 Flexible Architecture

The network architecture should be as flexible as possible to facilitate easy growth and to address requirements which will inevitably change in the future. Facilities must be included to measure network service levels and network usage, together with tools for management and control.

4.1.6 PTT Compatibility

Finally, in the international environment, it is necessary to understands the PTT regulations, which vary from country to country, and to design the network to ensure these regulations do not inhibit provision of necessary functions.

4.2 Design Approach

Perhaps the most useful way of discussing the extensive topic of network design is to suggest a possible design approach to address each of the objectives listed above.

4.2.1 Access to Services

A method widely adopted to enable users to access any service in the enterprise is to separate the network from the host processors on which the services are run. A front-end processor owns the entire network and all the workstations are connected to this processor through Communication Controllers. The front-end processor knows the location of every host processor and its function is to check the authenticity of the user and to establish a connection between the user's workstation and a service for which he/she is authorised. The user's initial session is with the front-end processor, but after the connection has been established, the user's session is directly with the host processor. The advantage of this separation is that changes can be made independently to both the network and the applications and this gives great flexibility. For expository purposes, in the material which follows, I will use IBM terms for the front-end network processor which is the Communication Management Configuration or CMC (IBM, GC24-1668) and for a Communication Controller which is 37X5 (IBM, G511-1096 and IBM, GA33-0021).

In separating the applications from the network, we have created what is called a Closed Network, in that workstations are connected to the CMC and not directly to the applications. Network security is provided by making the CMC responsible for access control. When a user logs-on, his indentity is checked by the CMC and if valid he is allowed to access any application listed in his user profile entry held in the CMC. The authorisation process may, of course, include other checks such as his credit rating. Further security can be provided by use of encryption on the lines. The data on the host processor would be protected by software such as the IBM product RACF (IBM, GC28-0722).

4.2.2 Connectivity

To provide maximum connectivity, it is necessary to design a network with clean interfaces allowing easy attachment. Wherever protocol converters are required to handle special workstations, they should be placed outboard between the 37X5's and the workstation. In the international service environment, it may be necessary to provide for a hierarchy of autonomous customer, national and international networks. These should be interconnected through clean gateways.

4.2.3 Network Service Quality

Most networks are configured on the basis of a wide-area or backbone network of nodes distributed geographically according to the volume of network traffic in each area. In order to ensure reliability, these backbone nodes are connected to form a fully or partially meshed network giving alternate routing capabilities; certainly it is unacceptable to have only one line connecting a node to this network. Since response times are limited by the slowest link in the chain, it is advisable to interconnect all backbone nodes with high speed lines, unless traffic is extremely low. Nothing undermines the reputation of the service provider more than poor response times. Use of high speed lines facilitates the use of the latest technologies, in particular digital circuits which are much more cost effective since they are relatively cheaper than analogue circuits, give fewer errors and allow higher line utilisation. To maximise accessibility of the services, the network must be available and supported for as close to 168 hours a week as possible. Clearly, if the network is owned by the CMC, it is advisable to have this processor backed up by a hot stand-by processor.

A valuable contribution to good service is to have a consistent approach to the Help Desk function, ensuring uniform standards and helpfulness. This can be enhanced by implementing an on-line support system allowing users to enter problems directly from their workstations. The system is best provided on a dedicated host to which the user can request connection via the CMC. The user defines the problem by means of a structured dialogue and the problem is then placed in the appropriate queue for resolution by staff skilled in that area. At any time, the user can query the status of resolution; the problem is not considered closed until the user has approved the solution. The system provides valuable information on the types of problem arising and the methods of solution. By linking the support systems in different countries, international problem determination is facilitated. The value of the system is also in providing an alternative when the Help Desk phones are all engaged; it must, of course, be used by the Help Desk staff.

As in all other areas of service delivery, measurement systems are needed for all elements of the network. They would measure for example availability, number of interruptions and response times; these are all discussed below in Section 7.1. Network accounting information can be collected on the 37X5's, where the number of characters transmitted and received can be recorded. Support systems should be included for network problem determination and network support purposes.

4.2.4 User Friendly Interface

One of the primary objectives for delivery of services is ease of use. Since the CMC is the first processor with which the user communicates, it is important that it provides a consistent interface giving a standard appearance for all services. The user, having satisfied the various checks for authenticity and legality, should be presented by the CMC with a clear menu of services which he is allowed to access. A very important goal for ease of use is achieved by implementing password propagation. This allows a user to access all those services for which he is authorised by supplying only one User ID and one password to the CMC. The CMC will then automatically log-on to each service requested and transfer the password to the appropriate service. In short, the initial session with the CMC sets the tone for the whole service and this must be as good as possible and provided in the user's own language.

4.2.5 Flexible Architecture

Inevitably the demands on the network will grow and so will the facilities needed; this requires a flexible and open-ended network architecture. In my experience, power and flexibility are achieved only by having a simple design. Normally this is the result of continuous iteration on the design, simplifying it at each stage. The correct design has probably been reached when the solution is so simple as to be obvious to other people and felt to have been achieved with little effort. Certainly a feature will be clean and simple logic and interfaces.

4.2.6 PTT Compatibility

When providing services on an international basis, one of the problem areas is that imposed by PTT regulations in each country. Although most countries are committed to liberalisation of the largely government-imposed controls, the rate of progress varies considerably and there is little consistency. The definition of value-added is a particularly variable item. In order to design an international network, therefore, it is necessary to maintain an ongoing dialogue with the PTTs in each country, both to understand their plans and to capitalise on new opportunities.

4.3 Network Management

For most networks, the challenge of management and control is at least as great as the technical challenges of function and performance. Accordingly, network management needs special attention, in particular accountability must be well defined.

In an international service environment, each Service Centre should be responsible for its country network, customer networks attached to the country network and international connections to other countries.

The owner of an international service problem should be the Service Centre owning the host service being used, and it is that centre's task to resolve network problems by working with all groups on which it has a dependency. In particular, Service Level Agreements should exist between centres with commitments for network availability, response times, service hours and problem determination and resolution.

There should be centralised responsibility for network architecture and development of all network software with emphasis on function, performance, management and control.

5 AUTOMATION

An increasing contribution is being made by automation to all aspects of Service Centre work. This is particularly true in the Operations area which has traditionally accounted for a large proportion of staff numbers (Simpson and Spooner, 1988). Therefore any manager of a Service Centre should continually assess opportunities for automation. In order to assist him to do this, I review below the objectives of automation, some of the principal application areas and the staffing and planning implications.

5.1 Objectives

The principal objectives of automation are as follows:

- Increased productivity of staff
- Improved service quality by reducing human errors
- Handling increased complexity
- Enhanced security
- Remote operation of systems
- Unattended operation of systems and network
- Improved responsiveness to users' problems

5.2 Application Areas

In my experience, the greatest benefits have been achieved through use of Automation in the following six areas.

5.2.1 System Console Consolidation

The most spectacular results have been obtained by system console consolidation, using packages which allow all systems owned by an installation to be run by one operator (IBM, GC22-9112 and IBM GC30-3463). In essence, the operator has a console attached to one processor which has connections to all the other processors to be operated; the processors can be local or remote.

To achieve this without overwhelming the operator with information and tasks to perform, the console messages received from each system are first subjected to detailed analysis. It has been found in most installations that up to 90% of messages are purely informative and require no action by the operator. These can be filtered out and suppressed. In examining the remaining messages which do require attention, many of the actions to be carried out are routine in nature requiring a level of judgement that can be automated.

The next step is to design Action Routines for as many of these as possible. In general, the Action Routines are Event-driven, Timer-driven or Threshold-driven, and can be implemented for automatic execution. They can also be initiated by the console operator. By Message Filtering and use of Action Routines, the actions required by the console operator are dramatically reduced. In this way, one operator can handle a large number of systems and theoretically there is no limit to this number. In practice, I have seen an installation in which one operator controlled well over 20 local and remote systems.

5.2.2 Network Control and Management

The same methods have been applied to Network Control and Management, with one operator controlling the entire network from one console (IBM, GC22-9112). This can be particularly valuable in coordinating network changes across multiple locations. Ideally one operator would control all systems and network elements from one console.

5.2.3 Unattended Operation

For unattended operation, the approach has normally been for the systems and network to be controlled by programmable workstations which can also monitor the status of all elements. In the event of significant problems, critical messages go to a screen in an area manned by security guards who can telephone appropriate Service Centre staff who are on call-out duty at home. In the unattended mode, there will probably be severe limitations on I/O operations.

5.2.4 Batch Processing

In the area of batch processing, software is available for job scheduling and control. Printed output volumes can be reduced by holding the data on spool files for a limited period to be inspected by the user, who would make the decision as to whether the information should be printed. Similarly, concerted drives to interview users will identify a surprisingly large amount of printed material that can be avoided. The point is that in many enterprises, a huge amount of printed output is created which is either thrown away immediately or of which only a tiny proportion is actually needed. Other measures are to send the output to a printer in the user's office area and ask him to control the printer. This normally reduces the volume quickly. Finally, if material has to be printed, it should be done in the location nearest to the distribution point; human intervention can be reduced, for example, by increasing the length of continuous stationary. Some companies are contracting printing out to an external print shop connected via telecommunications links.

5.2.5 Change and Problem Management

Systems exist which can greatly help change and problem management, providing facilities for use by those responsible and mechanising certain tasks, in particular data base management, to ensure consistency and insight. In some installations, users can log-on to a problem management application and communicate regarding the status of resolution.

5.2.6 Data Storage Management

Management of data storage is increasingly important, in that it is the dominant user of air-conditioned floor space, it represents a very large proportion of the hardware budget and needs significant support staff in the absence of automated tools. An example of a data storage management system is provided by the IBM product DFHSM (IBM, GH35-0092), which migrates data automatically to less costly storage when it has been inactive for some time and restores it on demand. In addition, incremental backup is provided where only data which has been changed is copied onto the backup media. This not only saves storage space but can be initiated automatically, saving staff.

5.3 Staffing

All the above automation is rapidly reducing the number of staff needed in

Operations and for some Installation Management disciplines. In other areas of the Service Centre it is likely that use of Expert Systems will prove valuable, the objective being to capture the knowledge and more importantly the techniques and approach used by the most skilful staff. Work has already been done in addressing the functions of the Help Desk, while Service Planning, Systems Support, Service Support and Operations Support are other potential areas. To my knowledge, however, progress with Expert Systems in the Service Centre has not progressed very far to date.

One obvious result of automation is that although it reduces the number of staff required, those remaining have to be increasingly skilled. Nevertheless, in those installations where most progress has been made in automation, the staff have been involved in analysing their own work. They have identified the more boring and repetitive aspects of the job and helped to automate them. In this way they have not only been more creative but have become enthusiastic advocates of automation.

5.4 Implemention Planning

Overall, automation is producing very beneficial results and is, of course, an ongoing process. It is, however, essential that the installation is well organised and has good management processes in place before embarking on automation. Very often the decision to automate acts as a catalyst for critical analysis and improvement of the current processes; certainly automating inadequate processes will severely limit success. In developing a plan, it is advisable at the beginning to target areas which have prospects of early success and can give credibility to automation.

6 MANAGING MULTIPLE SERVICE CENTRES

When IS owns Service Centres in multiple countries or locations, two issues generally arise. Firstly, is the continued existence of all the centres justified; and, secondly, assuming there is a need for more than one centre, what functions should be placed in each? The problem to be addressed is essentially how to allocate services to the centres in such a way as to provide optimal support for the users at minimal cost.

In this section the principal approaches are described. I then discuss two topics: key decisions to be made in selecting an approach and organisational considerations.

6.1 Principal Approaches

There are four principal approaches: centralised service, decentralised service, cooperative processing and regionalised service. The strengths and weaknesses of each are discussed below.

6.1.1 Centralised Service

In this approach, all user services are provided from one central Service Centre with at most a front-end processor in each country or location. Its strengths include:

- Economies of scale
- Full functions and uniform performance available to all users
- Single corporate data base
- Centralised architecture and design
- Concentration of scarce technical skills

This approach is particularly effective where applications are common with little local variation.

The weaknesses include the following:

- User management feels it has no influence or control
- The impact of a disaster will be much greater if services are centralised into *one* location
- Not possible to solve legal restrictions on cross-border services. (For example, Switzerland has laws relating to financial data and Sweden has laws relating to personal data which may prevent such services.)
- Performance probably less consistent for local users.

6.1.2 Decentralised Service

In this approach, each country or location provides the full range of services required by the local users. Its strengths include:

- Local ownership and control
- Applications tailored more closely to local requirements
- Operating data held locally
- Performance normally more consistent for local users

The weaknesses include:

- Overall cost may be greater
- Consolidation of corporate data bases more difficult
- Little portability of applications
- Functions and performance will normally vary between locations
- Difficult to attract and retain technical skills

6.1.3 Cooperative Processing

This term means that there is a centralised architecture and design for the total enterprise. Services are provided within this design and functions are placed both centrally and locally so that they cooperate and communicate to optimise the service provided to the users. Careful decisions are made as to placement of functions according to the requirements of the users. The strengths of this approach include:

- Economies of scale
- Some degree of local ownership and control
- Full functions and consistent performance are available to all users
- Single corporate data base with operating data held locally
- Common applications are run centrally while those needed in only one country/location can be run locally
- Centralised architecture and design
- Concentration of technical skills

The weaknesses include:

- Overall cost can be greater than the centralised approach
- Management of total corporate service more complex
- Technical skills may be difficult to attract and retain locally

6.1.4 Regionalised Service

Sometimes as a step towards centralisation, Regional Service Centres are created providing services on a geographical basis normally. The functions of such a Centre in an international environment would be to provide all the services within the country where it is situated and also to other countries which are adjacent or near to it or which share a common language. In addition the Service Centre may be nominated as a Centre of Competence for selected international applications, providing service to all countries. This responsibility would be allocated either because the Centre possesses expertise in those applications or because the corresponding data base is most logically centralised in that country. A further function of a Regional Centre might be to act as a Network Control Centre for the international network, able to take over control when required.

It is normal to establish several Regional Centres, primarily to ensure continuity of service by providing alternate network routing, plus backup for processing, data bases and network control. In addition there may be a limit to the practical size of one installation.

The criteria for assessing the capability of a centre to assume regional responsibilities in an international environment might include:

- Ability to provide high quality service
- Cost per unit of work delivered
- Availability of skilled personnel in the country together with the ability to retain staff and recruit more
- Volume of business in that country
- Existence of a favourable business environment in the country
  - PTT liberalisation policy
  - Labour relations
  - Legality of running services for 24 hours a day and 7 days a week
- Situation regarding cross-border traffic and charges
- Ability of 'Help Desk' staff to speak the international language of the enterprise, which is normally English

Establishing a regionalised service gives most of the benefits of a centralised service, except that there is no longer a single corporate data base image.

6.2 Key Decisions

In selecting an approach for the number and location of the centres and their respective functions, a number of key decisions have to be made.

The major decision to be made relates to data. Should there be one centralised Data Base or a hierarchy of centralised, regionalised and local Data Bases? Whatever the decision, it is clearly vital to ensure that currency and consistency of data are maintained at all times.

The Network should be designed to minimise the bandwidth required, consistent with the Service Level objectives. Continuity should be ensured by provision of alternate routes through the network. The philosophy should be to use the Network to access data where it resides naturally, rather than wasting bandwidth to move high volume data around.

Unless the users receive service on workstations which are channel attached to a processor, the availability and response times should not differ noticeably between local, regional or centralised services. Hence processing should be located wherever the data resides; however, if it is distributed among too many locations there will normally be excessive spare capacity overall.

The decision as to whether a service should be centralised will have to be taken service by service and depends on:

- The degree of commonality
- Service levels required
- Importance of local responsiveness

The choice of whether or not to centralise need not be the same for all services. It is very important to prepare a detailed migration plan for incremental centralisation of services, ensuring protection of all current services until migration has been achieved satisfactorily.

In general, centralisation will normally yield significant savings which are at their greatest if there is a large number of common applications, a high degree of decentralisation and very little automation in place. Most savings result primarily from a considerable reduction in staff numbers, but also savings in spare capacity and backup systems.

6.3 Organisational Considerations

Assuming there is a need for multiple centres either in different countries or in one country, I show in Figure 4 a possible IS organisation. This is based on the organisation charts included earlier in the chapter in Figures 1 and 2.

I have indicated those functions which in my view should be centralised with the letter 'C'; those which could be decentralised with the letter 'L'; and those which could be in either with the letters 'C/L'.

Centralised service can mean one logical centre in N physical locations, each the centre of competence for specific applications. Indeed, a meshed network of Regional Centres may be the best centralised approach. With the use of automation all these centres can be run remotely from one location in which all the technically skilled staff are centralised. This would require only a skeleton operations staff in the physical centres to handle those situations needing human intervention, such as Input/Output operations and out-of-line situations requiring buttons to be pushed. The location from which all the centres are run could be selected as a place to which skilled staff could be attracted or where they are already living. In this approach it is necessary to provide protection against a disaster resulting in loss of all technically skilled staff. The physical centres can be located where real-estate is cheap.

In an international environment, however, some functions and services will generally remain local, including:

- The 'Help Desk', a necessity in the international environment for reasons of language or even dialect
- Network Support to interface with the local PTT for resolution of telecommunications problems
- Local applications, in particular those with legal restrictions

7 MEASUREMENT SYSTEMS

It is virtually impossible to manage a Service Centre unless systems are installed to measure the quality of service provided, the resources utilised and the costs involved. To this end, it is essential to have expert staff working

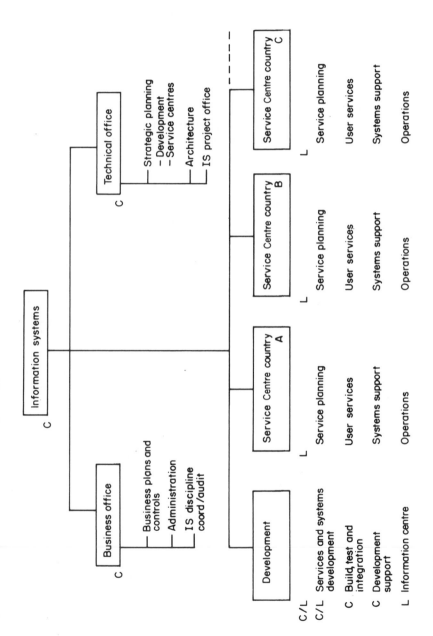

FIGURE 4

continuously to upgrade existing measurement systems and create reports which improve information, capture data which addresses new areas and provide better insight. These reports should be working documents used by management and staff to understand the current status, improve the service as appropriate and plan for the future. In the words of the author of Chapter 2 of this book entitled 'Exploiting IT—The CEO Sets the Tone', 'What happens is what you inspect rather than what you expect.' If the measurement systems are properly designed, they should become the *only* source of such information in the enterprise, in that the users should have complete confidence in the information provided and not feel constrained to make their own measurements. Only in this way can fruitless comparisons of incompatible information be avoided. As far as possible, all information on the quality of service provided should be available on-line to users; this is very instrumental in gaining acceptance and user confidence. The measurement systems discussed below cover the following areas:

- Service Effectiveness
- Service Efficiency
- Accounting

7.1 Service Effectiveness

This is normally addressed by measuring the quality of service provided against the objectives documented in the Service Level Agreements with the users (see Section 2.2). In this section, I give an example of the kind of information desirable in a reporting system and also discuss an approach to the crucial issue of how to measure the response times experienced by users without incurring unreasonable cost.

7.1.1 Reporting System

Wherever possible, the information should be presented in graphical form, preferably in colour, augmented by tables of values where appropriate. The system should be structured to produce reports at a number of levels of detail. From my experience, I have found the following three-level structure to be very effective.

(a) Management Overview   Covering key service parameters on a weekly basis over, say, the last 13 weeks for each processor. The parameters could include:

- Availability
- Number of Interruptions
- Response Time to Users
- Prime Shift CPU Loading

The audiences addressed are User and IS Management and the information should be entirely graphical. It is important for these graphs to be prominently displayed in the Service Centre.

(b) Service Level Report   This would be a more detailed report showing for each processor all service parameters on a weekly basis over, say, the last 52 weeks. It would be broken down by major sub-system and major application and provide both response times and batch turnaround times as experienced by the users. Other items would include CPU utilisation by shift, utilisation of the Network links, number of users and so forth.

The audiences addressed are Users and Service Centre managers and staff. The information should be presented graphically as far as possible with some tabular data.

(c) Weekly Report   This would include for each processor a graph for each day of the week covering the 24-hour period and plotting, for example:

- Response Time
- CPU Utilisation
- Number of Active Users

and indicating the percentage availability and numbers of interrupts for that day. The report would also contain summary tables for the week covering items such as those listed in Note 2.

This report is intended primarily for the Service Centre staff who are supporting the services.

7.1.2 Response Time Analysis

In addition to internal system measurements, a Service Centre must measure the response time experienced by a user at his/her workstation. Hardware features exist which allow the actual response times at the workstations to be recorded and processed. However, this data does not give a clear indication of what the user was trying to do; further, it is expensive to collect for all users. When a user complains about degraded response, the commands he/she is using may have changed and require more resource to process. In the case of a relational data base system, the command may be the same but the size of the table may be significantly bigger, automatically resulting in longer response times.

In providing interactive services, particularly when the users are remote or in different countries, it is essential to have an automated system to sample response times continuously at various nodes in the network. The method most widely used is to load a PC with scripts representing typical commands for each service. The PC logs-on to each service in turn, normally during Prime Shift, and records the response times for the scripts. Very often these scripts are divided into short, medium and long transactions. The continuous samples can record average response times and, for example, the 90th percentile cut-off.

The nodes selected are typically channel attachment to the hosts, the gateway from the installation, the nodes of the wide-area network, the country gateways, etc. The information gives an excellent health indicator for response on a continuous basis and is essential in analysing performance problems reported by users. With good geographical coverage, it is possible to identify quickly where the problem exists or to establish that the end-user has made some fundamental change.

7.2 Service Efficiency

While service effectiveness is concerned with the extent to which the services are delivered to the users responsively and with the agreed quality, service efficiency addresses the cost of effective delivery of services in resources and hence money. These can be measured by tracking over time such ratios as Work Units per person year or cost per Work Unit, where Work Unit is a generic term covering entities for which the user is charged. An example is shown in Figure 5, covering for a Service Centre the period 1975–83.

While the billable Work Units processed have increased at an annual Compound Growth Rate of 40%, the person years have decreased by 1%, giving a productivity improvement of 41% per person year. The expense has increased by 14%, which is much smaller than the growth in Work Units, resulting in a 19% annual reduction in cost per Work Unit. In this particular company, although the Service Centre expense was increasing, it was doing so at a smaller rate than the overall company expense. As a result the percentage spent on IS Services was decreasing annually by 7%. This would occur only in a Company where IS had achieved a very high degree of penetration.

It is even more effective if productivity and cost improvements can be expressed in business terms wherever possible to indicate the benefits accruing to the enterprise.

7.3 Accounting System

7.3.1 Objectives

The primary objectives of a Service Centre Accounting System are:

- To provide the basis for Charge-out for a Profit Centre or Cost Recovery for a Cost Centre

	1975 act	1976 act	1977 act	1978 act	1979 act	1980 act	1981 act	1982 act	1983 plan	CGR (%)
Billable work units (K)	210	460	628	932	1316	1642	1763	2306	3128	+40
SC person years	143	135	141	144	146	134	134	134	131	−1
SC expense ($m)	4.8	6.8	7.4	8.7	9.7	11.0	12.3	13.1	13.7	+14
K work units/person year	1.5	3.4	4.5	6.5	9.0	12.3	13.2	17.2	23.9	+41
Cost/work unit ($)	22.9	14.8	11.8	9.3	7.4	6.7	7.0	5.7	4.4	−19
Net SC expense as % of company expense	19.5	20.6	14.4	12.8	11.8	13.9	12.4	10.8	10.7	−7

FIGURE 5   Service Centre Productivity

- To facilitate forecasting
- To measure resource utilisation

7.3.2 Accounting Parameters

The number of parameters which the accounting system tracks should be as small as possible and preferably those selected should give repeatable results. To charge for a large number of elements adds complexity and administrative overheads; further, it gives a specious impression of precision in an area which is by its nature imprecise. For example, some years ago, a study of a number of European installations found that the parameters used ranged in number from three to over twenty. However, analysis showed that in almost all these installations, well over 90% of the recoveries came from two or three parameters.

The accounting parameters should be selected with the objectives of being:

- Understandable to the user
- Controllable by the user
- Needed by the service provider for forecasting and capacity planning purposes

In general, these parameters should address the main areas of expenditure, which are processing power, storage of information and network bandwidth. The first of these is measured by CPU time consumed, the second primarily by DASD occupancy in megabytes or gigabytes and the third either by the number of characters transmitted/received or by the number of Terminal Connect Hours.

The fact that the information stored on DASD is not active does not significantly reduce the cost and should be handled by migrating inactive data to less expensive media and/or use of compaction and compression. Although you can time-slice processing and network capacity across, for example, different time zones, this is not practicable with DASD occupancy. This therefore is a key area in which to make charges.

The cost of Network bandwidth includes the telecommunications lines and the associated hardware connecting it to workstations and processors. Terminal Connect Hours can, of course, put different demands on the network for each service used.

As an alternative, users are increasingly interested in being charged for the number of transactions processed, which is more understandable to them. To do this, each application has to collect the information and may have to classify a number of transaction types.

7.3.3 Differential Charging

Another refinement is to introduce differential charging, in which lower rates are charged for off-shift processing or low priority work. The motivation is to make it more attractive for users to use off-peak periods. Although there is a widespread belief that differential charging can be used to influence the users' work patterns, in my experience this seldom happens in practice.

However, there is one area where I do believe that differential charging is advisable and justified. In a large installation, the economies of scale are derived primarily from the big user departments and indeed they are the ones who assert with some degree of credibility that they could run their own dedicated installation cheaper. If all user departments are charged the same rate regardless of their contribution to economies of scale, then the assertion may well be valid. It is appropriate, therefore, to charge a cheaper rate for the big user departments through, for example, volume discounts. This does make the accuracy of workload forecasts much more important in order to plan the rates to be charged.

7.3.4 Accounting Reports

The Accounting System should provide Variance Reports, showing actual utilisation against forecast for both the current period (say a month) and Year-to-Date, covering

- Total Billable workload processed
  - By major service
  - By User Department
    - By major service
    - By user (if required)
- Total Non-Billable Usage
  - Housekeeping
  - Workload to install and support services

The workload and charges should be reported in total and for each chargeable parameter.

7.3.5 Capacity Planning

The Accounting System is essential for Capacity Planning since it provides the information which enables the User Departments to prepare their workload forecasts. It also includes the resources used by the services. Although the horizon of users is fairly limited, it is necessary to obtain their forecasts and if necessary to extrapolate from the accounting data to augment this information and prepare estimates of their workload. In order to complete a Service Level Agreement with a User Department, there must be agreement on the size of workload they wish to process. Equally, in order to create a coherent systems plan and investment strategy, the workload must be projected a few years ahead based on information from the Accounting System, the Service Level measurement system and knowledge of new services planned for introduction in the future. Fortunately, in most installations, 5% of the users utilise 75% or more of the processing power; hence attention can be concentrated on these users and the services they use and, if appropriate, the resources required by the remainder can be added as a percentage of the dominant 5%.

8 SUMMARY

In this chapter, I have tried to show how a Service Centre might address its mission of delivering IS services effectively to the end-users. The primary goals were identified as: responsive user support, high quality service levels and cost effectiveness. A strategic approach was described showing some of the key steps in addressing each of these objectives. I then suggested a possible IS Organisation to implement the Strategy and discussed three areas which have proved of great significance in most implementation plans; these were the network, automation and management of multiple Service Centres.

Finally, I expressed the view that in my experience the ability to manage a Service Centre effectively is largely determined by the quality of its Measurement Systems. These should be designed to give insight into actual achievement in comparison with objectives and also provide feedback both for control purposes and, where appropriate, modification of goals, strategy, organisation and the implementation plan.

NOTES

Note 1

Over ten years ago, a study in an installation I was managing indicated that on any given day less than 50% of the users logged-on to the systems and each user that did log-on referenced approximately 20% of the data sets he/she owned. In short, less than 10% of the data sets held on DASD were active each day. At that time, we were experiencing a data explosion and banks of DASD were being installed continuously to keep pace with demands. This resulted not only in expense but also, more seriously, the air-conditioned floor space available could not sustain this growth rate. The percentage of data active today in that installation would be nearer 5%. Clearly it was unacceptable to pay a premium price to store data which was largely inactive; on the other hand it was not possible to predict which data would be active on a given day.

As a result, development was started in conjunction with another location to develop a Data Storage management system which eventually became the IBM product DFHSM (IBM, GH35-0092). In essence this provides dynamic management of data sets, selecting inactive data which is then compacted and compressed to occupy less storage and migrated either to another area of DASD or to a cheaper medium such as Mass Storage. Data sets are automatically restored on demand to high-performance DASD for processing, the only delay occurring at the beginning of an interactive session while the data is restored. This led to spectacular savings in cost, floor space and staff.

Note 2

The detailed weekly service effectiveness report for Service Centre staff would contain summary tables covering such items as:

- Job turnaround time by Job Class broken down, for example, into:
  — Queue time
  — Execution time
  — Print time
- Resource utilisation
  — Channel activity
  — DASD activity by device
  — Paging activity
  — Lines output
- Sorted lists showing:
  — Biggest users by shift
  — Largest jobs
  — Programs using most CPU time
  — Users with worst response time
  — etc.

REFERENCES

IBM G511-1096 'IBM 3745 communication controller product and technology overview'.
IBM GA33-0021 'Introduction to IBM 3725 communication controller'.
IBM GC22-9112 'Systems and network operations automation using netview release 2'.
IBM GC24-1668 'Communication management configuration'.
IBM GC28-0722 'Resource access control facility general information manual'.
IBM GC30-3463 'Netview general information and planning manual'.
IBM GE20-0749 'A management system for the information business, Vol II, The information systems service mission'.
IBM GE20-0751 'A management system for the information business, Vol IV, Managing information systems resources'.
IBM GH35-0092 'Data facility hierarchical storage manager general information manual'.

BIBLIOGRAPHY

Jones,I.W.L.(1988) 'Effective IS resource management in a multi-national organisation', Paper presented at the UK Computer Measurement Group Management Strategy Conference, January.
Simpson,R. and Spooner,R.F.(1988) 'The automation of operations', Paper presented at IBM's IS Executive Institute, September.

Chapter 9
SECURING VITAL IT SERVICES

Steve Davis

1 WHY SECURE IT SERVICES?

1.1 IT Is an Essential Business Asset

In a book where the central theme is the creation of an environment for the imaginative and effective use of IT within an enterprise, a chapter on contingency planning is most appropriate. As the penetration of computer systems increases within an enterprise, so does its reliance upon the continued reliable operation of such systems. As such, the subject of contingency planning is a topic requiring attention in many enterprises and indeed this has long been the case.

For the purpose of this chapter, contingency planning for computer services will be defined as:

> The provision of agreed plans which, in the event of a significant problem with services provided by computer systems, will allow:
>
> — End users to continue with their essential business functions until the service is restored.
> — IS to restore the service in a timely and safe manner.

Contingency planning of course is not new and it pre-dates computers by many years:

> And here we must noate, that every Abbott kept a monastery registry (which they called a leger booke), of all material things belonging to the estates of their Abbey, and did likewise make another Leger booke of the same and deposit it in the hands of some neighbour—abbott thereby to prevent fraudulent dealing in erasing or altering, and to prevent the losse of theire bookes by fire or other accidents.
>
> Richard Gough
> *The History of Myddle*, c.1700

Managing Information Systems for Profit.   Edited by T. J. Lincoln
© 1990 John Wiley & Sons Ltd

Contingency Planning for computer installations gained impetus during the late 1960s and early 1970s as companies moved from batch to on-line processing. Further impetus was given by a number of well publicised disasters during that period. If one views the number of courses and consultancy offerings available on this subject today, it is tempting to imagine that all is well and that most companies are paying due regard to the topic. My experience suggests that this is not the case in many companies within the UK.

This feeling of unease is confirmed by a survey of 490 companies by Arthur Young (1987) which concluded that only 31% of the computer installations surveyed had a fully documented contingency plan. It may be that a considered decision that the level of computing within a company does not warrant a contingency plan is perfectly legitimate. In most cases, however, the 'no plan' option occurs by default. Even in those companies where a contingency plan exists I have found examples where the plan is unworkable, inappropriate, or untestable. Again, this is confirmed by the Arthur Young survey which found that only 16% of the 490 installations had fully tested their plan within the last 12 months.

Given the increasing dependence upon computing in many companies, the apparent lack of attention to this subject is disturbing.

1.2 IT Disasters Do Happen

It is not the intention of this chapter to invoke panic; the likelihood of a disaster happening is remote. However, they do occur and sometimes from unexpected causes! One company had its mainframe computer equipment destroyed by a lightning strike. The building housing computer equipment was struck by lightning, even though the building had a lightning conductor which protected the building by conducting the lightning to earth. Unfortunately, the earth for the computers was adjacent to the lightning conductor earth ... ! In another incident an extremely powerful radar system interfered with computer processing at a nearby site. Data was corrupted at the point where it was written to magnetic disk, rendering it unreadable. The obscure nature of the problem took a very long time to diagnose and resulted in considerable disruption.

Fire, however, seems to be the prime cause of loss. The widely reported fire at the Open University in 1987 completely destroyed a computer system and also resulted in the loss of some research data. There are other issues which may be external to an enterprise but could impair the ability of computer systems to function normally. In this context, recent industrial action by British Telecom and Post Office employees have alerted many people to the need to consider the *total* delivery chain involved in getting data from computer systems to its intended destination.

Other examples occasionally make the press headlines and although no reliable data exists upon which to assess the probability of a disaster occurring, the mere fact of their occurrence and the impact they cause suggests that it would be prudent to consider the eventuality.

1.3 You May Be Exposed and Not Know It!

Experience suggests that contingency planning is often poorly done. Accordingly, although a plan may exist it might not stand rigorous examination. Why is this? Some of the reasons are shown below:

- In many installations the development process does not consider the possibility of the application being unavailable for an extended period. Data backup and recovery procedures in the event of operational failure are normally provided, but real disaster planning is either ignored or considered tacitly to be the responsibility of computer operations.
- Often the main focus of attention tends to be on the development process. The general creativity of this process and the urge to achieve predetermined goals seem to create an atmosphere of optimism which is sometimes misplaced. This phenomena is not peculiar to IT developments:
  - The Titanic was thought to be unsinkable and hence carried insufficient life boats.
  - The Maginot Line was deemed to be impregnable; no secondary defences were thought to be necessary.
  - Failure probabilities for the NASA Shuttle programme were based upon theoretical component failure calculations rather than previous launch histories.
- There is often little interchange of skills between operations and development and hence operations management are rarely well placed to take on the contingency role thrust upon them. As many IS managers have a predominantly development background, there may also be a lack of focus throughout the rest of IS regarding the problems inherent in contingency planning.
- The creation of a contingency plan can be tedious and time consuming. It lacks the glamour and promotion prospects offered by development and is often staffed on the basis of availability rather than talent. It is generally a retrospective task following the completion of a development project, and yet requires the support of development staff. Such support is likely to put added pressure on development resource which is probably already facing a large backlog of work in direct support of the business. This can create friction and further impairs the process.
- Contingency planning can be a costly exercise. If done retrospectively, there may be little enthusiasm by IS managers to put forward a case which is likely to be viewed as additional expense with no apparent benefit to the business. In some cases the expense of providing a comprehensive disaster plan may

invalidate the original business case for an application. Thus even where disaster plans are produced there is often pressure to provide a minimum cost 'solution' which may look good on paper but in practice is likely to be unworkable.

Whatever the cause, the subject of contingency planning often has low visibility and priority. Users and senior management tend to consider the topic only when problems arise, rather than as part of the development cycle. Even when user management get involved the issue is often viewed as a highly technical 'computing' problem. All too often the subject only gets attention when a very serious problem arises in the daily operation of systems. At that point executive management focus on the subject and a realistic plan emerges; for an unfortunate and tiny minority this may be too late.

1.4 Weak Links May Exist in the Service Chain

Much of the computer equipment and internal operating system software on offer today have high degrees of internal resilience and thus are able to provide good levels of reliability. Computers designed specifically for very high availability have extremely sophisticated internal backup systems which can guarantee close to 100% availability over very long periods. High levels of equipment reliability are becoming the expected norm; there are, however, many other elements involved in the service chain. These include application systems, computer operators and telecommunications networks to mention a few! Application systems are often written within the enterprise and these are also becoming more reliable, although they often fall short of equipment reliability levels. The way in which applications exploit information technology may, however, leave an enterprise vulnerable to localised problems, causing significant disruption in the IT service provided to large numbers of end users.

Equipment, no matter how reliable, needs a specific operational environment and protection from physical threats and misuse. Equally, the way in which computer systems and services are designed needs to consider the overall resilience and security of the total service chain used to deliver an application system to the end user. Such issues are the responsibility of local management within the enterprise. Unless management take a pro-active role in the securing of IT services then the ongoing delivery of that service may be compromised. The general availability of reliable computer equipment does not alone guarantee a reliable IT service!

2 WHAT NEEDS SECURING?

2.1 What Resources Are at Risk?

The service chain necessary to deliver an IT service entails the use of a number of different resources. The resources used can be generalised into the main categories of computer equipment, the buildings and infrastructure necessary to support that computer equipment, telecommunication networks, people and data. Each of these resources are potentially vulnerable to a number of different threats, and a continuing problem with any resource will in time have some detrimental effect on service. A more detailed breakdown of these resources is contained in Appendix 1 of this chapter and the risks to which they may be vulnerable is considered in Section 3.4.

No matter how sophisticated the methods used to protect resources from loss, 100% protection can never be guaranteed. The timely reinstatement of resources made unavailable by a disaster is the major issue to be faced when considering contingency planning. The possibility of losing each of these resources should therefore be considered in turn and the lead times necessary for their replacement assessed.

2.2 What Are the Risks of Disruptive Events?

Discussions on the items which need securing often commence with a debate on the risks involved; the unlikely prospect of a jumbo-jet crashing on the computer hall often figures prominently in this debate! Unfortunately, reliable data on risk probabilities is in short supply. This is confirmed by reports from the National Audit Office (1987) entitled 'Computer Security in Government Departments' and from Coopers and Lybrand (1988) entitled 'The Security of Network Systems'.

The NAO report states that:

> NAO noted that one consequence of the lack of hard evidence about the level of computer crime (including fraud) in the UK is that estimates of its scale vary wildly, ranging from a few £ million to over £1 billion each year. But most of these 'authoritative' estimates are based on anecdotal evidence and come from those with a vested interest in the computer security industry.
>
> Information on the loss of computer capability through disasters is also limited. Data available on incidents outside government are largely anecdotal and impossible to substantiate, although NAO's review of published cases suggests that fire is the cause of over 50 per cent of serious disruptions to processing.

Despite this lack of hard data, most consultants seem agreed that the likelihood of disruptive events occurring can be ranked as follows:

1. Errors
2. Insider fraud/sabotage
3. Natural disasters
4. External threats

The Coopers and Lybrand report tends to support this view and shows data complied by French insurance companies which estimates the size of loss suffered, by cause. These figures show that errors cause the largest number of incidents but the smallest loss per incident, whereas deliberate actions have the smallest incidence but the largest cost per incident.

2.3 How Long Can You Survive?

Regardless of cause, any disaster is likely is to go through the same four phases shown in Figure 1.

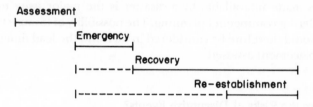

FIGURE 1   Disaster phases

The phases are defined as follows:

- Assessment phase—is the period in which senior management are made aware of the problem and a decision is taken of whether to invoke the relevant contingency plan. This phase should be subject to a strict time constraint in which the decision should be taken in order to obviate the possibility of management delays in the hope that things will improve. This phase may seem both trivial and obvious; however I can cite two examples involving the corruption of data in which management delayed invoking contingency plans and in both instances turned a potentially containable problem into a full scale disaster.
- Emergency phase—is the period between the cessation of computer services to the point where essential applications are again available for use. During this period, users of computer systems affected by the disaster will need plans which will enable the business to continue without recourse to the previously available computer service.
- Recovery phase—covers the period which commences with some computer systems being reinstated on an alternative computing facility through to the point where a full service is provided from that facility. The plan to achieve this transition should form the bulk of the IS contingency plan. (Note that for a few extremely time critical systems, the contingency plan may provide for an immediate switch to alternative facilities, hence bypassing the emergency phase.)

- Re-establishment—is the process by which the enterprise returns to a position comparable to that in existence prior to the disaster. If the disaster involved the total loss of computers and buildings, then clearly this phase could take many months to complete. Whatever solution is adopted for the Recovery Phase must therefore be capable of sustaining the entire computer processing needs of an enterprise over an extended period.

Figure 1 does not attempt to portray the relative lengths of time for each of the disaster phases. However, the time span of the Emergency Phase has a significant effect on the contingency plan solution adopted by the enterprise. The Emergency Phase can be considered as synonymous to 'Business Survival Time' and the definition of this time period is a major factor in arriving at the amount of money required in order to provide a contingency plan meeting the needs of the enterprise. Taking a worst case view of any potential disaster (i.e. a total loss of central computer equipment, buildings and some key skills), then the critical path to reinstate computer processing is as shown in Figure 2. The critical path as shown assumes no pre-planning.

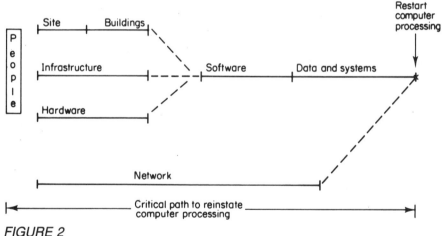

FIGURE 2

The relationship between the replacement lead time of that which has been lost and the length of the 'Business Survival Time' (or Emergency Phase) is critical when considering the need for a contingency plan. If the Emergency Phase is shorter than the total critical path shown in Figure 2 then expenditure will be needed to provide some level of duplicate facilities *in advance* of a potential disaster. The shorter the Emergency Phase, the greater the potential expenditure. The Business Impact Review described later in this chapter is designed to help senior management decide on the appropriate level of investment in such facilities.

2.4 Some Resources Are Expendable

The process of deciding upon an appropriate level of contingency cover and the production of a robust plan can be a time consuming exercise. In the absence of any direction or interest from the business, many IS functions either ignore the issue or concentrate on providing some degree of low cost cover for computer equipment and its accommodation. It is not unusual to hear people claiming to have a contingency plan only to discover that this consists of a contract with a supplier of portable computer rooms or for the use of a fully equipped fall back computer suite offered on a commercial basis. Clearly there could be a requirement for such facilities in the event of the destruction of existing computing facilities, but it is not the most important issue. Figure 3 illustrates this point.

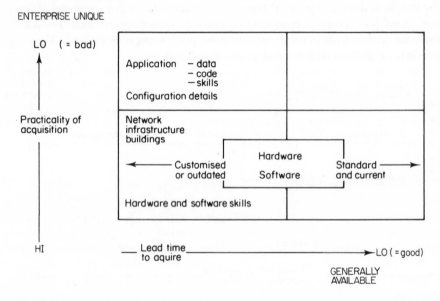

FIGURE 3   Availability of resources

The two axes on this matrix make a distinction between the practicability of obtaining that lost in a disaster and the lead time to acquire replaceable items on the open market. During this process it is useful to consider the degree to which the item is unique to that installation. For example, the current release of operating system software at any point in time will not be unique; the way in which an installation customises the release is likely to be unique to that installation. As a general rule, unique items present more of a problem to the contingency planning process and thus deserve greater attention; if they become unusable:

- They may not be capable of exact replication.
- The replacement/replication process will tend to be longer than that for 'standard' items.

In general, mainframe computers and data storage devices are not highly customised and hence tend not to be unique. Very new or very old equipment may prove to be the exception, but provided the software used is not unique to that particular generation of equipment, then the exposure is minimal. It is unwise to generalise for peripheral equipment; each device should be considered on its merits. Network processors and multiplexors tend to be more highly customised, and may be difficult to obtain in a timely fashion. A network consisting of leased lines will almost certainly be 'unique'; the use of dial-up lines will not. The network and the degree to which it is unique is a complex issue and depends upon the overall resilience of the network and its connection to central computers. One final consideration should be the quantities involved; very large quantities of any standard item could make it 'unique'. Electricity supply is an example of this point.

Similar logic needs to be applied to all other items shown in Appendix 1 (see Figure 9). From this it can be seen that items may be considered as being expendable if they can be reliably obtained in a lead time which will keep the critical path in Figure 2 shorter than the 'Business Survival Time'.

2.5 Secure Data at All Costs!

Many companies are now highly dependent upon large scale mainframe computing in support of daily business operations. In such cases there may be a tendency to concentrate on the timely reinstatement of inoperable equipment. This is an important issue, but remains secondary to the reinstatement or recovery of data. The business data maintained by computer systems will almost certainly be unique to an enterprise and *could not be reconstructed* from any other source. The integrity and continuity of business data is *the* key issue to be considered by any contingency plan.

It should be noted that the data issue is equally relevant to all sizes of computer from the smallest micro to the largest mainframe. If the processing being performed has relevance to the business operation then the data used by that process needs to be safeguarded. Data related to a computer system is likely to be held by both the IS and end user communities within an enterprise. End users are normally responsible for operating procedures concerned with the way they use the system and for any system-related data maintained externally from the computer. Although much data is likely to be held in computer readable format on magnetic media, items such as documentation, operating instructions and personnel details may well exist in hard copy only. When considering the data issue it is therefore important that all data is reviewed, regardless of the media used and the area responsible for its maintenance.

The requirement to copy and store duplicate data can be costly and is subject to some qualification. There is little point in regularly duplicating data which can be easily re-created, either from source or by simple reprocessing of other data. When considering disaster recovery, there may be some data whose usefulness degrades with time. If an extended recovery period is foreseen a value judgement is needed regarding the worth of such data after recovery.

It is likely that most enterprises making extensive use of computers will require some form of contingency plan, the main questions being the amount of time for which they could survive without computing and the degree of risk they are prepared to tolerate in their recovery plans. Unless the recovery lead time required is extremely short, then it is certain that most of the data described in Appendix 1 (see Figure 10) will need to be recovered as a prerequisite to the resumption of normal computer processing. In most cases the majority of this data will be held on computer readable media, and will be business related data and programs unique to that enterprise.

Although computer installations are normally extremely diligent at backing up data to cope with operational failures, such procedures may not be adequate to restore *all* the data held on an alternative computer configuration. The main issues to be considered in such an exercise are:

- That *all* documentation and data required to perform this exercise can be obtained from a location away from the main computer suite.
- That the process can be achieved despite the unavailability of some key skills.
- That data can be restored in a timely and consistent manner.
- That the configuration of the alternative facility cannot be guaranteed to exactly match that of the existing configuration.

The consistency issue is important and needs further explanation. When considering the copying and restoration of data it is essential that all data can be restored to a consistent and known point in time. A common problem to occur is for application program libraries to only be copied weekly, whilst the data maintained by an application is copied more frequently. If a change is performed which alters the format of application data then problems will occur if the changed program is restored between the time the change is implemented and the next copy of the program library is taken. This is a very simple example. In an environment where large volumes of data are stored and data interfaces exist between several applications the situation can become extremely complex. In such an environment, sophisticated and rigorous control may have to be implemented to control the copying and restoration of data.

Experience suggests that this can be a difficult exercise to achieve. As much of the data is likely to be irreplaceable, data recovery will be a requirement of *any* contingency plan, regardless of the method adopted to provide alternative equipment. As such, then it is an item of work that can be done ahead of any formal study.

3 WHAT PROCESS SHOULD I FOLLOW?

3.1 A Process for Contingency Planning

Although there are relatively few generic contingency planning solutions, the *detailed* solutions to be employed in providing a workable plan can be complex. It is useful to have a management process in place which will enable the production of a realistic solution matched to the needs of the business. A schematic of the general process is shown in Figure 4.

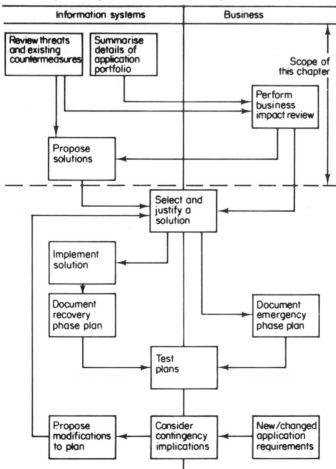

FIGURE 4 *Tasks and responsibilities*

This chapter considers the framework of activities needed to support a considered management decision process; Figure 4 is intended to guide management through the process and to ensure that each part of the process is carried out by the right functions within the enterprise, and at the correct management level.

In order to manage this process it is useful to have a project manager with sole responsibility for the exercise. Whether the project manager comes from an IS or business background is a moot point, the important issue is that he or she has sufficient time and management status to manage the task to a successful conclusion. The figure also shows the relationship between the various parts of the contingency planning process and this chapter, and indicates whether task responsibilities belong to IS or business functions. Probably the most important task required of business functions is to define the business impact in the event of a disaster. Before embarking upon this step it is vital to gain sponsorship from the Board of the enterprise so that the correct level of participation can be achieved. Unless the Board have confidence in the results of this exercise they will be poorly placed to make any value judgement when they are asked to review costed options aimed at providing a solution to the potential loss of computer support.

Finally, the time scales surrounding this process should be set with some caution. My experience suggests that from first contact with an enterprise to the point where a decision is taken regarding the selection of a solution, the elapsed time is likely to be in the order of 9 to 15 months. From there to the production and testing of a plan may take from 1 to 2 years to complete and entail several man years of effort.

3.2 Analysing a Disaster—The 'Contingency Cube'

Contingency planning for computers can be a complex area. There are many disciplines involved, from very technical software issues to general personnel considerations. It is also an exercise which is not performed often by the average IS person, and yet has to be explained in a cogent manner to senior management. The combination of these factors makes it difficult for those trying to understand the totality of the problem and then communicating the resulting issues in a simple way. It is perhaps this difficulty which prevents some people from addressing the issue. In attempting to solve this problem I found it useful to reduce contingency planning to a simple diagram and therefore developed the 'Contingency Cube' which is shown in Figure 5.

Whilst the 'Cube' was originally developed to explain contingency planning issues to Boards of Directors, with subsequent modification it has proved to be a useful tool not only to describe concepts but also to analyse potential threats and vulnerabilities facing an enterprise. The basic idea behind the cube is to define the resources involved in the operation of computer systems and to

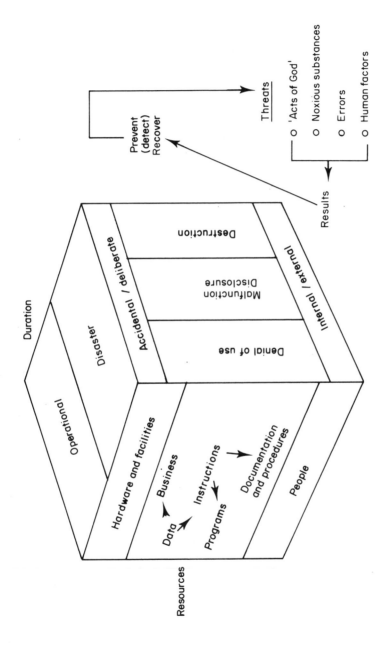

FIGURE 5 The Contingency Cube

review the events which may adversely affect those resources. From this can be derived the likely results and thence the impact to the enterprise of being without computer processing support over given periods of time. The three faces of the cube are described below.

3.2.1 Resources

The resources which form the service chain are categorised on the cube as follows:

- Equipment   ⎫
- People   ⎬ (plus materials and supporting infrastructure)
- Data   ⎭

The equipment element includes the computer and telecommunications devices required to deliver a service to end users, plus buildings equipped to house and support such equipment. Equipment is normally owned by the IS function; however the people and data involved in the process are likely to span both user and IS functions. A further breakdown of these resources is contained in Appendix 1 of this chapter.

3.2.2 Results

The second face describes the generic results of a disruptive event affecting resources:

- Denial of use—whereby all computer facilities are undamaged but cannot be used (e.g. lack of people due to a site evacuation for noxious substances, terrorism, etc., or industrial relations disputes, widespread sickness, extreme weather conditions, etc.).
- Malfunction—in some key aspect of the process, normally due to an error. The most serious (and likely) result here is the accidental corruption of data held within the computer application.
- Disclosure—which entails the release of sensitive data to unauthorised third parties. This is not strictly a disaster planning issue, but is an extremely important consideration and hence included.
- Destruction—of any or all major resource categories.

3.2.3 Time

The top face of the cube considers the time in which any abnormal event may represent a disaster to a given enterprise. This will be a combination of the extent of the problem, the length of time taken to restore computer services to normal and the criticality of the affected service. Problem durations are categorised as being either 'operational' or 'disaster', with the former relating to short term failures or equipment failures affecting specific devices where operational procedures can be expected to recover the situation. The time span in which the loss of computing would constitute a 'disaster' is likely to be different for individual enterprises. The failure of computer applications which directly support continuous flow processes in chemical or manufacturing companies are likely to cause a 'disaster' in a far shorter time span than in an enterprise where computing is confined to back-office administration. Over recent years the increasing use of computing in the finance, retail and distribution sectors has meant that in many cases a loss of computer processing could constitute a disaster in a matter of a few days, with failures of several hours posing a major problem. Clearly, the time factor has a major influence upon the sophistication and hence cost of the measures needed to recover from a computer disaster. The financial implications of the 'time to disaster' makes its definition an extremely important topic. A process for defining the 'disaster' lead time is described in Section 4 of this chapter.

3.3 Analysing Risk

Due to a lack of accurate and consistently recorded risk data, techniques have been devised which aid the average person in estimating risk probabilities. The performance of such an exercise relies heavily on individual perceptions of risk, and as such tend to be very subjective. One method used to reduce individual subjectivity involves the use of a group to produce a consensus view, and as such becomes expensive in manpower terms. There is value in listing all potential risks and performing a rough ranking in terms of relative probability of occurrence (e.g. is fire more likely than impact damage?, ..., etc.). It is also worth considering the possible effect of each risk because combined with the relative probability a view can be formed on the effectiveness of current prevention techniques.

The validity of attempting to perform a quantified assessment of risk is dubious as it relies upon people making subjective judgements outside their immediate experience. The numbers derived from such a process are sometimes then used to produce an annualised loss profile by risk category. This can be dangerous as the multiplication of two sets of unreliable numbers is likely to produce a large margin of error. It also tends to distract attention from the issue of whether an enterprise could survive a disaster should one ever occur!

Because of this lack of hard data the methods I have employed in considering contingency planning focuses more on the *impact* of a disaster, than the risk of its happening. Consideration of risk is limited to a ranking of threats in terms of their relative probability of occurrence. What evidence exists, suggests that the possibility of a computer catastrophe is remote, however the consequences may well threaten the existence of the affected enterprise. It can be argued that the definition of impact has a similar element of subjectivity, but in my opinion, it is more closely aligned to individuals' direct experience than that of defining risk probability.

3.4 Using the Contingency Cube

The cube can be used in conjunction with the lists in Appendix 1 to determine the vulnerability of an enterprise to specific threats, and also to ensure that critical data can be recovered in the event of a disaster affecting the computer facility. Both exercises can be usefully performed solely within the IS function and are best done *before* functions external to IS are exposed to the issues posed by contingency planning.

3.4.1 Vulnerability Analysis

Murphy's law is as applicable to computer systems as to any other activity and states that: 'Anything that can go wrong *will* go wrong ... and at the most inconvenient time.' Having understood the resources used in operating a computer-based process it is necessary to consider the potential threats to each major category of resource and then to derive the likely result. A problem with any of these resources or their prolonged unavailability will affect the continued reliable delivery of computer systems.

The generic threats shown in Figure 5 can be expanded as follows:

- Acts of God—natural events such as fire, flood, storm, disease, subsidence, animal/plant attacks, impact damage, etc.
- Noxious substances—such as chemicals, electromagnetic emissions, radioactivity, etc., which represent a danger to people, equipment or property.
- Errors—in the design or operation of equipment and/or computer programs and their associated control mechanisms.
- Human factors—such as revenge/sabotage, terrorism, industrial relations issues.

A vulnerability review is best undertaken by involving two or three managers who understand all aspects of the computer operation at a relatively high level. Such a review is likely to last between 1 and 2 days. During the review, potential threats from the above list are reviewed against the resources shown in Appendix 1 and a view taken on those resources which could be affected. It is important to consider the siting of computer equipment, the surrounding environment and any unusual social or political factors when assessing the relevance of potential threats to the enterprise. The impact of the threat on the affected resources is defined and current operational procedures reviewed to see if they could cope in a timely manner. This process therefore involves consideration of all three faces of the cube; each threat is considered against each *resource*, the *result* derived and the *time* to recover assessed. In effect each threat is given a discrete position on the cube.

Having deduced the threats to which the enterprise could be vulnerable, it is necessary to consider the risk of that problem occurring. As described in Section 3.3, the ranking of risks and impacts is normally done on the basis of high, medium or low; in some instances it may be possible to expand risk to a numeric ranking from most likely to least likely. When this has been done the adequacy of existing prevention and recovery techniques should be considered, taking regard to the extent of disruption caused by each threat and the risk of occurrence.

3.4.2 Recovery of Data

The 'data' section of the cube can be expanded as shown in Appendix 1 (see Figure 10); this can then be used in a 'data' audit where it acts as a checklist of all data which should be copied and stored in a safe place against the eventuality of loss.

The 'data' audit is straightforward but time consuming and is best achieved by setting up a small team comprising of operations and application development skills.

3.4.3 Outputs from Using the Cube

The combined output of these two exercises is:

- Details of essential data where backup is lacking or the current method is inadequate.
- A view of major vulnerabilities and areas where better protection from risk may be appropriate.
- Scenarios of the potential time without computer processing in the event of different types of loss. These should take into account any existing plans to deal with the situations foreseen.

These outputs contain some extremely sensitive information and hence those people chosen to do this work must be carefully selected. All output and working papers from the process must carry a security rating in line with the sensitivity of the information contained within them.

An important point highlighted by considering threats and their potential results is the need for multiple plans. A plan covering the loss of computer hardware will not aid the recovery of data corrupted due to a programming error. Equally a plan dealing with the results of data corruption may not be relevant to withdrawal of labour by key staff. Plans for all eventualities should consider both the IS *and* user actions which will be necessary. Moreover, the plans related to the loss of computing should be part of an enterprise wide plan which considers all problems which could have a severe impact on the well-being of that enterprise.

Although the cube is a relatively simplistic way of viewing contingency planning it has proved to be a useful tool, both as an aid to communication and as support to planning sessions.

4   HOW DO I REVIEW BUSINESS IMPACT OF A DISASTER?

The objectives of a Business Impact Review are to define:

• The maximum amount of time during which the enterprise could survive without computer processing (i.e. the length of the Emergency Phase).
• The potential losses sustained by the enterprise as a result of disaster, taking regard of current IS capabilities to restore computer processing.

There are a variety of ways to review the business impact of a disaster with no shortage of consultancy methods being offered.

4.1   Bottom-up or Top-down?

4.1.1   Bottom-up

Some techniques rely upon detailed interviews with end users of each computer application; these however tend to be protracted and hence costly. Bottom-up analysis in this way introduces the danger of engendering a parochial view of the relative priorities. For example, asking the Payroll Manager his opinion on the criticality of the payroll system is likely to produce a very predictable (and narrow) view that it would be impossible to operate without the system. The same question posed to the Finance Director may produce the answer that staff can be paid on the basis of the last good payroll run and all errors sorted out when computer systems are restored. An additional danger of the bottom-up approach is the tendency towards 'misplaced' accuracy. There are a large number of unknowns to be considered when attempting to quantify the financial impact of a disaster, most of which are matters of opinion. For example, the potential impact to long term sales prospects; by what percentage might they decrease? Arriving at such a figure will probably be a matter of informed management judgement, and as such open to debate. Having agreed a percentage there is little point in attempting to calculate the resulting financial impact to a level of accuracy greater than margin of error of the original estimate. If the impact review is conducted at too low a level there is a danger that figures are embellished beyond the point of reasonableness. In any event, experience suggests that these judgements are more appropriately made at senior levels of management.

4.1.2 Top-down

The top-down approach assumes that a business impact review is best conducted by involving senior managers with a wide business perspective as they are better able to take an informed view of the level of contingency plan necessary for the enterprise to survive in the event of disaster. Whilst these techniques appear more plausible, they frequently suffer from the lack of a formal process and can appear vague and lacking in direction. To overcome this I have found it necessary to design a formal process which is described in the next section.

4.2 'SESAME'—A Technique for Impact Reviews

The process for evaluating the impact of a disaster is a development of the SESAME technique which was originated by Dr Tim Lincoln (1986) for the cost/benefit analysis of installed computer applications. SESAME sets out to compare existing computer applications against a realistic alternative system which may be computerised, partly computerised or entirely manual depending on executives' perception of the best alternative system.

The original SESAME technique seeks to identify both the costs and benefits of application systems. In adapting SESAME for use in contingency planning I have ignored the costs of developing and running applications and normally use a comparison with manual methods as in most cases it is the only method open to the enterprise in the event of a computer disaster. It also differs from the original version in that cost impacts are categorised under standard headings and the costs of catch-up following the restoration of service are also considered. Both versions use standard questionnaires, each tailored to the specific needs of cost/benefit or impact analysis. The strength of the technique lies in the use of these questionnaires as they help direct the thinking of senior managers.

Experience suggests that SESAME can be applied in any organisation or industry type. The technique is easily understandable, relatively simple to use and is efficient in terms of manpower. The involvement of senior management is probably the most important factor in the successful completion of such studies, and over the years it has provided useful insights to executives on both cost/benefits and business impacts.

5 HOW DO I USE SESAME?

The study can be considered as consisting of four discrete phases; these are described in the following sections.

5.1 Specify the Dimensions of the Problem

This phase is normally done within the IS department as preparation for the study proper and consists of the following steps.

5.1.1 Specify Applications

The first task is to produce a *brief* precis of each application system which describes:

- Its basic business objectives and functions
- The operational environment
- Number, type and location of end users
- Processing volumes (in business terms)
- Major interfaces to other applications

Business Impact reviews normally consider the effect of a major outage at the main data centre within an enterprise. When producing the application precis it is important to consider those applications running at the data centre in question plus any applications running at remote locations but which are accessed via links which pass through the main data centre. Loss of the main centre may make access to such remote applications impossible. Any new applications planned for implementation over the next 2 to 3 years should also be included in this list.

5.1.2 Decide Granularity of Analysis

Having drawn up a list of all applications it is necessary to review the relationships between them in order to take a view of the 'granularity' of the total application portfolio. From this review it is possible to build a simple model showing which applications groups can be run without reference to other applications. The greater the number of stand-alone groups the better the granularity. In many computer installations today, applications are integrated to such a degree that it is difficult to take any given application and run it 'stand-alone'. There are valid business reasons for this trend, but it does complicate the 'contingency' issue.

The granularity review is important as much of the conventional wisdom on contingency planning encourages the selection of 'critical applications' to be run in the event of a disaster. There is little point in asking end users to review the relative criticality of individual applications if in practice they are so tightly integrated as to make stand-alone processing impossible.

5.1.3 Define Business Processes

The application inventory is used in a session in which the major business processes are defined and cross related back to application systems. At this point an 'owning' business function for each business process is defined and a preferred senior user representative proposed. The output of this process is a matrix of business process to application system, an example of which is shown in Figure 6.

System Process	1	2	3	4	etc.	Process owner
A	X	X				
B						
C			X			
D	X					

FIGURE 6   (Reproduced by permission of Blenheim Online Publications)

Depending upon the output of the granularity analysis, it may be necessary to show groups of application systems rather than individual applications on the matrix. Similarly, if the study involves a very large number of applications then it may be appropriate to group applications together as logical processing blocks and to make a value judgement as to which areas should be investigated in depth. In many cases it will be found that relatively few applications are dealing with the bulk of main line business operations.

When an agreed set of processes, applications and potential 'owners' exists, some lobbying may be required to test the suitability and availability of the preferred user representatives selected.

5.1.4 Review Key Business Indicators

Following the definition of business processes, key business volumes, values, staff numbers, etc., need to be obtained, reviewed and added per process. If these numbers are subject to fluctuations, common assumptions are needed to define, average or worst-case values as appropriate. It is useful at this stage to consider the history of changes in these numbers as they may provide a clue to the way in which computing has affected business performance. Future business plans over the next 2 to 3 years should also be considered.

5.1.5 Prepare Executive Presentation

Finally, the output from the process described in Section 3.4 needs to be reviewed in preparation for a Board presentation so that:

* A realistic outage time can be given in the light of existing IS recovery plans.
* The current status of IS prevention measures can be favourably presented.

When selecting the outage time it is usual to take a worst case view and assume the total loss of all central computing facilities, with a realistic recovery time in line with the state of IS readiness. It is reasonable to assume for the purposes of the impact analysis that end users would have access to hard copies of stored computer data taken at a point some time before the disaster occurred.

5.2 Initiate Study

This phase is designed to involve the general business community in the contingency planning process and has the following activities.

5.2.1 Obtain Executive Commitment

This phase is designed to gain the commitment of executives to the topic of 'Contingency Planning'. As the study will involve personnel from various user functions and from IS, executive sponsorship from within the enterprise is essential. The role of the sponsor is to define the terms of reference and scope of the study, publicise the study throughout the organisation and provide support in obtaining suitable team members.

5.2.2 Educate the Board

Having gained a suitable level of sponsorship the study is best started by a presentation at Board level. This provides some high level education on the concepts of contingency planning, describes the current status of IS systems and their ability to recover from a disaster, and outlines the objectives and conduct of the Business Impact Review. The presentation should also seek to gain agreement for the assignment of team members from the business functions and to the involvement of the Board in a review of the study findings.

5.2.3 Assemble Study Team

A team of around four to six people from within the enterprise would normally be required for 3 to 4 weeks to perform a study which covered all applications being run within an installation. The involvement of the senior user representatives is normally contained to 3 to 4 days with the expectation that some staff work may be required from lower levels within the representatives' span of control. Team members must be of a relatively high level, have a broad view of business operations and be qualified to judge both the internal and commercial aspects of a disaster. It is likely that all major business areas plus Finance and IS Development will need representation on the study. Normally the Study Leader would be from the client enterprise with guidance on the method coming from an external consultant.

5.2.4 Set Reporting Dates

Regular progress meetings are usually set up at this stage with the sponsor, and a date agreed for reporting back the study conclusions. A summary of the report is normally presented to the Board. Reporting back at this level tends to have a beneficial effect on study team motivation!

5.3 Analyse Impact of Disaster

This phase constitutes the major portion of the study and uses a small team of senior user managers to estimate the impact of a disaster.

5.3.1 Define Alternative Method of Operation

The first task in this phase is to brief the team on the background, objectives and conduct of the study plus their specific responsibilities. A re-run of the Board presentation is a useful way of achieving this. At that briefing the team is asked (as a group) to consider the way in which they would go about running the business for whatever period of time has been agreed as the 'disaster scenario'. When this post disaster *modus operandi* has been tested for practicality and agreed upon, it is formally documented together with any assumptions which have been made. This ensures a common understanding between all business functions of how they would relate to each other in this manner of operation. At the conclusion of this session users are asked to consider:

- The business and financial implications of running their business process without the support of computer systems
- The maximum length of time this method of operation would be viable

- The impact and length of time taken in catching up, following the restoration of computer processing
- The affect of planned new computer applications or business ventures on their ability to run the business without computer support

Standard questionnaires are used to guide team members and to ensure the consistency of their answers. Experience has shown that it is rare for users to be unable to identify alternative manual systems and to specify both the impact on resources and the business.

5.3.2 Establish Costing Basis

The potential impacts of running in 'disaster mode' can be categorised as shown below. The exact spread of cost depends upon the length and cause of the service outage (e.g. additional manual resource is only realistic if a very long outage is predicted).

Example cost categories are:

- Direct costs
  - Additional labour costs (plus accommodation, training, etc.)
  - Cost of extra supplies and services
- Loss of business
  - Inability to service existing business
  - Failure to capture new business
  - Customer dissatisfaction
- Loss of control
  - Poor statistics for decision making (late/inaccurate)
  - Inventory increases/stock-outs
  - Bad debts/credit control
  - Vulnerability to fraud
  - Incorrect payments/billing

(Reproduced by permission of Blenheim Online Publications.)

As well as considering the costs accruing during the period when computer systems are unavailable, it is also necessary to consider the costs of recovering the situation when normal processing is restored. Such cost categories are difficult to generalise, although the updating of pre-disaster computer data, the making good of delayed business outputs and the gradual restoration of the *status quo* generally appear as line items.

In some cases, costs can be derived from past statistics. Loss assessments are cross-checked by the Study Leader and are also reviewed and challenged in a group session with the whole team present. When a final set of costs has been agreed upon by the study team, they are summarised and subjected to a final review with senior management.

5.3.3 Define Criticality

If appropriate, application systems are ranked by criticality within the constraints of granularity. The studies to date have covered a range of business sectors but in all cases the business processes, which could be broadly described as 'maintain incoming cash flow' and 'support existing customer commitments', have featured as being critical ... perhaps not surprisingly!

Finally, this phase of the study is used to determine the maximum amount of time for which the enterprise can survive without computer processing. This is based upon a consensus view from the team on either the viability of maintaining the business operation in disaster mode or of the ability of the enterprise to survive the financial aspects of the disaster. This tends to be an iterative process as experience has proved that it is often the impact of bringing application systems up to date following the disaster which is the constraining factor.

5.4 Present Findings

This is the final phase of the study and involves a formal presentation of the study results to the Board.

5.4.1 Present to Board

The output of the study will typically be a presentation to the Board of Directors covering the following:

- Detailed analysis of the potential costs likely to be incurred in the event of 'loss of service' in the current environment
- An assessment of the maximum time for which it would be practical for the enterprise to survive without computer systems
- A summary of the most critical application systems ... if appropriate!
- An assessment of implications of predicted growth and additional function
- A review of the applicability of current IS recovery plans in the light of the maximum survival time defined by the study

5.4.2 Propose Further Actions

In the event that current IS recovery plans are unable to meet the needs of the business, then a follow-on study should be proposed. This study will take as input the maximum survival time agreed by the Board and consider potential solutions which will meet that time constraint. The output of the study to consider solutions should also be reviewed at a future Board meeting.

6 WHAT STRATEGIES CAN I USE TO DEAL WITH A DISASTER?

Having defined the nature of potential threats and the resulting business impact, it is appropriate to consider the strategies available to deal with a possible disaster affecting computer processing.

6.1 Minimise Cost, Impact and Risk

There are three tactics which may be adopted in this category:

• Acceptance of the risk (i.e. do nothing!)
• Insuring against the eventuality with a policy covering the direct and consequential losses
• Use of a high integrity site (i.e. maximum protection from physical threats)

The 'do nothing' case minimises costs in the short time, whereas the insurance case minimises the financial impact of a disaster. The high integrity site seeks to minimise the chances of a disaster affecting the IT service.

High integrity sites can be categorised as having good physical security (fences, security guards, restricted access, etc.), high impact resistance (e.g. an underground bunker) and are designed to minimise fire risk (e.g low flammability furniture, no smoking, sophisticated fire detection and extinguishing equipment). Such sites are often well away from other buildings, main roads, railways and other known risks (e.g. subsidence, flight paths, chemical plants, etc.). They house computers and essential personnel connected with computer operations only and have no external signs or notices which would indicate their purpose or to whom they belong.

This should not be regarded as a definitive list of the attributes of a high integrity site, but merely to define the term more fully.

Each of these options have some merit; however careful consideration is required before adopting any of them as the destruction of computing facilities would lead to a considerable lapse before processing could be restored.

6.2 Duplicate Facilities

There are potentially a large number of options available in this category; these have been reduced to the matrix shown in Figure 7. The matrix covers equipment and data only; a separate plan would be needed to cover the loss of people. Taking a worst case view that the disaster involved the total loss of equipment, data and people, then the people plan would be a prerequisite to all other activities. In practice this is a remote possibility and is rarely catered for. The options shown on the matrix will only work where the base data (particularly application-maintained data) retains its integrity.

The vertical axis of the matrix represents the resources which may have to be replaced in a timely manner. The horizontal axis of the matrix represents the

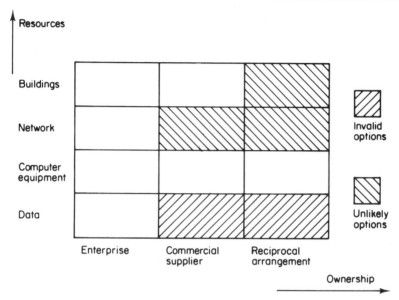

FIGURE 7

potential sources available to replace lost items in a timely manner, immediately after the disaster. The hatched boxes show those options which are invalid or unlikely. The invalid options apply to data; in almost all cases this will have to be replaced from within the enterprise.

In theory all other options are valid, although reciprocal agreements between enterprises are normally limited to the short term use of essential computing facilities. Similarly, the provision of duplicate network connections is normally a permanent operational feature and owned by the enterprise; however, suppliers are now emerging who offer portable telecommunication equipment which can be supplied at short notice. The most common forms of commercial arrangement are for the use of empty rooms suitable for the immediate installation of large computers or for the dedicated use of a computer 'bureau' providing an immediate backup service. These options are often referred to as cold or hot site solutions. Another variation of the empty computer room is the portable computer room whereby a suitable building can be erected on a preselected site within a matter of days.

The deciding factors for most enterprises when selecting a solution in this category are the time in which processing can be re-started and the degree of risk involved in each option. This is best illustrated by considering the 'cold' site option. In such a case a room is available capable of immediate occupancy by replacement computer equipment. Depending upon the amount and age of the equipment to be replaced and the degree of optimism of the assumptions used, a wide range of lead times for resumption of processing can be arrived at. In reality, there is insufficient evidence available to make an informed judgement and no real way to test the theories propounded. Despite the uncertainty around the exact lead time of different solutions there are three generic solutions, each one of which represents a step function in expenditure on duplicate facilities. This is shown in Figure 8.

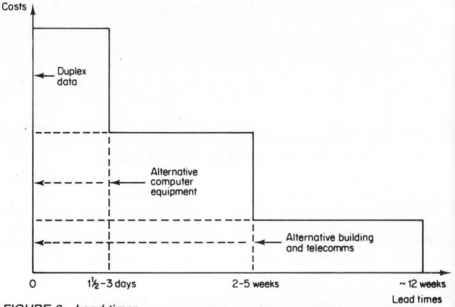

FIGURE 8   Lead times

The lead times shown in the figure represent the time between a disaster being declared and the point at which computer processing can recommence. Thus, if an enterprise has the need to recover from a disaster in less than one and a half to three days then the 'duplex data' option should be considered. This solution requires that the same data is being maintained simultaneously on two computers which are far enough apart to obviate the possibility of both being affected by the same physical threat. In many instances the data on one machine may be a short time behind the other machine in terms of currency.

The lead time shown is based upon a large mainframe configuration, and represents the time taken to reload backup data and to verify its accuracy and consistency.

If a recovery time of less than 2 to 5 weeks is required, then duplicate hardware should be considered (i.e. I consider it unlikely that a mainframe configuration could be obtained, installed and data reinstated in under 2 weeks). The range of 2 to 5 weeks is personal opinion and has a large spread due to the great variety in the size of mainframe computer operations and the age and degree of customisation of the equipment used.

Similar logic applies to the duplicate building and telecomms option, and, again, the lead time is personal opinion and will vary depending upon circumstances.

6.3 Maximise flexibility

If the need for duplicate facilities includes the requirement for duplicate equipment then the cost of providing contingency is likely to be significant, especially if enterprises opt for an 'in-house' solution. A further problem faced by some people is the ratio between the critical and non-critical work being run on their computers, as often critical work represents a far greater load than the non-critical. This section describes possible methods for minimising these problems.

6.3.1 Look for Strategic Opportunities

If the IT services on offer include support to the developers of new applications then it is likely that this service will not be considered to be critical in the event of a disaster. In many instances, however, the development service will consume a significant proportion of computing resource, 30% being a fairly typical figure. If this service is put onto a separate 'contingency' machine which is capable of supporting all production work in the event of a disaster then the contingency machine will have a significant amount of spare capacity. This capacity could then be used at a marginal cost to provide a greatly enhanced development service with the possibility of productivity gains within the development group. A similar argument can be used to mount an end user computing service for non-critical work.

Other examples concern the strategic value connected with the siting of a second computer centre. In one instance it was used as a method of attracting scarce technical skills due to its location; in another it was used to reinforce an enterprise's commitment to establish a marketing base in another country.

6.3.2 Centralised Versus Decentralised

When considering recovery options the topic of a centralised mainframe versus multiple decentralised minicomputers often arises. The minicomputer option is sometimes proposed as a self-sustaining contingency option in place of a mainframe.

The use of minicomputers at a number of widely dispersed sites does offer greater flexibility and the advantage that the loss of a single minicomputer is less disruptive than the loss of the mainframe. Assuming that the minicomputers and mainframe are all fully loaded and performing the same job, then, clearly, less redundant capacity needs to be reserved for contingency purposes in the minicomputer case. However, the use of minicomputers in no way reduces the need to back up the data stored on these machines and to store this backup well away from the processing site. The backup requirement is sometimes missed by those arguing the minicomputer case!

6.4 Combined Strategies

In practice, many enterprises use a combination of the general strategies covered in this section. One combination commonly adopted is to use a commercial 'hot' site for immediate fall-back for a period of up to 8 weeks and in that time have a portable computer room built and equipped at a predetermined site. Another is to use a high integrity site, sometimes containing two discrete computer rooms separately supplied with electricity, water and telecomms, with a further and remote 'cold' site attached to a node on the network. The theory here is that the high integrity site greatly reduces the risk of it being rendered totally inoperable, with the cold site as a fall-back *in extremis*. In the case of enterprises operating continuous flow processes, a combination of central mainframe and distributed minicomputers is sometimes adopted with the minis able to run for several days without needing to communicate with the mainframe.

There are doubtless many more permutations which can be arrived at from the various options described and indeed there may well be other options. Neither is there any shortage of people prepared to help in proposing solutions; the key issue with contingency planning is to ensure that management understand the size and scope of the problem before *anyone* considers the solution!

7 SUMMARY

Contingency Planning for computer systems is a topic deserving attention of senior management, both within and outside the Information Systems function. It is primarily a *business* topic rather than a technical *computing* topic requiring management to make value judgements on risks and costs, and as such a 'do nothing' case could be a valid outcome of the management decision process. Whilst a decision to have no plan is a valid option it should not be the default unilaterally adopted by the IS function.

The delivery of a reliable computing service depends upon the continued availability of people, equipment and data, each of which is vulnerable to multiple threats. It follows therefore that multiple plans are necessary to cope with different contingencies. This coupled with the complexity of producing a sound plan and the potential expenditure involved means that the process may well extend over many months and involve both IS and user personnel. The recovery of data in a timely and consistent manner is a complex process and is likley to be a mandatory part of all contingency plans. It is therefore worth starting this exercise before seeking direction from the business.

Little reliable quantitative data exists regarding the risk of an enterprise suffering a computer-related disaster; however, an understanding of the *impact* of a disaster is more important than a quantified definition of risk. A business impact review conducted by senior management is the best way of deciding upon the need for a contingency plan. Such a review will need sponsorship from executive management. The SESAME technique represents a proven method of conducting an impact review and is simple to use and efficient in terms of manpower.

Finally, there are a large number of possible solutions to the problem of securing IT services; a prerequisite to the consideration of *any* solution is a clear view of the dependence of the enterprise upon IT.

APPENDIX 1—DETAILED BREAKDOWN OF COMPUTER RESOURCES

The key resource items in the 'Contingency Cube' (Figure 5) are further analysed in the following diagrams. These diagrams should not be regarded as being exhaustive; however they do represent a useful way of breaking down a complex operation into a series of understandable and manageable chunks.

Equipment

Figure 9 (below) describes the elements to be considered. The diagram assumes a central processing complex, attached to a teleprocessing network serving end users at the centre and at a number of remote locations, and running a number of batch and on-line applications. The use of multiple central processing sites and/or the user of departmental minis and micros may complicate the contingency issue; they do not invalidate the process descriptions in this section. The equipment element of the process also

	Computing	Networking
Delivery mechanisms	Central processors Storage devices Peripherals	Front-end processors Multiplexors and lines Terminals
Support mechanisms	Infrastructure: heating, cooling, buildings and fittings	
	Services: water, electricity, gas.	
	Consumables: paper, ribbons, tapes, etc.	

FIGURE 9

includes all the ancillary support equipment and services necessary to support the main computer equipment.

Data

The 'data' component of the process considers both data related to the operation of the total process (i.e. 'process' data) and the data maintained by the process for the end user as part of a business function (i.e. 'business' data). The maintenance of business data is the primary objective of the overall process.

Process data		Business data
Documentation		

Application
  − Specification
  − Modification level
Operating systems
  − Components
  − Levels
Computer / network
  − Configuration
  − Connection
  − Equipment
      specification
Data index
  − Identity
  − Media
  − Location
Contacts
  − Internal personnel
  − Suppliers
Control procedures
  − Change and problem management
  − Standards
  − Measurements
  − Accounting , ... , etc.
		Application
		  − Input data
		  − Stored data
		  − Output data

Instructions		
Programs/parameters/ execution control	Operating procedures	
Application Operating system Housekeeping	Computer operations Users	

FIGURE 10

'Process' data can be subdivided into 'Supporting Documentation' and 'Instructions'. 'Documentation' specifies the nature of the process and the equipment necessary to run it. 'Instructions' covers computer instructions necessary to run the application(s) plus operating procedures for users and operators. These procedures will cover the direct operation of the total process, equipment, general purpose software (e.g. network and computer operating systems) and the application(s).

The various constituents of 'data' are shown in Figure 10.

People

This element represents the availability of the correct skills to operate and maintain the process. It should be noted that people may play a dual role in any process as either the originators or beneficiaries of that process. This illustrates the need to consider both the IS and user aspects of computer processing. A review of skills is equally valid within and outside an enterprise; applications may be supplied and maintained externally as an example.

Figure 11 shows the categories needed.

```
┌─────────────────────────────────────┐
│ People skills/numbers               │
├─────────────────────────────────────┤
│ Originators / maintainers           │
│ –      Application                   │
│            –    Users                │
│            –    Developers           │
│ –      Operating system             │
│ –      Equipment                     │
│ Providers                            │
│ –      Computer operators*           │
│ –      Network operators             │
│ Beneficiaries (end users)            │
└─────────────────────────────────────┘
```

* For the purposes of this table the term computer operator is taken to include all other operations support staff, data preparation, etc. In practice some of these functions may be performed by end users.

FIGURE 11

REFERENCES

Arthur Young (1987) 'Management awareness of computer risks—a European survey'.
Coopers and Lybrand (1988) 'The security of network systems—Report 5, Summary and recommendations'.
Lincoln, T.J.(1986) *Do Computer Systems Really Pay Off?*, Elsevier Science Publishers B.V.
National Audit Office (1987) 'Computer security in Government Departments'.

Chapter 10

COST-JUSTIFYING CURRENT USE OF INFORMATION TECHNOLOGY

Tim Lincoln and David Shorrock

1 AN EVOLVING PROBLEM

Computer systems have evolved very rapidly over the past few years as technology has become cheaper and more powerful, communication networks more pervasive and managers more aware of the strategic potential of Information Technology (IT). First generation systems installed in the 1960s tended to be static, limited in function and usually localised in their impact. Increasingly, however, systems are becoming flexible, evolutionary and integrated with key corporate business processes ranging from R&D through manufacturing to sales and services.

The fact that current systems often have a fundamental impact on the way in which business processes are performed, rather than just supporting their administration, means that they can now be a major influence for organisational change. This trend can confidently be expected to continue in the foreseeable future. Developments in the field of expert systems, image processing, video and communications technology, and the establishment of more information services agencies will all mean that the impact of information technology will increasingly extend not only beyond departmental limits, but also beyond corporate, community and national boundaries.

Such evolution has already added a dimension of complexity which tends to overwhelm the traditional techniques used by managers to establish the costs and benefits of computerisation projects. These techniques typically focus on the now rather quaint concept of computers as tools for cost displacement rather than the improvement of organisational effectiveness and competitiveness.

In a recent report, Earl and Runge (1987) stated that 80% of successful 'competitive edge' applications surveyed completely bypassed the normal management approval processes. Reasons offered for this were the difficulty in predicting with any degree of certainty the costs and benefits of such systems, and the perceived need to go ahead on the basis of managerial 'hunch', or

Managing Information Systems for Profit. Edited by T. J. Lincoln
© 1990 John Wiley & Sons Ltd

strategic insight, if the anticipated benefits of the system were to be realised quickly.

It has become apparent to those working in this field that conventional cost/benefit analysis techniques lag behind the capabilities of modern computer systems. They are unable to predict the full impact of systems on corporate performance. In organisations placing high emphasis on formal investment appraisal the lack of confidence engendered by this inadequacy acts as a brake on the expanding use of technology.

Experience shows that there is no easy prescription which, once followed, will enable managers to anticipate accurately, or even evaluate after the fact, the ultimate financial impact of complex computer systems. However, many Information Systems (IS) and Financial Directors still seek such prescriptions. Accordingly the time seems to be right to review current techniques and make some recommendations about how they might be improved.

2 CASE STUDIES

The following brief casestudies drawn from recent consulting experience illustrate the type of problems which can arise.

2.1 Closely Coupled System/Organisation

A large supermarket chain had recently implemented an on-line computer system to support distribution. The original cost/benefit case was felt to be unsatisfactory and senior management were uneasy about the level of benefits being achieved. Accordingly a post-audit was requested to review the new system's financial impact.

Under the previous system supermarket managers ordered goods directly from main suppliers using an overnight batch system. This was inefficient since the potential economies of large scale ordering were not being realised. Accordingly the new system was installed to enable supermarkets to place orders via high speed data links on regional distribution centres. The centres were then able to order economical quantities directly from suppliers and offer improved levels of service to individual supermarkets.

Analysis showed that for all practical purposes the computer system could not be considered separately from the distribution process. Attempts to analyse the implications of managing the process without the use of the system were judged by executives to be artificial and meaningless. The conclusion was reached that the costs and benefits of the on-line system could not be realistically assessed in isolation of the costs and benefits of the new distribution process.

2.2 Evolving Common Systems

A major utility operating across a large number of districts was in the process of implementing a system which integrated ordering, billing, account queries and associated customer services. Unfortunately, early development was plagued with delays leading to considerable uncertainty about final costs and schedules. Following a number of senior management changes it was decided to commission a study to review actual costs and benefits incurred to date and to forecast the likely outcome after full implementation. At the time of the review only three sites were live and it was planned that the remainder should be phased in over a period of about 3 years.

Management felt that the most appropriate yardstick against which to measure the new system was the set of existing computer systems which supplied similar but less integrated function in the majority of sites. Investigation showed that when the new system was commissioned the intention had been to freeze development of existing systems and the original business case was developed on this basis. Unfortunately because of the delays, this intention had not been fullfilled and existing systems had had to be enhanced with functionality of the sort envisaged for the new system. Indeed a mild form of rivalry arose between different development teams with the result that senior management were receiving inconsistent and sometimes conflicting advice.

The result of this was that the benefits of the new system over the existing ones were diminished. Districts observed this happening and, because they had freedom to decide when they would implement the new system and whether they would install enhanced versions of existing systems while waiting, the comparison base for the post-audit became most complicated. The study team had therefore to make assumptions about development schedules of both the new and existing systems, the functionality of both systems at different time periods and individual district implementation strategies.

The situation ultimately became so complex that it proved extremely difficult to arrive at unambigious cost/benefit figures. Communicating meaningful conclusions in simple managerially acceptable terms was an even greater challenge.

2.3 Top Management Ambivalence

An Insurance Company installed a new computer for handling the major part of its reinsurance business, replacing a partly computerised system. The new system was designed to provide a cost-effective and disciplined means of processing payment of premiums and claims and reconciling broker accounts, etc. Fairly easily calculable cost displacement benefits were indeed obtained, such as reductions in clerical staff, improvements in cash flow and savings in time taken for production of standard reports. Accordingly, when management commissioned a cost/benefit post-audit it was felt to be a reasonably straightforward task.

During the analysis the study team became aware that since installation further system benefits had become apparent. These mainly arose from the ability to support underwriting decisions by rapid production of non-standard reports. There was an ever-accumulating volume of data on claims, brokers, classes of business, etc., generated both internally and from the external industry networks with which links were being established. These were of direct relevance to the underwriting decision-making process. Furthermore they would become of increasing value in future years as anticipated business growth was likely to exceed the company's ability to recruit and train new underwriters. The potential for automated decision-support systems as training aids and an increasingly effective substitute for underwriting experience was very significant.

Unfortunately, whilst it was generally accepted that all these secondary benefits were being realised to a greater or lesser extent, it proved impossible for the study team to persuade underwriting managers to quantify them. This reluctance stemmed from three factors: firstly, the degree of subjective assessment involved; secondly, the difficulty of breaking down the decision-making process into its component parts to arrive at a reasonable assessment of the impact of the computer at each stage; and, thirdly, the natural reluctance of managers to commit themselves to figures against which their future performance might well be judged!

In the absence of any pressure or encouragement from top management on the underwriters to conduct such an exercise there was no way in which the study team could apply rules of thumb to substitute for the managers' intimate knowledge of their jobs, and therefore of the likely benefit of the new support facilities. The benefit analysis concluded on a somewhat unsatisfactory note. Cost displacement benefits had been quantified, and a positive though unspectacular return on investment calculated. Secondary benefits, which were felt to be far more significant, were identified but not quantified and it was realised that the picture was far from complete.

---

3 KEY ISSUES

As illustrated in the above casestudies, cost/benefit analysis of computer systems can lead to confusion, contention and waste of time. At the root of the difficulties described are issues which affect all studies and which have always existed. The difference nowadays is that they do so in a much more profound way and can therefore no longer be ignored. In the experience of the authors the key issues to be taken into account are the following:

1. Many Cost/Benefit studies have confused objectives.
2. Computer benefits and Organisational benefits are increasingly closely coupled.
3. Computer systems are increasingly closely inter-linked.
4. It is becoming more difficult to define credible, viable alternatives to computer systems: meaningful comparisons are therefore hard to make.

5. It is very difficult to predict the nature and speed of evolutionary change in systems.
6. Different measurement methods can lead to differing conclusions.

Each of these issues will now be described more fully.

3.1 Confused Objectives

Many, perhaps most, cost/benefit studies are prompted by a concern articulated in terms of 'value for money'. If the study is attempting to forecast the future impact of computing the question posed might be 'Will I get value for money from this investment?' If a post-audit is involved the question could be 'Have I obtained value for money from this investment?' In both cases it is assumed that 'value for money' is an unambigious concept which demands no further clarification.

Unfortunately in the experience of the authors this apparently simple concept often conceals more than it reveals. Examples abound where more specific concerns lie at the root of executive interest and the following examples illustrate questions which became apparent only after the study started:

Pre-implementation reviews:

1. Why should we not continue to invest in the current system?
2. Will the new system actually save money?
3. Will the new system ever deliver tangible benefits?
4. Do the users understand what they will get?
5. Is the proposed system strategically right?
6. Does the projected return exceed the weighted cost of capital?

Post-implementation reviews:

1. Is my level of expenditure on the system reasonable?
2. Why is my budget increasing when computers are getting cheaper?
3. Is the system delivering the benefits that were promised?
4. What do I have to spend/do to get more benefits?
5. Are other organisations doing better?
6. Am I getting a reasonable return on my investment?
7. Has the system been competently implemented?
8. Should I fire my IS manager?

Some of these questions are very specific while others are generalised. To answer them adequately demands different techniques and different skills. You would not expect, for example, the same skills required to answer a purely financial question relating to return on investment to be appropriate for a question requiring extensive managerial judgement. And yet because of the imprecise nature of the 'value for money' concept it is not uncommon to find junior financial analysts straying into judgements of managerial competence.

Failure to focus on the specific issues that require attention will result in time-wasting at best and grossly ill-informed decisions at worst. However there are a number of factors which make it difficult to clarify precisely what the key issues are. Firstly, executives who believe the issues are straightforward do not take kindly to being taken through the thought process required for clarification. For example the authors have been told, with a certain amount of irritation, that cost/benefit analysis is very simple—all you need to do is to record the costs, analyse the benefits and compare the two. A degree of tact and detachment is useful in dealing with this situation. Secondly, a cost/benefit exercise is a learning process for the people involved, including executive sponsors. As the analysis unfolds it is quite normal for additional questions to be asked which were not anticipated and which require a different form of analysis. Thirdly costs and benefits can be contentious and have political implications. Accordingly it is quite normal to have to deal with hidden agendas and game-playing. Recognising such situations and knowing how to deal with them requires a level of experience often found lacking in cost/benefit study teams.

3.2 Computer Benefits Versus Organisational Benefits

It is often argued that there are broadly two categories of benefit to look for from computer systems: cost displacement or avoidance (relatively easy to assess) and more qualitative improvements to do with speed and quality of information and improved levels of service (much more difficult to assess and requiring managerial judgement to do so). In either case it is assumed that benefits, however difficult to quantify, are at least directly attributable to the computer system.

Unfortunately computer systems are, as we have seen, often difficult to disentangle from their managerial and organisational context. When a system is introduced as part of, or concurrently with, a major reorganisation, cause and effect relationships can become blurred. If centralised buying, integration of sales and service and automated underwriting, as described in our case studies, were all impossible without computer support, does this mean that the whole of the benefit of these new ways of doing business should be attributed to the computer? Common sense suggests that the other components of the management system—the new organisation, the training, the methods and procedures, new managerial initiatives—all, in varying degrees, contribute to increased efficiency and effectiveness. However proponents of a system will often ignore this and argue that all benefits flow from the computer while less convinced executives will view this claim with scepticism. The result? Claims, counter-claims, delays and indecision.

3.3 Linked Systems

The scope of most modern computer systems is seldom limited to a single department, function or business process. Because of this failure to identify clearly the boundaries of the system(s) under review invariably leads to wasted effort and lack of focus. The dilemma is that the very systems which are in most need of cost-justification are often those for which the definition of precise boundaries is most difficult.

Many systems have direct links to other systems with critical data and function interdependencies. The further this mutual dependency extends (in other words the more genuinely integrated the systems are) the more complex the overall pattern of both costs and benefits becomes. This inter-dependency is seen very clearly in, for example, manufacturing systems where design, sales forecasting, production planning, production control, manufacturing and inventory control are increasingly inter-linked.

It is essential that the implications of any linkages to other systems be understood. The boundaries of the system under review should be defined and agreed with senior management. The decision of whether to include or exclude a particular system or feature which has linkages to the prime system under review may be far from straightforward and can fundamentally affect the outcome.

But the issue is more complex even than this. Linkages can apply both within an organisation and between totally separate business entities. 'Just-in-time' manufacturing is an example of an increasingly widespread improvement in efficiency and competitiveness which is impossible to achieve without direct computer links into suppliers' inventory, ordering and delivery systems. Indeed many major manufacturers are now making the ability to interact with their own computer systems a pre-condition of supplier certification. Other examples of computerised integration between companies, their suppliers and customers are to be found increasingly in retail, banking and insurance, often driven by industry-wide initiatives. Increasingly, external agencies are providing these links.

Many of the systems which exploit these linkages are merely extensions of ones originally intended for internal use and were therefore justified on the basis of internal benefits. Such benefits as they have achieved when used internally are often of little consequence when compared with the strategic advantages derived from the outside linkages (Earl and Runge, 1987). As this process of interlinking systems continues, justification of computer projects will become more a matter of strategic positioning in relation to markets, customers, suppliers and less a matter of purely internal efficiency.

Thus it is unwise for a cost-justification exercise to attempt an assessment of the benefits of such strategic systems in isolation. They constitute such an important element of corporate strategy that the only measure of their success or failure is overall corporate performance.

3.4 Alternatives to Computer-based Systems

Once it is known *what* is being assessed, the next fundamental question is 'With what is the system being compared?' or as an economist might ask 'What is the counter-factual?' To illustrate this, how could the benefits of marriage be assessed without knowing what state it is being compared with? Is it celibacy? living in sin? free love? or some other states that could be mentioned but are perhaps better left unspecified? The selection of the comparison basis will essentially depend on the issues of acceptability, function and service levels. These are discussed further below.

The comparison base *must* be something which management can accept as a feasible (indeed the most likely) alternative to the computer system under evaluation. The comparison must also be consistent with the accepted work pattern of the people involved. The difficulty here is that what seems feasible at the start of a study often comes to seem unrealistic or naive as the investigation proceeds and people become aware of the full extent of what the alternative would entail. The classic case is of course where a manual system is initially assumed reasonable, then found to be hopelessly impractical because of the size of the workforce needed to complete tasks within an acceptable time frame.

In addition to the question of feasibility that of function must also be carefully considered. Computer systems almost invariably contain a lot of new functions—things which simply were not attempted previously because they were too lengthy, error-prone or cumbersome. Two approaches are possible to deal with this. For ease of comparison, the starting assumption could be made that the alternative system could, given the appropriate resources, perform the full range of new system functions without significant deterioration in critical service levels. If this assumption is made, the basis of comparability is essentially one of cost. The alternative approach is to accept that strict equality of service levels is not possible and that the computer unique functions or levels of service are clearly 'benefits' (or perhaps 'disbenefits') of the system. In this case some more sophisticated form of analysis than simple cost displacement is called for since we need to assess the ultimate value of doing something we have never been in a position to do before.

It is therefore necessary at the outset to establish which functions are to be considered 'do-able' and which critical service levels are achievable by the alternative system and which are not. The essential dilemma here is that frequently the closer the service level of the comparison base is made to be, the more unrealistic the comparison appears. However the further apart the service levels are, the greater the difficulty in quantifying the benefits.

Experience has shown that the definition of an acceptable comparison base can raise very severe difficulties. It is often found that the more successful a system is the more difficult it can be to suggest a practical and acceptable alternative. In the last resort if an acceptable alternative cannot be found, the costs and benefits of the system under review cannot be meaningfully analysed.

3.5 Predicting the Pace of Evolutionary Change

A key problem related to the comparison base issue (but distinct from it) arises from the fact that the world is not static and that systems evolve over time. Consequently any analysis of costs and benefits which extends over time must take evolution into account. One would expect to see, for example, estimates of maintenance and perhaps enhancement costs together with estimates of associated benefit improvements. This is especially the case where flexibility, or capability for change, is identified as a key system benefit.

Evolution of course applies not only to actual, 'real' computer systems, but also to the 'comparison base' systems which may be manual, an existing computer system or an hypothetical system. Generally speaking it is the comparator system which causes most problems when estimating the impact of evolution.

Where the comparison base is a manual or clerical system there is a temptation to assume, probably because such systems are familiar and easily understood, that they are static and unchanging. Whilst it is true that manual systems are not normally the subject of formal, planned maintenance in the sense that computer programs have to be, it is nevertheless shortsighted to assume that they do not change or that such change does not cost anything. In many sophisticated organisations there are of course 'O&M' departments, but even where such departments do not exist, there will inevitably be change and at least some productivity improvements over time through the normal process of management. This needs to be taken account of; it is usually unrealistic to assume that if, for example, X clerks processed Y transactions per day two years ago this processing rate will remain static forever.

Where the comparison base is a previous generation computer system assumptions have to be made about the amount and type of maintenance and enhancements it would be reasonable to expect to have done on it had it not been replaced. Under normal circumstances historical maintenance costs can be used as a guide. However, in the world of rapid technology change it is quite common to find that the hardware or systems software underpinning an application has become obsolete, in which case the investment required to maintain an existing system becomes virtually impossible to estimate.

Where the comparison base is a hypothetical computer system the method of analysis is essentially the same, but the increased number of assumptions that has to be made obviously tends to make the exercise more academic. Most difficult of all is the situation (as in the public utility case quoted) where multiple implementations with different schedules, levels of functionality and business environments are involved.

Experience has shown that assumptions concerning the evolution of both the real and comparator systems are amongst the most important and the most difficult to make in a practical study. Perhaps because of this, a high percentage of business cases reviewed by the authors do not attempt to explore these issues and consequently have very dubious conclusions.

3.6 Measurement Issues

There are a number of measurement issues which arise during cost/benefit analysis which at first sight seem trivial. In fact the situation often arises when small changes in the way costs and benefits are measured can significantly affect the outcome of the analysis. In the experience of the authors the issues which give rise to most confusion are related to:

1. The time period over which costs and benefits will be measured
2. Whether overheads are to be included in the analysis
3. Whether avoided costs can be legitimately classified as benefits
4. Which ratio, or other measurement, best represents the results of the analysis

These issues are discussed further below.

3.6.1 Duration

It is often forgotten that time is a boundary which needs definition in a cost-justification exercise, and slight changes in start or finish points can dramatically change its outcome. Manipulation of time boundaries is therefore one of the many ways in which analysts can be economical with the truth.

The two most important dates to be defined are of course the start point of the analysis and the finish point. However, the granularity of the analysis can have a subtle impact when 'Discounted Cash flow' techniques are used. Although apparently less open to debate the start point of analysis is not always obvious. For example, should analysis start when a system was first suggested, or when work first started, or when a firm Board commitment was made? The simplistic response is to start at the point when costs are first incurred, but what about R&D costs or pilot systems. Should they be considered sunk or taken into account? Such decisions can make or break a cost/benefit case.

Similarly a decision must be made about how far the analysis should look into the future—over the expected life of the system or some shorter period? If the period is less than the expected system life should a residual value be included in the analysis? Some categories of costs and benefits will be known with much greater precision than others simply because of the different planning horizons employed for different types of activity. Computer system benefits are closely associated with business activity which is difficult to predict more than a few months ahead. Computer costs, however, are often known with greater precision and some categories of computer related costs (e.g. buildings) may be predictable for up to ten years ahead. Since a meaningful analysis must compare benefits and costs over the same time duration a compromise is needed and here lie fertile grounds for contention.

There are no standard rules for defining these dates but many companies feel that a horizon of between three and five years from the time when a definite decision was made to proceed is about right. The analyst must decide which dates he thinks are reasonable and should seek management agreement before the analysis is completed. In cases where real uncertainty exists, the use of sensitivity analysis is the only solution.

3.6.2 *Extent*

At some point during cost/benefit analysis the question always arises 'Should only direct resource costs be taken into account or should we also include associated overheads.' This is sometimes seen as a technical issue to be decided by the accountants—until managers realise the dramatic effect that the decision can have.

It is very tempting when considering a relatively small subset of a major system to take the view that since it has little impact on the overall cost of computing (unless it lies at the margin of some step function requirement for increased computer capacity) it need not carry its share of the total cost. Taking this view has two consequences. Firstly, applications producing only marginal benefits can be very easily justified if excess hardware capacity is available. A single such justification need not matter but the greater the number of applications implemented using this rationale the more absurd it becomes. Secondly it can prove impossible to justify needed increases in hardware capacity if their cost is judged solely against the benefits of the individual application triggering the upgrade.

The danger of marginal costing, and its potential for gross distortion of cost data, will be self-evident to experienced accountants. To the general businessman, however, it sometimes needs to be pointed out very clearly as a potential danger. This is not to say that marginal costing is in all cases wrong, but that due consideration should be given to the relative size of the systems in question, the expected life of the application, the number of people affected and the amount of space and other overheads involved before deciding whether marginal or full costing should be used. At the very least it is essential that both actual and comparator systems are costed in a consistent manner. The help of neutral financial professionals can be of great help in ensuring that this is done.

3.6.3 Reduced Versus Avoided Costs

It is not unusual to draw a distinction between reduced costs and avoided costs and consider both as legitimate benefit areas (IBM, G509-2214). Reduced costs are considered to be an actual reduction of headcount or other cost category from the current level whereas avoided costs are a claimed reduction from the level that would apply at some stage in the future if the system were not implemented.

Many managers take a jaundiced view of avoided costs, claiming that they are impossible to control and that accountability cannot be assigned. This view is understandable since business cases for automation are often based on headcount and other growth scenarios which are patently absurd. Claiming a computer system will avoid some or all of the extrapolated costs derived from such scenarios simply invites derision.

On the other hand, to accept only cost reductions as legitimate benefits appears unrealistic, particularly in an expanding business. To do so is to suggest that costs can be held constant in the future regardless of business volumes and activity.

The answer to this apparent dilemma lies in the quality of forward plans in the business. If the company has very little idea, and no plans, as to future costs then avoided costs will always appear suspect. If on the other hand plans are well established to the point of having firm commitments on cost budgets then an avoided cost has real meaning and can be controlled. Examples of the latter situation are to be found in organisations having a strong planning culture, particularly where headcount is concerned. Even in such organisations, however, firm plans rarely exist for more than twelve months ahead and avoided costs beyond this period should only be claimed after very careful consideration.

3.6.4 Ratios

A cost/benefit study will identify time flows of costs and benefits of the system under review compared with an alternative system. It is usual to convert these time flows into a single financial measure which can be compared with the same measure from other investments. The question arises therefore as to which measure is to be used. The pros and cons of alternative measures are dealt with in a wide variety of standard accounting texts (e.g. Weston and Brigham, 1978) and we will not repeat the arguments here. It is perhaps worth making the point, however, that no one single measure is perfect and each has its own strengths. In the work we do we always report the financial performance in terms of payback period, mean benefit/cost ratio and internal rate of return. The first two are easily understood but rather misleading in that they take no account of the time value of money; the last is arguably the most meaningful single figure to use but is commonly misunderstood. As with most consultancy work a compromise between accuracy and understandability is required which will differ between managers and organisations.

4 BENEFIT ASSESSMENT

For the reasons outlined in the section above, the assessment of computer system benefits has always been contentious and recent developments are making the situation worse. There are in fact three issues which tend to merge but it is useful to consider them separately. These are:

1. Forecasting benefits
2. Prioritising investments
3. Ensuring benefits

which are considered further below.

4.1 Forecasting Benefits

There are a number of techniques employed to forecast future benefits of proposed computer systems and a review of these will perhaps be helpful. They are described below in descending order of their ability to produce hard data.

4.1.1 Pilot New System

Where very major investments are involved it is common to pilot a new system in a limited geographical region or function so that the system can be proven and any bugs removed. At the same time system costs and benefits are usually measured so that they can be extrapolated to the whole organisation.

Piloting can produce very convincing benefit forecasts and has helped companies make major investment decisions. However there are disadvantages of expense, time and practicality (Strassman, 1985). Expense is a concern because pilots, if they are to be fully representative, will require the full range of function and therefore carry most of the development costs. Time is a concern because pilot evaluation implies a monitoring process covering the period prior to implementation to a time when users have learnt to use the system effectively. Thus the benefits to be gained from full implementation will be delayed considerably. Practicality is a concern because it is sometimes impossible to pilot certain benefits. In particular where benefits rely on major organisational change or on very wide use of system (e.g. electronic mail) pilots can be of limited value.

4.1.2 Prototype New System

Prototyping as a development technique is well known and fairly widely used. The objective is to implement a 'quick and dirty' system which will allow a user to gain experience with the facilities quickly and cheaply. Very commonly the result is a changed or enhanced set of requirements which forms the basis for the full operational system. In a similar way to pilots, prototypes can in theory be employed to evaluate potential benefits before making major investment decisions although we know of no cases of prototypes being used exclusively in this way.

Under the right circumstances prototyping can provide some measure of the benefits likely to accrue from the system. However because prototyping frequently leads to changed system requirements extrapolation is not always straightforward. Experience has also shown that prototyping carries the risk that users once given a 'quick and dirty' system will be reluctant to sanction the additional expense of developing a production system. They will therefore lack the security, integrity, reliability and documentation that a 'proper' system should provide as a matter of course.

4.1.3 Rely on User Assessment

User assessment relies on forecasts of potential benefits based on known system specifications. This is probably the most widely used of all systems' appraisal techniques and has high credibility. User assessments are consolidated by systems analysts for forecasting purposes and are also sometimes used as a basis for budgetary planning.

The technique, however, brings with it inevitable 'game-playing'. Because of the uncertainties involved users will always bid low, especially if they believe that their resources or targets may be affected. As the benefits become more intangible this characteristic becomes more pronounced. In the limited cases where computer systems are being used merely to automate an existing process, user assessment is not a bad guide since the benefits of such systems tend to be directly measurable. However to the extent that organisational change is a design objective of most major systems individual user judgement influenced by local experience, tradition and vested interests cannot be relied on.

It is therefore not surprising that in those cases (of which the authors are aware) in which benefit forecasts based on user assessment have been compared with post-audited achievements, there is very little correlation between the two.

4.1.4 Start from Existing Achievements

The assumption made here is that if installed systems can be shown to have produced specific returns then this provides a useful starting point from which to estimate the likely benefits from similar systems in the future.

This approach has a certain appeal: where the systems concerned are in the nature of generalised facilities such as office automation, analysis of previous experience is often the best if not the only guide. Indeed the marketing literature for office automation places heavy emphasis on figures illustrating productivity improvements when performing standard office procedures in real life situations.

Experience of more specialised applications is, however, much more difficult to translate from one environment to another. Even where there is a high degree of similarity between both systems and environments the credibility of reported case studies is often suspect and it is difficult to overcome deeply held executive prejudice merely by quoting other companies' experiences. The situation would be much easier if there were a wide range of authenticated post-audits which could be used as a recognised database to which adjustments could be made to accommodate differences in scope and business volumes. IBM, through the audits conducted in the UK using the SESAME technique (IBM, GE15-6140-0; Lincoln, 1986), has acquired a database illustrating the range of financial returns from a variety of applications. However the sample is as yet too small and the variety of applications too wide for the data base to be of general use for purposes of comparison.

The most likely source of usable databases will probably be initiatives undertaken by or on behalf of specific industries. There are already signs that this is beginning to happen; IBM's own industry Marketing function in the United States and elsewhere is accumulating increasing amounts of data on performance improvements resulting from installation of standard industry applications. Much of this data is being incorporated in the IBM ISIS programme (IBM, G520-6497-00) which is aimed at helping customers to better understand their opportunities for profitable investment in information technology.

Meanwhile some larger companies are conducting internal post-audits to learn from their own experience of computing and apply their conclusions to the forecasting and management of future systems benefits. Used with other evidence, reliable case studies can significantly enhance senior executives' confidence that IT can produce reasonable returns and it is a great pity that more studies have not been conducted and published.

4.1.5 Link to Business Objectives

This technique has grown considerably over the last few years and there are now many variants. They all use the argument that if a system can be shown to directly support a key business objective then there is a prima-facie case that the investment will be worthwhile. The link to the business can be via, for example, business processes, critical success factors, value chains and competitive advantages. Examples of these techniques are given in Chapters 4 and 7 of this book dealing with 'Linking IS Strategies to Business Objectives' and 'Gearing IT in the Office to Business Needs'.

There is no doubt that formally linking IS investment to business objectives is an effective way of capturing senior executives' attention and obtain their commitment. It can also assist in the process of clarifying and prioritising strategic objectives when other approaches have failed. However, two limitations of such techniques must be born in mind. Firstly, their use demands a level of top management commitment and involvement which can be difficult to achieve. The role of the sponsor of the study proves to be vital in sustaining the commitment and ensuring follow-on action. Secondly, such technques only result in hard numbers if they are followed up by more detailed study.

4.1.6 Utilise Management Judgement

Ultimately an element of senior management judgement is involved in all system investment decisions involving significant company resources. Examples vary from companies relying on an IT Director with a proven track record to steering committees charged with taking a corporate view. These judgements sometimes take into account user assessment and hard experience but frequently these days depend on acts of faith.

Mature management judgement can be very effective and should not be underestimated. It is, for example, probably the best way of taking company culture into account. However judgement is often clouded by politics, functional or professional bias and past experience, which can be positively misleading if it is not tempered by an awareness of change. The need for continuous updating of decision-makers' understanding both of the business environment and of the potential of IT is therefore paramount.

4.2 Prioritising Investments

Once a system's costs and benefits have been assessed the question of its priority in relation to other IT investment proposals arises. This can be quite a complex process and rarely is done purely on the basis of ROI.

Buss (1973) argues there are four prime factors to be taken into account, namely financial benefits, business objectives, intangible benefits and technical importance. He advocates an eight-step approach involving the preparation of matrices comparing levels of investment on a high to low scale against each of the four prime factors. Another example of a matrix-based approach is that used by Price Waterhouse (Informatics, 1988) which has on one axis investment benefit categorised as productivity improvements, minimising risk or expanding the business, while on the other the company's investment orientation categorised as infrastructure, business operations or market influence.

An alternative approach which has been used with IBM classifies projects into the following three types in order to assign gross priorities.

1. Essential Business Requirement—unavoidable expenditure, e.g. statutory requirement
2. Payback Projects—costs and benefits can be measured and will be incorporated in the sponsor's operating plan
3. Opportunity Investment—new ventures with high potential returns which are difficult to quantify and often have higher than usual risk

Category 1 projects would normally be assigned highest priority. Category 2 projects would be rated, initially at least, according to ROI while management judgement would be used to assign priorities to projects in category 3. Assignment of projects into these three categories has proved to be helpful in clarifying management thinking. For example, once a number of projects has been assigned to category 2 it is a straightforward process to determine their relative priorities. However it would be a mistake when using this approach to give a category 2 project a higher priority than one in category 3 without taking into consideration the fact that different qualitative criteria are involved.

4.3 Ensuring the Benefits

It is one thing to forecast benefits; it is something else to ensure benefits actually materialise. This is particularly so when non-specific 'benefits' such as increased organisational flexibility or improved decision-making are claimed. It is not difficult to argue for almost any major new system that it will indeed provide such features but until they have been exploited and measured the claims can only be regarded as pious wishes. Unless a deliberate and systematic effort is made to plan and manage benefit achievement these wishes are likely to remain unfilfilled. There are three techniques in common use to ensure benefits claimed actually materialise and these can be categorised as budget commitments, performance measurement and charge-out.

4.3.1 Budget Commitments

The procedure is that, at the time an investment decision is made, a user will agree that the defined benefits will be automatically incorporated within future user budgets. Thus if a headcount saving is forecast, the headcount budget will be lowered by an equivalent amount and management can be reassured the benefit will be realised. Whether this is done as a direct result of the system is often open to question but the technique does have the effect of concentrating the mind wonderfully!

Minor variants on the technique are to be found in terms of the timing of the budget adjustment. At the extreme this can be done immediately the investment decision is made, but a rather less drastic approach is to phase the adjustments according to the system implementation schedule. In the latter case user budgets have to be subject to a rigorous planning and commitment process for if the budget for future years is not defined precisely a designated adjustment will not have too much meaning.

4.3.2 Performance Measurement

Many companies do not have the strong planning culture which is necessary for a budget commitment process to work effectively. Even where such a culture does exist something more is required to manage the realisation of the types of benefit which cannot be reflected in departmental financial or headcount budgets.

It is often too easily assumed that qualitative benefits—those to do with raising service levels or improving customer satisfaction for example—simply cannot be measured because they have not direct quantifiable financial effect. In reality there is a wide range of performance indicators of a non financial nature which can be used if only the trouble is taken to record and measure them.

The choice lies broadly between measuring some end result—by conducting periodic surveys of the affected population's opinions about the overall effect of the system—and measuring some more tangible factors which are known to have an important influence on this end result. If the desired aim is improved customer satisfaction, for example, this could be measured either by market research or by measuring such things as the company's response times to emergency calls, percentage of fulfilled orders, product reliability statistics and so on.

Of course it takes time and effort to install and maintain measurement systems; observations need to be made over extended time periods to establish trends and if it is not immediately obvious which indicators are relevant some research may need to be done beforehand. The point is that management's view of what is measurable should not be limited by the present accounting system.

4.3.3 Charge-Out

Realistic and effective charge-out of computer services can be used to force users to carefully consider whether a system is worth the estimated cost. From a corporate viewpoint benefit forecasting is then something left to user judgement: if users feel that a system will help to meet their targets and is affordable then they are free to commission it. It is, however, important that charge-out procedures are consistent, understandable and easy to administer; otherwise they can generate excessive internal disputes which cloud users' judgement of the value of IS investments.

The three techniques described above are well proven and in widespread use. However they do tend to encourage rather localised and short-term views of benefits. To realise the potential of the typical 'strategic enabler' system something more is required.

As argued by Applegate, Cash and Mills (1988), 'management should not just react to technology but they should use it to change the organisation'. One of the major recommendations emerging from audits carried out by the authors in the recent past has been for the creation of a benefits management sub-project, reporting at the highest level, to institute processes which will ensure:

1. That a corporate and cross-functional view is taken of the opportunities that computerisation provides
2. That appropriate measurements and improvement targets are identified before implementation
3. That accountability for realisation of benefits is assigned to line managers as part of their operational objectives
4. That appropriate project review or steering committee mechanisms are in place to set policy, approve targets and review performance

The achievement of a corporate or cross-functional view of computer potential is not easy. The establishment of management systems designed to focus on business processes rather than functional management has been an important part of the Quality movement in industry in recent years. So far progress appears to have been slow and uneven, but there are indications that considerable improvement in the quality and effectiveness of Information Systems support is ultimately achievable if this effort is sustained. Regardless of the approach used to ensure Information Systems benefits the method of managing their implementation is vital. Careful consideration needs to be given in setting up a benefit management process which defines and achieves the desired objectives in a manner which takes into account corporate culture and practice.

5 SESAME GUIDELINES

Experience suggests that there is no perfect or ideal solution to the problems inherent in cost/benefit analysis. However, over the years the authors have refined a cost/benefit technique termed SESAME which, if used with care, will enable the analyst to avoid the type of mistakes discussed in Section 3 of this chapter. In view of the evident need for flexibility and open-endedness, SESAME does not follow strict deterministic procedures but rather adapts to suit individual circumstances. This flexibility places high demands on the analyst who will need considerable experience of dealing with complex, unstructured issues. Given this experience the following guidelines help the analyst cope with the wide variety of situations which can arise.

1. Ensure the proposed study has an appropriate sponsor and review with him what objectives he, and other people involved, may have for the study. Document these objectives before the study starts and refer to them as work continues. Beware of studies which appear to have inconsistent objectives or hidden agendas.

2. Define the benefit areas expected from the system and agree the measurement criteria to be applied. These criteria should embrace not only the immediately measurable benefits but also the less tangible and even those which were not foreseen. Unless this is done studies will tend to focus on financial savings to the exclusion of other, possibly more important, benefits.

3. Consider carefully whether or not the system under review can credibly be considered in isolation from its organisational environment. This can present difficulties. Most systems change the way users behave to some degree; indeed this is how benefits are generated. However the larger the change in organisational behaviour the more hypothetical it can seem to consider the costs and benefits of the system as opposed to those of the organisational changes. At some point management may consider that isolating the system in this way is too artificial and that the analysis carries no credibility. Such a point was reached in the supermarket case study described in Section 2.1 of this chapter. If this point is reached the analyst has no choice but to extend the scope of the analysis to include the effect of the new organisation or to recommend the study is abandoned.

4. Evaluate the linking or integration of systems and select acceptable system boundaries. A trade-off often has to be made between analysing a group of interrelated systems which logically belong together but are too big to analyse and focusing specifically on a particular system which is easier to analyse but whose costs and benefits have interdependencies on other systems.

5. Ask the question 'What will this system be compared with?' and ensure that the sponsor and other influential people accept that a realistic comparator has been selected. Beware of artificial comparators chosen specifically to make the new system look good or bad. Document the reasons for choosing

the comparator and ensure all key players understand and concur with the reasoning.

6. Select carefully the period over which the system will be evaluated and identify the major changes to be taken into account during this period. Ensure that the impact of change on both the system and its comparator is thoroughly evaluated. Examples of changes may include legislation, organisation, user requirements and system obsolescence. Document the changes which will be taken into account and if appropriate explain why other changes are to be ignored.

7. Ensure that the measurement criteria employed are as neutral as possible. Where non-financial criteria are used make sure that they are measurable and that management accepts their relevance. Measurements should ideally be an integral part of the operating procedures for the system and new measures should not be necessary. Where financial measures are appropriate, use a variety of methods as detailed in Section 3.6.4 of this chapter and point to the pros and cons of each in order to give as complete a picture as possible.

8. Ensure that an appropriate study team is deployed with the skills, availability and commitment required to cope with the issues identified above.

9. In situations where analysis can be done before implementation, try to reduce the area of uncertainty by careful use of pilots, periods of parallel running and other techniques.

6 SUMMARY

This chapter has explored the issues surrounding investment appraisal of Information Technology. Cost justification is a standard commercial practice and its application to IT may appear straightforward. In practice, however, the pervasive nature of many applications and the progressive integration of IT into the infra-structure of the business complicates the process considerably.

The three case studies described provide indications of the problems that can arise. The review of the fundamental issues involved provides insights into their sources and nature, and strategies for their resolution are described. Specific guidelines are given to assist the cost/benefit analyst.

It has been argued that cost-justification of IT is 'a child of its time', in other words was necessary once but has now outlived its usefulness. In light of the problems described in this chapter this is a seductive argument; if it were true it would make the analyst's life much easier. Experience however does not support the claim. Far from being a diminishing requirement it appears that senior management are increasingly requiring a business case to support new IT investments and indeed proof that existing investments have actually achieved tangible financial benefits.

There is therefore a continuing requirement for a professional credible approach to providing such justifications. Where such analyses are required we hope that this chapter will throw some useful light on the inherent problems. Unless analysts rise to these challenges there is a real danger that senior executives will be inhibited by their natural caution and fear of uncertainty from exploiting the full potential of modern technology.

REFERENCES

Applegate, Cash and Mills (1988) 'Information technology and tomorrow's manager', HBR, November/December.
Bus, M. D. J. (1983) 'How to rank computer projects', HBR, January/February.
Earl, M. J., and Runge, D. A. (1987) 'Using telecommunications based information systems for competitive advantage', Research and Discussion Paper, RDP 87/1, Oxford Institute for Information Management, Templeton College.
IBM G520-6497-00 (1988) 'IS investment strategies: making a difference on the bottom line'.
IBM G509-2214 'A business case for DP resources'.
IBM GE15-6140-0 'Computer systems profitability assessment in manufacturing'.
Informatics (1988) 'Going for IT', July.
Lincoln, T. J. (1986) 'Do computer systems really pay off', *Information and Management*, **11**, 1, August.
Strassman, P. A. (1985) *Information Payoff. The Transformation of Work in the Electronic Age*, The Free Press.
Weston, J. F., and Brigham, E. F. (1978) *Managerial Finance*, 6th ed., Holt, Rinehard and Winston.

Chapter 11
DEMONSTRATING THE IS CONTRIBUTION

Bill Amos

1 INTRODUCTION

Questions concerning the value of the contribution of IS to the performance of an enterprise are raised ever more frequently by senior executives. Those questions may simply be prompted by the sheer size of the annual expenditure on information technology and its supporting infrastructure, but are also often triggered by the lack of available evidence as to the nature and extent of the IS contribution.

Before proceeding I would like to offer the following definition.

> DEFINITION. For the purpose of this chapter the Value of IS will be defined as the contribution to business performance of the accumulated investments in systems, technology and IS infrastructure.

An ability to demonstrate regularly the value of the IS contribution to business performance may be an essential ingredient in the creation of management confidence so necessary to embark on imaginative new uses of systems on which the future success of the enterprise may depend. The seniority of the managers who raise the concern demands that it be treated seriously, so it is interesting to note that such questions still, in so many cases, beg an answer.

This chapter will examine the nature of the concern and consider some past attempts to address it. It looks at circumstances that may give rise to the concern and, from many approaches reviewed by the author, recommends a way to assess the value of IS. It also suggests strategies for measurement of IS performance and resource utilisation that are necessary to support, and ensure a clear understanding of, the value of IS so assessed.

The ideas expressed will be of interest to executives responsible for managing systems as well as to any executives who have ever questioned the contribution of IS to their own business performance.

Managing Information Systems for Profit.   Edited by T. J. Lincoln
© 1990 John Wiley & Sons Ltd

2 SENIOR MANAGEMENT CONCERNS

There is much evidence that senior managers are concerned about the financial performance of IS (Gale, 1980). There are two aspects to this: firstly the immediate justification of future IS investments and secondly the on going demonstration of the accumulated value of all of the investments to date in IT-related hardware, software, buildings and people. The first of these is addressed in Chapter 10 of this book and this chapter will focus on the second of these concerns.

As IS investments are likely to have been made over a large number of years, any estimate of the value of IS must not be invalidated by the fact that hardware is regularly replaced as new advances in technology are introduced, and major business applications are modified or replaced to keep pace with changing business requirements.

Returning to the source of interest in the Value of IS, the managers who are concerned are certainly conscious of the increasing levels of investment in IS and realise that IT is no longer an exclusive domain of the IS community. They see implementations of IT by business managers outside of IS and recognise that the rate of change in the field of IT is so rapid as to make it exceedingly difficult for them to become or remain meaningfully involved.

Perhaps frustration at not being sufficiently involved prompts questions which focus primarily on financial aspects of IS performance. These questions take a number of forms such as 'What is the IS contribution to the bottom line?', 'Are we getting value for money?' or 'How does our IS spend compare with our competitors?'. These usually mean that there is a good awareness of IS expenditures but a less than clear idea of the related benefit—even in respect of major new projects and investments.

Another form of the question may be 'Why do we continue to increase IS spending?' Here there is often a desire actually to reduce the level of IS investments without having the knowledge or confidence to select the areas to reduce. In many examples like this senior managers frequently also complain that IS managers baffle them with science when arguments in support of technology investments are presented in technical terms that are fully understood only by experts.

On a more positive note the question is occasionally posed in a form such as 'Are we spending the right amount on IS?' In this case there is usually an understanding of the benefits arising from systems and perhaps a willingness to raise the level of IS investment in order to capture a greater share of these benefits; or more importantly to direct IS investment into areas that could bring competitive advantages which may be difficult to quantify using conventional approaches.

Experience suggests that IS managers attract questions from their superiors concerning financial payback to a greater extent than managers of other functions. There appears no comparable focus in management literature aimed at the legal, marketing, personnel, procurement, etc., functions although similar questions could equally be asked of them.

The following factors may offer an explanation of this phenomenon:

1. Since the IS business is relatively young, computers having entered commercial use to a significant degree only in the 1960s, many of today's top executives 'missed out' on the experience of managing IS. They were already well advanced in their chosen careers by the time this new function was born and as a result they *lack familiarity* with it.

2. There is certainly *greater visibility* today of IT issues. Media attention, in the general press as well as in specialist literature, continually focuses on the uses and abuses of systems. As already mentioned, the levels of investment in IS have grown to the stage where the annual budget for a typical IS organisation constitutes a significant part of the overall expenditure of an enterprise.

3. In many organisations the IS function is *not well integrated*. It is viewed as a separate, difficult-to-manage component of the business. Unfortunately this view is often reinforced by IS managers who continue to express the performance of their function in terms that bear little relation to the business of the enterprise. Excluding IS from the business planning cycle also discourages integration. Within IBM Europe, for example, it is only since 1983 that planning for IS was included as an integral module of an overall country business plan. Previously IS had been treated as a separate entity with a separate sequence of plan reviews.

4. Many top managers continue to view IS as an expense item and make little attempt to consider the benefit side of the equation. As IS managers have been *unable or unwilling to demonstrate the value* of the IS contribution to the business then their credibility in this area has been eroded.

5. *Top management may feel estranged from IS* and believe IS to be out of touch with business issues. This may be due, in part, to poor management of expectations by IS managers and confirms the opinion—frequently incorrect—that IS is run by managers who are technicians and not businessmen.

6. Finally, a poor record of *managing the achievement of claimed benefits* from IS projects may have generated scepticism about IS performance. Of course, managing the achievement of benefits is a responsibility that must be shared, not only by IS management but also by the sponsoring user manager and indeed by senior general managers.

Arguably the most serious of these factors has been the inability or unwillingness of IS managers to demonstrate convincingly the value of the IS contribution to the business. This has in turn reduced the confidence of top management to make strategic IS investment decisions—with potentially serious consequences for the continuing success of their enterprises.

3 SOME APPROACHES TO DETERMINE THE VALUE OF IS

Many attempts to demonstrate IS value have been based on some kind of cost/benefit analysis, usually featuring a cost displacement approach. A number of powerful techniques have been developed to perform this task, and Figure 1 shows some of the more important of these.

←——Past time ———		———Future time ———→
PIMS (1)	P	
VALUE CHAIN ANALYSIS (2)	R	
	E	ISIS (3a)
SESAME (3b)	S	
SPS (3c)	E	SPS (3c)
	N	SIM (3d)
	T	SAS (3d)
	T	ATT (3e)
EPDP (3f)	I	EPDP (3f)
	M	ENTERPRISE INFORMATION ANALYSIS (4)
	E	

FIGURE 1

1. Amongst those that evaluate the effects of installed systems are PIMS, a program which includes a maintained data base and is conducted by the Strategy Planning Institute, Cambridge, USA. This approach has been further developed by Paul Strassman (1985) to highlight the contribution of management to business results, the 'management value add', as well as the contribution of installed technology.
2. The value chain analysis approach of Porter (1985) evaluates the contribution of each of the component parts of a business strategy, and can include the contribution of technology.
3. A number of methodologies developed and/or used within IBM have been applied successfully in both North America and Europe. These include:
   a. ISIS (IS Investment Strategies). This methodology produces a financial comparison of a company with its major competitors, examines the

existing portfolio of applications, identifies areas where a high return on additional investment may be expected and prepares the supporting business case.

b. SESAME (Systems Effectiveness Study and Management Endorsement) (Lincoln, 1986) applies primarily cost displacement techniques to evaluate the benefits of installed systems.

c. SPS (Satisfaction and Priority Survey) uses opinion survey techniques to establish subjective user and IS assessments of the importance and effectiveness of installed systems. Analyses of major agreements and disagreements between user and IS perspectives is used to prioritise future IS investments. The approach is based on the User Needs Survey (Alloway, 1979).

d. SIM (Systems Investment Methodology) and SAS (Strategic Application Search) are used to determine the coverage of systems already implemented and to identify the most productive new areas for future investment.

e. ATT (Application Transfer Team) studies specify in detail the system requirements of a particular business area and generates the associated business justification.

f. EPDP (Executive Planning for Data Processing) also uses a cost displacement approach to quantify the benefits of installed applications and to examine areas for optimum future investment.

4. Enterprise Information Analysis (Parker, 1982) proposes a financial justification based on a taxonomy of intangible costs and benefits, and risk and uncertainty associated with technological change.

Many of these methodologies have proved to be very valuable in supporting individual project justifications. However none provides an adequate evaluation of the IS contribution according to the definition given at the beginning of this chapter.

In particular the emphasis on quantifying the *benefit* of future systems may create a restrictively narrow view of 'value'. Sponsors or users of proposed systems may be unable, or reluctant, to declare all of the potential benefits, and those who are only indirectly affected by a system may decline to acknowledge any quantifiable benefit at all. Accordingly, even detailed calculation of the return on investment (ROI) almost always understates the eventual potential contribution of a project. Estimation of the value of multiple systems presents particular problems since the aggregated ROI calculations may fail to reflect the collective effect of systems on the supported organisation, by overlooking perhaps improved organisational efficiencies that arise from increased availability and accuracy of information.

A common weakness of some of the techniques identified in Figure 1 is that they do not always recognise the role of systems investments in the overall business performance of the enterprise. They fail to capture the ongoing contribution of IS as an integral part of the business since they ignore the value of *the IS Base* that may have been established and enhanced over many years.

4 CHANGING NATURE OF SYSTEMS

One reason why many of the techniques referred to in Figure 1 do not meet our specific requirement of demonstrating the ongoing contribution to the business may be that they do not recognise the changing purpose of systems.

At the outset of the use of computer systems almost all applications were justified on the basis of *saving money*. As the purpose of many of the systems was to displace labour, the benefits were easily assessed by traditional cost benefit analysis (CBA) techniques. Systems that improved the efficiency with which an organisation met its objectives were satisfactorily evaluated in this way.

However, over time, as the range of business functions supported by computer applications spread, the objectives of new systems changed. No longer is the purpose only to save money but now systems are expected to *make money*. Technology and systems are now used to differentiate products, to reposition companies in their field of operation and even to change the structure of an industry. This is illustrated in Figure 2.

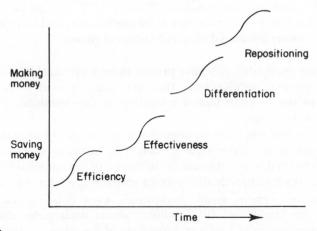

FIGURE 2

Traditional CBA techniques alone may be inadequate, in these situations, to calculate accurately the value of expected advantages, due in part to the intangible nature of the benefits and/or because, without the use of systems, a particular business area would simply not have been entered. Such systems

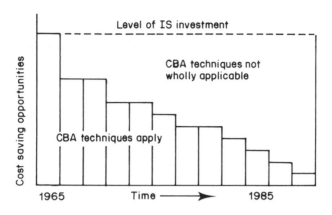

FIGURE 3.

may be considered as belonging to a 'Post-Business-Case' stage of development. This is illustrated in Figure 3.

In these circumstances, potentially valuable IS investments may not be supported by top management because the familiar financial techniques fail to provide the necessary justification. Sound business vision and strength of management's conviction may be the only factors that can be relied upon to justify investment. If this is the case, familiarity with the potential of the technology and the issues involved in applying it will certainly enhance the confidence required to make decisions.

If we accept that it may not be possible to demonstrate in advance the returns available from many of the uses of systems and technology today—and since absolute quantification of benefits may not be possible in any case—then concerns about the value of IS must be approached differently. A climate has to be created in which top management has enough confience in IS to feel able and encouraged to make important decisions on future systems investments.

This *Climate of Confidence* can be created by ensuring that IS becomes a fully integrated function of the enterprise and by communicating relevant information on the performance of IS in terms that other business managers understand. By such actions it can be shown that IS really does contribute to the business performance, top management's perceptions can be altered positively and many of their concerns and misconceptions about IS can be removed. The creation of this climate can reduce significantly concerns over the value of the IS contribution. However, it must be recognised that this is a long-term approach and when the IS contribution *is* a serious concern a short-term response is usually needed.

The approach taken must apply to what I referred to as the 'Post-Business-Case' stage of systems development, where value is not only the calculation of short-term benefit but reflects in some way the ultimate performance of the enterprise. It must also take into account the judgements of senior (non-IS) executives on the suitability of IS applications and services provided and should reflect the particular characteristics of the industry. It clearly must contain enough quantification to satisfy the expectations of the executives who raise the concern and, I believe, must display the measured or assessed value in perspective with other relevant measurements.

The question then is, '*What other measurements?*'

5 IS MEASUREMENT STRATEGIES

At this point it is worth considering the other side of the coin, as it were, and examine situations where the value of the IS contribution is not questioned.

Here the work of J. Rockart and others provides a valuable lead (Rockart, 1982). In this study of the critical success factors of a number of senior IS executives he based his selection on the high reputations they enjoyed among their peers and with their superiors. In those cases where the IS contribution was rarely if ever called into question, Rockart found that IS management had already established a high level of credibility with top management. All of the managers studied enjoyed a close reporting relationship and rapport with their Boards. They took care to demonstrate continually good IS performance, to be seen to exercise sound judgement and never were responsible for unpleasant surprises. As a result top management developed confidence in IS management's ability to control the significant levels of IS expense involved and had confidence in the IS measurements supplied to them.

Paradoxically, this is precisely the environment that we concluded earlier was essential as a basis to be able to demonstrate successfully the IS contribution.

There is of course one other circumstance where the value of IS is not questioned, although it does not offer much guidance. This is where IS managers have simply been lucky! Whether or not their departments are performing well, either the company's dependence on IS has not been recognised—yet—or in their enterprises IS is not yet strategically important, as defined by McFarlan and McKenney (1983).

In summary, then it appears that the value of the IS contribution *is not questioned* when:

1. IS is well managed and this fact is recognised.
2. IS may be poorly managed but this is not recognised.

The value of the IS contribution *is questioned* when:

1. IS is poorly managed and recognised.
2. IS may be well managed but this fact is not recognised.

In this context I use 'well managed' to mean delivering reliably and cost effectively a range of IS services to agreed committed service levels, thereby ensuring a high degree of client satisfaction. Similarly, 'recognised' implies an awareness of the performance of IS by the senior managers of the enterprise.

'Poorly managed' implies absence of many of the characteristics described above with, perhaps, additional evidence of unsatisfactory audit comments and almost certainly a visibly aggrieved set of clients looking for alternative sources of IS service. The term 'not recognised' indicates that, whatever the actual performance record of IS, little or no awareness of it exists amongst senior business managers.

Returning to the question of 'what other measurements?' are needed to create the appropriate context in which to consider the assessed value of the IS contribution, the four situations outlined above and illustrated in Figure 4 provide some guidance.

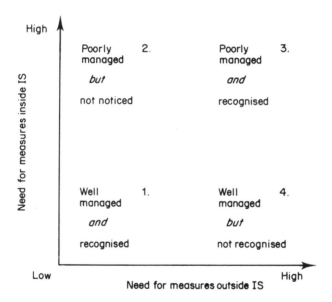

FIGURE 4

For each of these situations a different measurement strategy is required. The measurements tracked in each case will be customised to fit the specific needs of the situation. The emphasis may be on a set of measurements for use internally by IS personnel or to provide user and top management with a set of meaningful indicators.

Thus in the case of a well managed but unrecognised IS organisation there clearly is a greater need to demonstrate performance to management outside the function and to include in the measurement program,for example, data to allow comparisons to be made with other similar IS organisations.

On the other hand, a poorly managed function that has not been noticed as such has a greater need to focus on internal performance measurements to initiate corrective actions. Only when performance has been improved should the offer of performance information to an external audience be considered. My experience of examining the performance of a number of IS organisations in Europe indicates that IS managers have been slow to recognise the importance of a carefully selected measurement strategy. The objectives of the measurement program selected will vary according to the nature of the situation, as follows.

5.1 Well Managed and Recognised

Here the objective is *Constant Vigilance*. The situation is always under control and measurements are used to enable the early detection of possible problems and to shape the expectations of top management. The value of IS is understood and considerable freedom may be exercised to track and publicise measurements to support changes in IS strategy and directions.

5.2 Poorly Managed but Not Recognised

Here the objective is *Detailed performance analysis*. The situation is not under good control and there may be frequent service interrupts. Detailed measurements should be used within IS to identify the root causes of problems and to initiate corrective actions. The priority is to fix internal problems and so long as there is no pressure to do so, the external audience may be addressed later when performance has been improved.

5.3 Poorly Managed and Recognised

Here a carefully chosen measurement program is *Essential for Survival*. It is mandatory to demonstrate regularly to top management, and within IS, that obvious problems are being tracked and root causes determined and resolved. Measurements must be shown that will convince senior user management that the situation is being improved as a result of the actions taken, and every opportunity taken to offer information that will alter their negative perceptions of IS.

5.4 Well Managed but Not Recognised

In this case everyone closely associated with IS knows how good a performance is delivered and the need is for an external *Publicity Campaign*. Measurements that focus on particular IS strengths can be used to draw favourable comparisons with other IS organisations. However, comparisons with other organisations must be treated with caution due to possible differences in definition of factors measured. Attention may also be focused on continuous improvement trends or sustained high levels of service. Such an organisation is in an excellent position to enlighten top management about the value of the IS contribution.

So, depending on the perceived performance of IS, we can determine the other measurements that are required to provide the appropriate perspective for the assessment of the value of IS.

To ensure this perspective, it is useful to publish an annual statement of the IS support to the business, modelled on the annual report of an enterprise as required under the UK Companies Act.

6 ASSESSMENT OF IS VALUE

For the purpose of this chapter it is assumed that:

1. The IS function is an indispensible part of the enterprise (this may not always be perceived by top management!) and IS services and applications are key components in the overall business infrastructure.
2. The other functions in the enterprise are responsible to formulate and manage business strategies for overall corporate improvement.

This section will present an approach to the assessment of IS Value which has been found to provide sufficient quantification to satisfy management expectations and takes into account top management opinions.

The approach described here is based on one suggested in the 'Prism' report (Index Group and Hammer, 1987) on the subject of IS measurements. It recommends the calculation of a value of IS defined as the 'Degree of Automation' and is expressed in 'Automation Value Points'.

The degree of automation is calculated by summing the product of the following three separate factors for each key function in the organisation:

1. The business significance of each function determined, for example, by the cost to the enterprise of revenue impacts and measured by a relative points value allocated by the senior manager in the organisation
2. The impact of installed systems on the functions supported determined by the scope of activities covered by, and effectiveness of, the systems as assessed by user management
3. The quality of installed systems determined by their reliability, currency of development techniques used and ease of maintainability, as assessed by IS management

The sum total of the points allocated provides the 'Automation Value Points' measure, but as this is an artificial factor the author suggests applying the calculated result, as a percentage, to a unit of measure appropriate to the business, such as units of production, etc.

The three factors specified above give rise to a new set of questions designed to help the executive better understand the contribution of IS and these new questions can be answered using established methods.

1. What is the relative importance of the constituent functions within the enterprise ? This question can be approached, as suggested in the Prism report, by soliciting the view of the senior executive. A hypothetical example of such an allocation is shown below for a company which develops, builds, markets, distributes and services its products:

Relative significance of functions

Function	Significance (%)
Development	8
Manufacturing	12
Distribution	15
Marketing	20
Procurement	10
Finance	10
IS	10
Customer support	15
Total	100%

Although subjective, this part of the 'Prism' approach has merit in that it involves the views of the top executive in the area where subjectivity is greatest.

2. How important are IS systems to the function(s) supported ?

3. How robust and easily maintainable are the systems ?

Questions 2 and 3 may be addressed by the User Needs Survey (Alloway, 1979) or by other simply constructed 'Opinion Survey' methods. Question 2 is answered by user management by considering the scope of their business activities covered by IS systems, their degree of dependence on these systems and their satisfaction with the level of service delivered.

Question 3 is answered by IS management taking account of the consistency of performance of the system and its ease of maintainability.

4. How well does IS deliver, install and operate systems ?

   This question is answered by one of the customised measurement programs identified in Section 5 of this chapter.

5. How well does the collection of functions—the total enterprise—perform ?

   The answers to Question 5 are, of course, revealed in the statements and data included in the annual report of the enterprise.

Having obtained an executive assessment of the relative significance of the different functions to the overall business and by asking the heads of the using functions about the functional fit of their supporting systems and their extent of dependence on these systems we can deduce a numeric value for the system impact. A similar numeric value for the quality of the systems can be obtained by questions posed to the IS manager.

Taking the estimates obtained in this way, multiplying them together for each identified application and function, and finally multiplying this result by the relative significance as assessed by the senior executive we can arrive at an assessment of the value of IS as shown in Figure 5. We can define the

	Development	Manufacturing	Distribution	Marketing	Procurement	Finance	IS	Support
				Major functional areas				
Significance	8	12	15	20	10	10	10	15
Applications or services (impact × quality)								
Application 1 Application 2 Application 3 Application 4 etc.		0.7 × 0.8		0.7 × 0.4 0.5 × 0.8 0.5 × 0.6	0.6 × 0.4			0.7 × 0.8
Totals		6.7		13.6	3.0	2.4		8.4
Sum of impacts = 34.1								

FIGURE 5

IS contribution to the business as being represented by the total sum of the impacts.

It only remains to agree the unit of measure for the value of IS that is appropriate to a specific enterprise or business and to express the assessed value in it. This could be revenue earned, units produced, etc.

Thus the hypothetical calculated value in the example (Figure 5) may be applied as a percentage factor to the NBT profit of the enterprise or as a percentage of units of production, as appropriate to the business of the enterprise. In this way also the contribution of IS is directly linked to the overall business performance of the enterprise.

However, it is important not to place too great an emphasis on a numerical result containing, as it does contain, such an element of subjectivity. This can be avoided by presenting the result in a framework within which this assessed value of the IS contribution is less likely to be taken out of context and/or misinterpreted.

7 PLACING 'IS VALUE' IN PERSPECTIVE

In order to more clearly inform the intended audience it is suggested that the report be modelled on a typical company annual report. A suggested list of contents is given below followed by comments on the purpose and use of each section.

1. Financial position
2. Computing capacity
3. Support to user functions
4. Key IS performance indicators
5. IS staffing and experience
6. User satisfaction survey results
7. Strategic impact of IS
8. Future directions and opportunities

7.1 Financial Position

Given the underlying financial aspect of questions about the Value of IS it is appropriate to start with an outline of the financial position indicating how the year's IS costs were incurred and, assuming a cost centre or profit centre practice is employed, how these costs were allocated amongst the client functions. Significant differences from previous years and detected trends can be commented on.

The enterprise's investment in systems can well be illustrated by showing the IS expense and IS capital outlay per company employee over the past, say 5, years together with ratios of IS costs to company revenues and IS costs to total enterprise costs. Comparisons may be drawn with corresponding data from other similar or competitive organisations, if available. A report, commissioned by IBM UK Ltd, and published by the Oxford Institute of Information Management (1989), is part of an initiative to give wider circulation to this kind of information.

An excellent expression of the contribution of IS is to show *trends* in unit costs of doing business, e.g. the cost of an invoice or sales order processed or the cost of an inquiry transaction over time.

7.2 Computing Capacity

As a key role for IS is the provision of computing power to the enterprise then prominence must be given to information about available capacity.

Given the layman's unfamiliarity with concepts such as MIPS (millions of instructions per second) and gigabytes of disk storage space then graphs showing growth rates of these measures may mean little to managers outside of the IS community. However impressive graphs of these absolute measures may be, it is again better to express them in terms of units of computing power and storage capacity *per enterprise employee*—and do not forget to include an explanation of the terminology employed!

Given the current dramatic trends commonly found in this area, comments linking capacity growth to increases in business volumes, for example, or the introduction of new IS services will be helpful.

The number of VDU and other terminal devices installed is also important data and the ratio of enterprise employees per terminal installed is a good indicator of the extent and rate of penetration of technology within the organisation.

The opportunity may also be taken to illustrate how use of state of the art technology takes advantage of manufacturers' improving price/performance to keep cost increases below the increase in absolute capacity required.

7.3 Support to User Functions

Having commented on the overall cost of IS services and support and having indicated what this has acquired in terms of equipment, it is certainly pertinent to comment on the new services and projects that IS has implemented or is developing for the client functions.

In view of the comments in Section 4 of this chapter it is desirable to distinguish between efficiency-oriented applications that have directly calculable returns on the one hand, and on the other those projects aimed at acquiring or maintaining competitive advantage for which benefits may have to be expressed more subjectively.

Systems described in this section should be restricted to key projects only—defined by size of implementation effort or size of expected benefit, if known. For each project give a brief statement of the new function provided and *either* a description of the identified benefit with details of projected ROI and payback period *or a statement by the sponsoring user executive of the expected benefit to the enterprise!*

A histogram showing the *relative* costs and benefits of the referenced projects gives a useful indication of IS support to different user functions, and if the data is available, it may also be helpful to include graphs showing the situation to date in terms of the average break-even period and average internal rate of return achieved by IS development projects.

7.4 Key IS Performance Indicators

Having shown *what* (is being provided by IS), *for whom* and at *what cost* it is timely to turn to *how effectively* the IS organisation is performing.

Notwithstanding the recommendations on measurement strategies given in Section 5, there are a few indicators of IS internal performance which should be included in the report.

With the theme of demonstrating the IS contribution still very much in mind, the percentage of service level agreement commitments achieved, the number of MIPS supported per IS employee and the size of installed application base (in function points or lines of code) maintained per IS support person are useful indicators of service performance and efficiency (see also Chapter 6).

To illustrate performance at delivering new application function, the total of new function points—or lines of code—delivered per IS development person should be shown. The quality of new application code delivered can be demonstrated by the number of recorded errors per thousand new function points or new lines of code (see also Chapter 8).

Comments relating demonstrable development productivity improvements to investment in new development tools or techniques are very informative and should be included where relevant.

7.5 IS Staffing and Experience

At this stage some indication of the size of the IS community, its distribution by age, sex and/or qualification and experience is appropriate. This can be given by showing changes in IS headcount over, say, 5 years along with numbers of new hires, highlighting the percentage of university graduates and perhaps a breakdown by sex if relevant, e.g. to indicate compliance with equal opportunity policy—or leglislation.

Distribution by age and/or IS experience may be included, especially if it is considered necessary to draw attention to, perhaps, a skills imbalance and support a case for increased IS recruitment.

Another indicator of an enterprise's investment in IS, and a key to future success, is the number of days devoted to training—both technical and management—and the associated costs. This data should be included and interpreted.

To maintain perspective, the ratio of total enterprise population supported per IS person may be shown.

There is a good opportunity here to draw attention to any meritorious achievements of individual IS employees (or groups of employees), such as awards gained or other recognitions by the enterprise, the IS profession or the community.

7.6 User Satisfaction Survey Results

Assuming that a survey technique like the one referred to in Section 6 has been used, this report is an excellent vehicle to convey selected information to further illustrate the IS contribution.

Publicise positive comments from users and highlight the users' opinions of IS strengths. Comment also on the perceived weaknesses of IS and indicate any corrective actions planned or undertaken.

Comment on any major services or applications that users found unsatisfactory, and explain the root cause and the corrective action taken. Highlight services or applications that were highly rated by users and draw attention to their importance to the following section.

7.7 Strategic Impact of IS

It is in this section of the report, having set the scene with appropriate information, that we reveal the result of the exercise to assess the contribution of the IS function to the enterprise. A brief description of the process used may be given, illustrated with tables such as shown in Figure 5 in Section 6 of this chapter. This will show the senior executive's assessment of the relative significance of the business functions along with the survey results giving the opinions of the senior user managers of the impact of IS services and applications on their operations. When factored by the IS manager's statement of quality, then a table such as Figure 5 may illustrate the method used to arrive at the assessment of the IS contribution.

The result obtained will therefore be seen against the background of the preceding profile of IS infrastructure, and a final perspective may be added by quoting highlights from the business results of the enterprise. Commentary linking the achievement of stated enterprise objectives to the IS activities already referred to will complete the picture.

7.8 Future Directions and Opportunities

This final part of the report may be used to draw conclusions from the key messages of earlier sections such as business areas revealed by the survey to require increased IS support, or to underline areas for future technology investments.

Information regarding new advances in technology that are relevant to the business are valuable and a brief outline of the IS support strategies planned for the coming years will go a long way towards setting the correct level of expectations with regard to future IS performance in the minds of the readers.

8 SUMMARY

The approach described combines an executive opinion on the relative importance of the functions in the organisation, a survey to provide user and IS views on the importance and quality of installed systems, as well as an analysis of the strengths and weaknesses of IS.

It derives an assessment of the value of the IS contribution to the business which together with other selected measurements is compiled into a report which can be produced on an annual basis. The objective of this report is to provide a detailed profile of the established IS infrastructure and support—not just a set of numbers.

Organisations that decide to follow the approach recommended in this chapter can expect to introduce modifications according to the practices they have already established. This has been the experience of the IBM France IS function which began to pilot the approach in December 1988 and who relied on the company's defined key business indicators to identify the applications of importance. Modifications will be influenced by availability, or otherwise, of expertise in the component parts of the process, e.g. the survey methodology and the willingness of senior executives to assign relative importance to the different parts of their organisation.

Experience of conducting similar exercises indicates that the effort required to complete such a study would be of the order of 2 to 3 man-months. Actual effort will vary according to how many of the suggested measurements are in regular use and to the techniques finally selected.

Discussion of the approach with senior IS managers has revealed a desire to be able to issue a report like the one described but which is, sadly, not matched by enthusiasm to embark on the activities required to achieve it. I suspect a historical and deep-seated aversion to publicity, rather than lack of resources, to be the root cause of the situation. Hopefully readers of this chapter will become convinced of the advantages to be gained by regularly applying the methodology and producing a report along the lines suggested.

The principal advantages are to enlighten senior management about IS and to better manage their expectations with regard to IS. It is also an excellent motivator of IS employees, and by highlighting system problem areas can provide valuable guidance in setting priorities for future IS investments.

In addition, for those enterprises that really do successfully exploit systems and technology to enhance their competitive position, extracts of information from the IS report may be included in the official annual report of the enterprise to enhance their reputations as leaders in the use of IT. A rare example of this was the annual report of IBM France in 1986, a large section of which emphasised the activities of the IS function and its support to the business.

REFERENCES

Alloway, R.M. (1979) *User Needs Survey (c)*.

Gale, B.T. (1980) 'Can more capital buy higher productivity?' *Harvard Business Review*, July/August.

Index Group Inc. and Hammer and Company (1987) 'Measuring and improving IS performance', Final Report, September.

Lincoln,T. (1986) 'Do computer systems really pay off?', *Information Management*, **2**(1) August.

McFarlan, F.W., and McKenney, J.L. (1983) *Corporate Information Systems Management— The Issues Facing Senior Executives*, Dow Jones Irwin, New York.

Oxford Institute of Information Management (1989) 'The Utilisation and Efficiency of IS. A Comparative Analysis'.

Parker, M.M. (1982) 'Enterprise information analysis; Cost–benefit analysis and the data-managed system', *IBM Systems Journal*, **21**, 1.

Porter, M.E. (1985) *Competitive Advantage*, The Free Press, New York.

Rockart, J.F. (1982) 'The changing role of the information systems executive; a critical success factors perspective', *Sloan Management Review*, **24**, 1.

Strassman, P.A. (1985) *Information Payoff—The Transformation of Work in the Electronic Age*, The Free Press, New York.

Note Added in Proof

The Automatic Value Points approach is disclosed by kind permission of Index Group Inc. and Hammer and Company.

INDEX